Modern
English
Society

Modern English Society

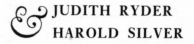

JUDITH RYDER
HAROLD SILVER

Methuen LONDON

Contents

Contents

vi Contents

Illustrations

Acknowledgements

The authors and publishers wish to thank the following for permission to reproduce the illustrations appearing in this book:

Radio Times Hulton Picture Library, for Nos. 1, 2, 6, 10, 12, 17, 18, 19, 23

The Mansell Collection, for Nos. 3, 4, 5, 7, 8, 9, 11, 13, 15, 16

Aerofilms Limited, for Nos. 20, 25

Keystone Press Agency Limited, for Nos. 21, 24

Michael St Maur Sheil, for No. 22

Rex Features Ltd, for Nos. 26, 27, 29, 30, 32, 33, 35, 36

Popperfoto, for No. 28

Press Association Photos, for Nos. 31, 34

Terry Williams, for No. 37

Note on the second edition

Since the first edition of this book was written in the 1960s considerable social, economic and political changes have taken place, in Britain and internationally. In the first edition we attempted, broadly speaking, to devote a number of chapters to the historical background to the Britain of the 1950s and 1960s, and a number to contemporary society. Now that the Second World War, and even the 1950s, are distant history or an indistinct memory to many of the possible readers of this new edition, we have felt it necessary to continue the historical narrative through the period since the end of the war. The discussions of contemporary society now take the form of case studies set in this narrative. Although the intention of the book is therefore the same as in the first edition – to put together some aspects of the sociology and history of modern England – the structure of the latter part of the book has been changed. We hope that the changes will not only bring the book up to date, but provide a perspective on the recent past that will be helpful to readers.

Critics of the first edition rightly pointed to large areas of omission – including the social impact of science and war, religion and agriculture. Apart from the fuller discussion of the Second World War we have been unable to respond to these criticisms of omissions, of which we warned readers ourselves. The book would have been unmanageable in size had we done so.

There are also wide areas of international economic and political change that we would have liked to deal with more fully, especially political tensions surrounding Vietnam, American politics and policies, the Middle East and Europe in the 1960s, and the world economic difficulties of the mid-1970s. We hope, however, that we have pointed firmly enough towards such contexts to enable readers to pursue their own investigations and make their own judgements. Reviewers of the first edition pointed to the difficulty of going beyond a combination of sociology and history to effect a proper marriage. We hope that readers will at least find this a useful working partnership.

Judith Ryder and Harold Silver
Chelsea College, 1977

Introduction

Our aim in this book is to set some distinctive features of contemporary English society in their nineteenth- and twentieth-century contexts.

Although our historical starting point is the process of change taking place at the beginning of the nineteenth century, we are concerned more centrally with the social transformations of the Victorian period: the growth of industry and towns; changes in the structure of employment; the development of large-scale systems of public administration, commerce and finance; the emergence of popular social movements and a democratic franchise; the appearance of public health and welfare policies; and the rapid expansion of communications. All of these had their origins in the eighteenth century, in the disruption of the more settled order of communal existence which resulted from the complex events we have come to know as the Industrial Revolution. They are developments which have had a continuing influence on English life, and we have tried to account for the changing nature of this influence at different stages in the late nineteenth and twentieth centuries. The discussion of contemporary Britain in the later chapters of the book is of a society with dominant industrial, urban and political characteristics. It is these contemporary contours that the historical discussion is intended to clarify.

This approach indicates our interest in demonstrating the links between the methods and emphases of the social historian and those of the sociologist. We have tried to show that, in their common concern with the changing network of social relations, the social historian and the sociologist can benefit greatly from a sharing of each other's terminology, data and techniques. We believe that if the resources of both are combined the meanings of concepts in everyday use can be more clearly grasped. Social history means more than an antiquarian interest in the manners and appearance of society, and more than an effort to make history reconstruct a sketch or 'fabric' of the past. We take it to be fundamentally concerned with human behaviour and action, with underlying changes in ideas, ideologies and attitudes. Recent trends in the history of population changes and of the family provide important examples. Social history entails an interest in the emergence and influence of ideas in relation to other social phenomena: labour and educational history have provided good illustrations of this interrelation. Social history has often been coupled with, but has increasingly broken away from economic history – which has become more involved with the historical application of economic theories and models. Social history is primarily concerned with the group, with the evolution of group relationships, and with the adjustment of policy, action and principle to social reality as the participants have seen it.

Sociology is concerned with many of the same issues, but from a different perspective. Sociologists, for instance, ask the following kind of question: What are the relationships between individuals and groups in a particular society? How are these relationships organized into institutions, such as the family, the economic and educational system, the political and legal structure, custom and morality? How are these institutions interrelated within a given social order? How does this order differ from other varieties of social order – in different societies or in previous historical periods? What are the mechanisms by which a given social order is changing, or prevented from changing? What are the effects of changes in one set of institutions on the structure of other parts of the society? How do individuals and groups perceive and interpret the social system, its institutions, its changes? How do they react and organize accordingly? In investigating such issues the sociologist often has to cope with economic, political or psychological considerations. But even while using the observations of other specialists to clarify his analysis, the sociologist has his own distinctive viewpoint.

Although sociology shares many of the concerns of social history and, in particular, a concern with asking significant questions about changing patterns of social movement, the difficulties of their relationship are obvious – and are reflected in this book. Both sociology and history involve rigorous – many would say scientific – analysis, though the common meaning of this is not clear, and has long been a subject of dispute within each of the disciplines. The question of how far history and sociology can use each other's methods is complicated by the fact that neither sociologists nor historians have as separate groups each employed the same approaches or held the same assumptions. The nature of 'facts', the process of the selection of data and questions, the role of the observer – these and other salient issues are matters of deep conflict within both sociology and history. None the less, it is our view that both historical and contemporary analysis can benefit from sharing – if nothing else, from sharing uncertainties about how to study society.

We go further than this, in asserting that it is right and proper to attempt an analysis of contemporary social structure by looking for both historical and sociological explanations of continuities and discontinuities, change and stability. 'Society' is a key word in our everyday vocabulary, a key concept in our attempts to understand ourselves and the way we live, and a key notion in relation to which we pass judgements and take political or other kinds of social action. It can only be clarified by glimpsing its meaning in the past and by understanding some of the processes by which it is constituted in the present. For each of us, it represents a marriage of abstraction and experience.

In this book we have tried to use our conception of social history and sociology to expose some of the structure and workings of a given society – modern English society. This is a necessary effort at approximation. Every historical and sociological analysis is the best we can do at the time, with the resources available, with the insights we think most useful and significant, with the research techniques open to us, with the questions in mind that seem most important at the moment, overcoming the theoretical and other difficulties as best we may. There is no such thing as *the* sociology of modern England or *the* history of modern England – there are many of both, including yours and each of ours. To reach as closely as possible towards a 'reality' that is useful for the moment there is every reason why at least one version of sociology and one version of history should share their data, aims, methods and hesitations.

This kind of approach to the description and analysis of society we take to be a kind of awakening; a critical and debunking activity. Not unlike poetry, as defined by Shelley in *The Four Ages of Poetry*, it makes 'familiar objects be as if they were not familiar', purging 'from our inward sight the film of familiarity which obscures from us the wonder of our being'. It is not so much that sociology and social history are pursuing certain kinds of knowledge as directing attention to certain kinds of question, and in the process confronting the settled assumptions of commonsense belief.

Asking questions about a particular society – especially about the society we actually live in – cannot be a neutral exercise. At the very least, it involves some selectivity and a judgement about which questions matter most. We accept, therefore, and in writing this book have been consciously aware of writing out of, a particular intellectual 'commitment'. For us, this has meant a commitment to unprejudiced analysis; a refusal to bow before empiricism pure and simple, and a constant attempt to detect the conceptual, ideological framework within which we all work.

We are sceptical about efforts to demonstrate that we are moving steadily into a homogenized form of society troubled only by international economic and financial maladjustments, intruding ideologies, indolent workers and doctrinaire radicals of one variety or another. Somewhere embedded in our analysis is a suspicion that radical students, child poverty campaigners, convention-breakers, rebels and protesters of many kinds are closer to understanding the reality of our society than are their critics (not all of whom are on the political right). We do not believe that we are all middle class now, or that our society has come near to solving the problems of democracy or welfare which demanded solution after the Second World War. We believe that, in spite of the considerable advances made in specific directions, our society continues to tolerate major injustices. We are cynical enough to consider that the system of government has been distorted to the point at which democracy as it is and as it might be has been seriously undermined. In short, we have to confess that the world we analyse in this book seems to us a disappointing place.

While following a broadly historical framework, we have looked for the points at which it is most helpful to consider broader questions of social analysis. In the last five chapters in particular we have selected case studies which are intended to enable the reader to refer across from historical to sociological discussions – and to see at what points in time certain kinds of sociological discussion have become prominent. The book could have been organized in other ways – thematically, for instance, following through the progress of particular ideas, structures and institutions. Such an approach would have risked separating related data too sharply. Since this is not a work concerned primarily with theories of sociology or history, and could not therefore have a structure of theoretical issues, the most workable framework was a historical one, seeking to facilitate the progress from historical to contemporary analysis.

We have confined ourselves fairly strictly to the implications of the word 'English' in the title of the book (though there are some developments, such as regional questions, which cannot be tackled without reference beyond the borders). Major historical differences in, for example, the administrative, Poor Law and educational systems of Scotland have made it impossible to try to trace the story alongside that of English society. Wales has, by and large, shared the administrative structure of England, but an account of the particular history of, say, Welsh education and culture would have involved us in discussion far beyond a manageable frame of reference. In broad outline the basic trends in urban and population growth, and the main aspects of contemporary society we consider, apply to a considerable degree throughout the United Kingdom.

There are other omissions. We have still found it necessary to omit any real consideration of the history of agriculture, of crime and punishment, of religious beliefs and forms of worship. Similarly we have had in later chapters to omit as detailed an account of the contemporary social services as is given in their earlier history – which is used to illustrate the forces which have influenced modern attitudes towards social analysis and social policy. We have tried throughout to ask significant questions and to suggest some useful perspectives, historical and contemporary, on modern English society.

Part 1 English society from the early nineteenth century to the 1940s

The following chapters discuss aspects of industrial, urban, political and social change that help to explain some key features of contemporary society looked at in Part 2.

1 The making of nineteenth-century society

Economic change

Three major processes have dominated the course of developments in British society during the nineteenth and twentieth centuries: the growth of industry, the growth of cities, and changes in the forms of political organization and public administration. It is with the impact of these developments, and with the society that has been shaped by them and by responses to them, that we shall be mainly concerned. Our emphasis must be placed first on the radical changes experienced by the first nation to undergo the process of sustained industrialization.

The sequence of events which marked the transition from pre-industrial, predominantly rural, eighteenth-century Britain was a complex one. There are symbolic events which act as milestones in the process: the various technical advances in the cotton industry in the 1760s and 1770s, the harnessing of steam power to drive machinery in the 1780s, the first population census of 1801, the end of the Napoleonic wars in 1815, the opening of the Liverpool–Manchester railway in 1830, the first Reform Act of 1832, the Poor Law Amendment Act of 1834, the beginnings of

Chartism in 1836, the repeal of the Corn Laws in 1846 and the Great Exhibition of 1851. The Industrial Revolution of the late eighteenth and early nineteenth centuries was not, however, as abrupt and as all-pervasive as the term (and some of these events) make it at first sight appear.

There is, of course, an inevitable time lag between discovery and application in a society with poor technology and communications, and in which human beings are not adjusted to the expectation of constant change. Watt's steam engine, for example, was built in 1769: a steam engine was first used to operate a spinning mill in 1785. The power loom was invented in 1787 and became economic in the cotton industry at the beginning of the nineteenth century, but the climax of the hand-loom weavers' fight for survival did not come until the 1830s and 1840s. The first Factory Acts, covering pauper apprentices, were passed in 1802 and 1819, but not until the Act of 1833 introduced the principle of inspection were even the beginnings of an effective system of factory regulation laid. In many important respects industry disrupted family economy and family structure. Child employment, for example, was nothing new, but its intensification, in factory conditions, made it a representative, socially disruptive feature of early industrial Britain. There was at work here what Neil Smelser discusses in terms of the 'structural differentiation of the family', and yet the process, he stresses, was drawn out long beyond the establishment of the factory system. Parental control over children *in factories* was still a reality into the 1830s.[1] The ripples of abrupt events are not always as large and as far-reaching as might be expected. Agriculture remained the largest single employer of labour for most of the nineteenth century. The first 'middle-class reform' of Parliament, in 1832, did not materially alter its class composition. Nor, it must be remembered, is change itself always as abrupt as it appears. There were manufacturing industries and factories before the Industrial Revolution. There were local Improvement Acts (and improvements) before the first national Public Health Act in 1848.

In a number of critical respects, however, we are dealing in the early nineteenth century with a *changing* society of an entirely new kind. Pre-industrial society was not without social mobility, although such mobility was only marginal, and in very real ways this was a static society. Peter Laslett argues that what he calls the 'one-class society' of pre-industrial England knew a certain amount of mobility, and yet *structural* change was negligible.[2] Although the eighteenth century was not a totally static society, people behaved predominantly as if it was. After, say, 1790, Britain did not suddenly become a mobile or an open society, but the ripples of radical ideas and action made it clear that more people were beginning to behave as if it ought to be.

Although the industrial revolution, writes a historian of the period,

> did have some massive social effects, one thing not included in these effects was the coming of some altogether new and 'open' industrial society. Instead, what we are faced with is more the breakdown of an old type of *social structure*, a transformation in the cultural organization of the labour community.[3]

Economic growth had in the past been 'either painfully slow or spasmodic' or 'readily reversible'. The extent of economic growth and stagnation in pre-industrial England is far from clear, but before the second half of the eighteenth century people 'had no reason to *expect*' growth. The ordinary man 'saw little evidence of economic growth within his own lifetime and no improvement that could not be eliminated within a single year by the incidence of a bad harvest or a war or an epidemic'.[4]

Eighteenth-century Britain had none of the national movements and organizations which in the nineteenth century became agencies of change. 'In the eighteenth century the characteristic instrument of social purpose', says T. S. Ashton, 'was not the individual or the State, but the club.'[5] Nor was it, he could have added, the *movement*. The radical tradition of the eighteenth century did not find form in the organized popular political and social movement typical of the nineteenth, but in the extra-parliamentary association, aimed at the correction of an abuse. Popular action might take the form of disturbance or riot, strike or petition, but it was not general or sustained. Eighteenth-century labour disputes and reform agitation were not imbued with the sense of purpose and solidarity which marked, for example, political radicalism, Chartism or trade unionism in the nineteenth century.

Social and political change

The breakdown in the stability of English society can be traced most clearly from the 1790s. We shall return to the economic bases of this change; it is with aspects of social and political change that we are first concerned. The outbreak of the French Revolution in 1789, whatever routes it later took and whatever responses it later provoked, was the point around which not only new radicalisms but new ideas in many fields began to take coherent shape. Political radicalism, the programme of principled argument for the reform of the ossified aristocrats' and landowners' parliament, and for a wider measure of popular representation, had its most recent roots in the agitation which had begun at the end of the 1770s, and which had been directed towards the enfranchisement of the property owners. 'Representation co-extensive with direct taxation' had become, together with annual parliaments, one of the main slogans of the more radical reformers. No one had contributed more than Major John Cartwright to the demand for 'pulling down a Despotism and reinstating public Liberty',[6] but the appeal was to ancient rights, to a concept of 'the People' which nineteenth-century reality profoundly altered, and to 'a recovery of lost liberties from a diffusion of knowledge'.[7] This was an eighteenth-century Enlightenment approach that was to run down into the sands of working-class experience, especially in the 1830s. It was part of the disappearing world of the extra-parliamentary association and the political club.[8]

With the organized, vociferous political movement, including the pioneer London Corresponding Society founded in 1792, the modern political world began. A tradition of popular radicalism was born and a step towards a more alert society was made. With the realization that it was possible for the popular will to assert itself, for tyrannies to be overthrown, for democratic principles to prevail, new aspirations became possible and explicit in the 1790s. Tom Paine's *Rights of Man* (1791–2), William Godwin's *Political Justice* (1793) and Mary Wollstonecraft's *Vindication of the Rights of Woman* (1792), for example, were public and influential expressions of a range of newly activated responses to a lack of rights and justice. Popular, organized political radicalism was one of the results. The body of rational analysis and objectives built up by the eighteenth-century Enlightenment, together with emergent Benthamite efforts towards social reform, came to be accompanied by popular movements, formulating new, precise and far-reaching aims. Action and Utopia became, for a long moment of British history, intertwined.

Human aspirations began to be defined on a wider front. The movements which, in the 1830s and 1840s for instance, sought to humanize industrial society and to achieve a greater measure of popular democracy were torn between two priorities – political action and social organization, parliamentary reform and, for example, the re-ordering of society on the basis of co-operative communities or trade-union co-operative production. It was too early in the 1790s for alternatives to be defined in this way, but alongside (and very frequently within) political programmes, objectives were being defined which indicated how far and how quickly it was possible to travel from the stable society. Around subjects like landownership, popular education, marriage and the status of women, the role of the press and the nature of power – not only in the State, but also, for example, in the Church – new forms of articulate opinion made a dramatic appearance. Society as a whole was not, of course, captured by such opinion. Articulate attacks on aristocracy, on privilege and landownership, Mary Wollstonecraft writing on women, Godwin on the State and Paine on human rights, for example, were heard by significant percentages of the population. Their impact was wide enough to make it impossible for assumptions about a hierarchical society ever to be held so impregnably again. Even if social mobility were still a fact of marginal transition from

landownership to aristocracy, from commerce to landownership, from aristocracy to the Church or the Church to aristocracy, from craftsman to master, it was now also an idea in
the market place. You are no longer, men were told, trapped
within the limits of a prescribed status. You have rights, and
you can, as men in society, aspire to be educated, to change
your conditions, to make independent judgements and con-
test the rules and usages that paralyse you. The response
showed that the new political and social radicalisms were
making explicit the objectives which men were already
beginning to formulate for themselves. The responses, of
course, were twofold: broadly speaking, they were those
of the unprivileged, whom they suited, and among sections of
whom traditions of radical ideas continued to be strengthened into the nineteenth century, and those of the
privileged (with distinguished exceptions), whom they did
not suit, and who framed, or acquiesced, in the reactions
and oppressions of 1794 and after. Out of these responses
and situations came compromises and failures. Popular
reform was impregnated at different stages with a sense
not only of idealism or protest, but also of failure and betrayal.

Social attitudes

By the end of the eighteenth century social tensions had
taken on a new dimension. The trials of the radical leaders
in 1794, the organized anti-radicalism of the following years
and the Combination Acts of 1799 and 1800 were the
reverse side of the development from the isolated calls of
'Wilkes and Liberty!' to the organized effort of popular
reform. They both mark the opening of new political and
class confrontations. In addition, however, to political
organization, social aspirations and the opposition they
encountered, an important new focus of discussion is also to
be found at this point – the need for social conciliation, the
need to guard against the upheavals that would result from
allowing new developments to run their course. New
developments related not just to new ideas and objectives,
but also to an awareness of social realities – the unregulated

growth of new industries and towns. The focal point of the early discussion was education.

Amid the bewilderments and uncertainties of the new tempo of social change, discussions of education had entirely new terms of reference. The increasing diversification of skills taking place as a result of new forms of organization in agriculture and industry, the harnessing of new technologies and the exigencies of urban life were leading to social interdependence on a wider scale. The emergence of nation-wide popular movements, the increasing importance of the press as a means of mass communication, and the new scale of social administration needed to cope with the new problems, were only some of the associated factors influencing the discussion. Urban growth and urban poverty, in particular, provoked the question of social defence against urban ignorance. This was the first crude debate about mass communications.

The debate took place between those who argued that popular education fomented discontent and taught people to aspire beyond their stations, and those who argued that a measure of education, enabling children to read their scriptures and to learn the rules of social obedience, was a necessary form of social self-protection. The Sunday School movement which spread at the beginning of the 1780s, and the monitorial schools which grew out of the beginning made by Joseph Lancaster in Borough Road in 1798, were attempts to come to terms with the realities of the new society. The Charity Schools of the eighteenth century had been a limited exercise in the education of the children of the worthy poor in elementary literacy, simple skills and obedience. The monitorial schools, in which a single teacher, spreading rudimentary knowledge downwards through child-monitors, could teach, or rather govern, a school of hundreds, even a thousand, were more appropriate symbols of the onset of mass society. Sponsored by the Church (through the National Society for Promoting the Education of the Poor in the Principles of the Established Church) and the Dissenting bodies (largely through the British and Foreign School Society), they set the scene for the later debate between the advocates and antagonists of

State intervention in education. Involvement by the State did not, in fact, occur until the first vote of government funds in 1833, and did not result in a consensus between the parties involved until the first national Elementary Education Act in 1870. Against every effort to promote popular education in the period from 1790 to the 1830s, however, some form of resistance was offered. Methodists, for example, who ran Sunday schools and interested themselves in education were labelled insurrectionaries. During and following the Napoleonic wars all who educated were accused from some quarter or other of undermining the stability of society. The expansion of the provision of elementary education, therefore, from the end of the eighteenth century, was a matter of voluntary effort.

Adjustment to all these new social realities was not easy; the dimensions of the problems were unprecedented, and the scale of the response required new ingenuities and imaginations to begin to cope with them. The Speenhamland Poor Law system of 1795, which sought primarily to relieve agricultural poverty by supplementing wages on a scale of benefit adjusted to the price of bread, was one of the symbolic gestures of the old society, a society which could still see itself bound by the responsibilities of community. The period between 1795 and the new Poor Law of 1834 was that of the Napoleonic wars and their aftermath, of slowing down or breakdown in handicraft industries, of towns mushrooming beyond the credibility of men, and social problems which seemed almost insoluble. It was consequently the period of the Utopian solution, of the millennium-round-the-corner. In religion, in political reform, in social organization, there were men searching for *the* answer. For all radicals, there was The Vote. For Joanna Southcott and Richard Brothers there was a Second Coming. For Robert Owen there was Co-operative Community. For phrenologists there was a proper understanding of the Mental Faculties. All were fanciful, but in their proper context none was ridiculous. And after the Berkshire Justices in 1795 had made Speenhamland synonymous in the eyes of some with the encouragement of idleness, the millennium which relentlessly gained the

1 *Lancastrian monitorial school, 1829*

ascendant among influential philosophers, economists and
Whig and radical politicians in their discussions of poverty
and the road to a more just society, was *laissez-faire*.

The important point about *laissez-faire*, with its
philosophy of State non-intervention and the self-
adjustment of relationships (in industry or in the market), is
that it evolved, through Adam Smith, Bentham, Malthus,
James and John Stuart Mill, with various convolutions, as
British society's first widely accepted philosophy of *change*.
It recognized the changing society, and offered what it considered a rational, humane basis for social policy. It was
never total in its opposition to collective intervention (and
usually, for example, considered education a proper subject
for State action) and never courageous enough to pursue the
full logic of its views (both Malthus and Edwin Chadwick
would have liked to abolish poor relief, but in fact advocated
a policy of deterring people from applying for it). The
utilitarian philosophy of *laissez-faire* was a complex compromise. Men should be left free. Legislation should enable
them to be left free, and prevent interference with their
freedom. A framework of rational central government and
legislation was therefore necessary, even if it appeared to
contradict the doctrine of self-interest. A. V. Dicey, in his
Law and Public Opinion in England in the Nineteenth Century
(1905), a book which for a long time dominated analyses

of social policy in the nineteenth century, saw it as a
philosophy of individualism, in contrast with the collectivism which grew out of the legislation enforced by 'Tory
humanitarianism' (of which Lord Shaftesbury was the
prototype), and which was ultimately, Dicey considered, to
turn into the misguided doctrines of socialism. But Dicey
did not see the flaw in Benthamite *laissez-faire*.[9] It was not
thorough-going:

> There is no real reconciliation between the argument of
> the natural, and the argument of the artificial, identity of
> interests. The one supposes that every individual by
> promoting his own interests promotes those of the whole
> society. The other supposes that there are some
> individuals who by promoting their own interest damage
> those of somebody else. The maxim, 'the greatest hap-
> piness of the greatest number', was a confession that the
> two arguments could not be reconciled, for it admits by
> implication that the interests pursued by each individual
> do not necessarily lead to the 'greatest good for all'.

Benthamism therefore had a 'great internal contradiction': it
led 'either to complete bureaucracy or complete anar-
chism'.[10] In practice it led to an inescapable compromise,
encouraging the individual to pursue his own interests, but
national and local government to promote collectivist solutions. The 1834 Poor Law Amendment Act, the 1835
Municipal Corporations Act, and the Factory Acts of 1833
and after were *laissez-faire* compromises of this kind. Bentham had said in effect that existing forms of State regulation were harmful because they did not promote a harmony
of interests. 'He wanted to sweep most of the existing
regulations away, and he believed that most things would be
better unregulated than ill-regulated as they were.'[11] Or, it
should be added, as they *might be*. Any form of regulation,
therefore, was a departure from pure doctrine, and departures were many in the society which saw itself to a large
degree as a *laissez-faire* State.

The features we have suggested so far offer a tentative
picture of some of the processes of change, largely in terms
of human aspiration and assumptions about status and mob-

ility; they also indicate some of the awareness of these new
processes of change, which had not been present to any
significant extent in the Britain of, say, 1780. There were, of
course, other sources of momentum, and an intricate point
of historical discussion is the relative priority to be given to
one factor or another in determining the growth of industrial Britain. This attempt to establish priorities is characteristic of any historical or sociological discussion. The role
of will and consciousness, of the religious and philosophical
assumptions by which people's lives are governed, the role
of economic laws and of the ownership of the means of
production – all such widely different considerations are
involved in the discussion of, for instance, the causes of the
Industrial Revolution or of class relations in the twentieth
century. Marxism has stressed economic-productive determinants as decisive in social change. Modern sociology,
both Marxist and non-Marxist, has suggested a wider range
of determinants that need to be considered in this process.
Our discussion of the nineteenth century will indicate those
points at which theories about society itself were changing.

The Industrial Revolution

The economic facts of the Industrial Revolution, suggested
Max Weber, are meaningless without an understanding of
the framework of belief in which it took place. He saw the
central fact of modern capitalism as having its foundations
in certain, largely Calvinist, assumptions about the desirability of profit – assumptions which make worldly activity
possible, and which therefore explain the important role of
nonconformity in early industrial and commercial expansion. The kernel of the argument about Protestant
asceticism runs as follows:

> ... asceticism looked upon the pursuit of wealth as an
> end in itself as highly reprehensible; but the attainment of
> it as a fruit of labour in a calling was a sign of God's
> blessing ... the religious valuation of restless, continu-
> ous, systematic work in a worldly calling, as the means
> to asceticism ... must have been the most powerful

conceivable lever for the expansion of that attitude toward life which we have here called the spirit of capitalism.

What this attitude did, Weber suggests, was sanction the acquisition of wealth, at the same time as *imposing restraints on its consumption*. The inevitable result was the accumulation and productive investment of capital. 'The Puritan outlook . . . stood at the cradle of the modern economic man.'[12]

Weber's thesis, which has been widely debated, underlines one set of factors in the early development of industrial society. There are many others which can be seen to have directly affected industrial improvement and expansion.

Changes in agriculture affected developments in a series of ways, most obviously in making it possible to supply a larger population, differently distributed. Historians have had to modify some of the ideas that used to be held about the reasons for the dramatic improvements in agriculture that took place in the second half of the eighteenth century, and about the effects of the enclosures movement. Neither, it is certain, took place so abruptly or had the abrupt effects that were for a long time assumed. The agricultural revolution of the eighteenth century released 'the latent powers of the soil on a scale that was new in human history; but it was not accomplished by means of a mechanical revolution'. Nor, it is suggested, was this achieved through 'a ruthless reduction of the rural population as a prelude to the formation of an industrial proletariat . . . there is no reason to think that the labour force engaged in agricultural operations fell'. The revolution lay in the manner of farming, the spread of 'alternate' agriculture, a process accelerated in the second half of the eighteenth century. Even though the processes were perhaps more cumulative and less dramatic than previously thought, this departure from traditional practice.

marks a new agricultural epoch, and its acceleration in the second half of the eighteenth century in the form of the classical enclosure movement and the first unmistakable steps by the agricultural pioneers towards 'high farming', mark the opening of the Agricultural Revolution just as surely as factory production marks the dawn of a new industrial age. From this time, the Agricultural

Revolution reveals itself as an indispensable and integral
part of the Industrial Revolution . . .[13]

Of the Industrial Revolution itself we can do no more
here than construct a simple economic-historical model.
The cotton industry, unlike the woollen industry, was
unhampered by regulations; it had available supplies of raw
material, available supplies of labour, a suitable climate in
both Lancashire and Scotland, and convenient resources of
water and fuel. It made the leap forward which was most
dramatic in social terms. Cotton was also the industry in
which technical innovation was most sought and achieved,
and it was able, slowly, to harness the power of steam. Coal
was a traditional industry and capable of expansion.
Estimated production in 1750 was 4·8 million tons, and by
1800 it had more than doubled (to 10 million tons). By the
end of the eighteenth century cotton had made a visible
impact on the economic geography of Britain, and
precipitated the great concentration of population in northern England that was an outstanding feature of Britain's
nineteenth-century history, affecting both the redistribution
of population inside England, and immigration into
England, most notably from Ireland. The impact of coal
was in this respect less direct, although it became increasingly a focus of awareness of the nature of industrial society.
By the 1860s Matthew Arnold could complain that coal had
been spoken of as 'the real basis of our national greatness; if
our coal runs short, there is an end of the greatness of
England . . . what an unsound habit of mind it must be
which makes us talk of things like coal or iron as constitut-
ing the greatness of England'.[14]
    The role of the iron industry was, in the short run, less
spectacular, but in the long term more fundamental to industrial growth than cotton. Henry Cort's puddling process
made cheap wrought iron available from the beginning of
the 1780s, enabling fifteen times as much iron (of high
quality) to be produced by the same amount of power, in
the same time. The ancient use of timber gave place to coal;
coal and iron together made a fundamental contribution to
the new sort of 'greatness of England'.

Innovation and invention obviously played crucial parts in the cumulative processes that led to the industrial breakthrough of the last decades of the eighteenth century. Equally obviously, each of the industrial developments we have mentioned, and all of the technical developments within them, had repercussions of a major order inside and outside the industry concerned. Arkwright's water frame (1769) for spinning meant factory production in an entirely new sense. Watt's steam engine (1769), later developed with rotary motion (1781), made it possible to erect mills in towns. Cort's puddling process not only contributed to the expansion of the coal industry, but, at a later stage of industrial growth, made railways possible. There was, therefore, at the end of the eighteenth century a cluster of inventions and technical developments, in agriculture as well as industry, which contributed saliently to the processes we describe as the Industrial Revolution.

There is, however, a complex of other economic and commercial factors to be borne in mind. There were skills and resources available to be utilized, experience of banking (the number of country banks rose from 100 in 1780 to 370 in 1800) and business enterprise to be drawn upon. There were during the eighteenth century periods of accelerated capital formation. There were periods of good harvest, and there was an upward trend in population.

A vital link in this interwoven set of developments was transport. On the basis of roads industrialization could not have gone so far so quickly. From the first Turnpike Act of 1663, attempts at improvement in road conditions had been slowly made, but the results were uneven, often short-lived and frequently non-existent. The completion of the Duke of Bridgewater's canal linking Worsley and Manchester in 1761 (which reduced the price of coal in Manchester by half), and then of the extension linking Manchester and Liverpool, opened an era of canal construction which was long enough to play a considerable part in the process of transforming Britain's undeveloped 'interior'. Between 1760 and 1840 the length of navigable waterways in England and Wales nearly trebled. With the advent of the canals 'England ceased to be hollow'.[15] Britain in general also ceased, economically, to be a confederation of relatively self-dependent regions. The history of industrialization, in the view of H. L. Beales, 'is the history of integration – the unification of the single society'.[16] The construction of a canal network did more than anything else to fill up the 'hollow' and at the same time made a major contribution to economic development by providing a source of experienced manpower for the building of the railways. The Industrial Revolution may have been, in its first phase, predominantly a change in methods of production, but the canal system was an indispensable feature of it.

The details which add up to the Industrial Revolution, therefore, included but were not entirely conditioned by scientific and technical advances. Such advances do not in themselves explain the revolution. Only in conjunction with other considerations, including the history of British overseas trade, the Protestant ethic and resources of human ingenuity, do these advances explain what made Britain the first industrial nation.[17]

Population

As the first population census was taken in 1801 and as information culled from sources before that date is defective, the discussion of population trends from the late eighteenth century presents a double set of problems. The first is simply to try to reconstruct population changes, and the second is to account for them.[18]

Population trends in their broad contours, and in the related questions of family and social structure, the growth of towns, occupational patterns and styles of life, are of central importance to analyses of social change.[19]

It is likely that the population of Great Britain at the beginning of the eighteenth century was of the order of 6·5 million. In 1750, at the beginning of the upward trend that was to be maintained right through the nineteenth and twentieth centuries, it was about 8 million. The census of 1801 reported a population of 10·5 million. In the next twenty years over 3·5 million were added to the population. Despite reservations about these figures (including the unreliability of the early census returns) it is certain that conditions conspired from approximately the 1740s to produce the possibility of a sustained increase in population. There had been increases in population, of course, in previous centuries, but these had been 'speedily cancelled by a single peak in the death rate. The difference was that the growth that we date from the 1740s was *not* reversed and indeed it accelerated to unprecedented levels in the 1780s and went on accelerating to a peak rate of growth in the decade 1811–21.'[20]

An increase (or decrease) in population can be the result of only two factors – birth rate and death rate (leaving aside here the third and less significant factor of migration). Prolonged controversies have raged around the likely contribution of one or both of these factors to the upward population curve of the eighteenth century. For a long time it was held that significant influences towards a fall in the mortality rate were the most likely explanation, especially as only a slight fall is necessary to have considerable long-term repercussions. It was held that improved food supplies, resulting from a sequence of good harvests, partly from improved farming methods, as well as improved hygiene and medical facilities, were the main contributory causes. Medical history no longer confidently upholds this view, although attempts are still made to demonstrate that health factors influenced, or may have influenced, a decrease in the death rate.[21] Other explanations relate to a higher birth rate, since it is known that population grew in this period even where there was no improvement in or access to any medical facilities:

It would seem . . . that increase in population, even in England, must have been largely a rural phenomenon deriving from causes to be found in the countryside, where access to doctors, hospitals and clinics would be least easy. This endorses the lesson, not only of Connaught but of other parts of Ireland as well, that there could be large increases of population in areas in which the improvement of medical facilities in the late eighteenth and early nineteenth centuries were unlikely to have had much effect.[22]

The discussion is being carried primarily into local studies. Alan Armstrong's study of York, for example, suggests, on the basis of 'somewhat insecure statistics', that between about 1750 and the 1820s mortality fell. The evidence available 'gives little support to the idea of rising fertility as a motor of population growth' in this period.[23] It is not yet possible, however, to make national deductions from such studies – and indeed national pictures of family and social structures, as well as of population trends, may continue to be difficult or impossible to draw.[24] Other factors that have been discussed in relation to the population growth have included the demand for agricultural labour, the 'family allowances' built into Speenhamland poor relief, the age of marriage and resistance to epidemic. Edward Thompson, pointing to the weakening of taboos against early marriage, the decline in 'living in' among farm servants and apprentices, genetic selection of the most fertile and other possible explanations, reflects that 'the arguments are complex and are best left, for the time being, with the demographers'.[25]

Industrialization and democracy

Industrializing (and urbanizing) Britain was rooted, therefore, in profound processes of social change. We have glanced at some starting points of the enormous developments that were to take place in population, the economy and society between the end of the eighteenth century and the middle of the nineteenth century.

Between 1801 and 1851 the population of Great Britain doubled, to attain nearly 21 million. In 1780 some 40 to 45 per cent of the labour force was employed in agriculture, and some 25 per cent in mining, manufacture and building. By 1851 the figures were 21 per cent and 42 per cent respectively. Urban problems were coming more and more into prominence. By the end of the 1830s government had committed itself to the regulation of poor relief, to the assistance and inspection (though not control) of education, to the protection of child and female (though not adult male) labour. By the 1850s the growing commercial and professional middle class had added new public schools and London

University to the traditional public and grammar school network (plus Oxford and Cambridge), which was unable, or unwilling, to cater for the new demands. Scotland, of course, had its parochial schools and four universities, though all of these underwent their decline, crises and inquiries in the early nineteenth century.

The date chart of the first half of the century would be, to cover the range of our interests, immense and meaningless. Even to look for the stepping-stones across the 1840s, for example, would take us through the Improvement Acts, particularly in Lancashire, to the Public Health Act of 1848. It would take us through the Mines Act of 1842, prohibiting labour by females and children below the age of ten underground, the Ten-Hour Act of 1847 (and the related Act of 1850), and the attempts to regulate the employment of boy chimney-sweeps (one of the many Acts was passed in 1840, although the practice was not successfully ended until 1875). It would take us through the Bank Charter Act of 1844, which restricted note-issue in England and Wales to the Bank of England and strengthened Britain's role as the commercial and financial centre of the world. A detailed look at the first part of the century would take us through periods of economic activity which have been described in the following terms:

1815–21, *peace and breakdown*: after mounting prosperity from 1811, a hectic postwar boom, followed by a crash in 1819.

1821–36, *recovery and expansion*: the biggest relative increase in industrial output of the century, a rise in real incomes, the vigorous promotion of trade and industry, a decline in prices (continuing until 1853).

1836–42, *critical depression*: the boom in railway and shipbuilding breaks in 1836, a fall in real incomes (followed, from 1842–73, by a period of 'growth by leaps and bounds').[26]

By mid-century Britain, as it has been variously described, was the 'Industry State', the 'Fuel State', the 'Workshop of the World'.

An economy, a society, in the early stages of industrialization, does not move forward uniformly or rhythmically. Across the early nineteenth century stretch the trails of enormously uneven economic and social developments. There are forms of social improvement and of social disaster, subtle and brutal changes in patterns and standards of life. The ways in which the growth-points we have established carry through into mid-Victorian Britain will emerge if we take one example, that of the notion of democracy.

Without defining this concept in detail, we take it to refer to three things: the way power is, or is not, diffused through society, and the extent to which those who exercise it are accountable; the right and ability of individuals and groups of individuals to dissent; and the ability of the individual to develop and express himself adequately within that society. 'I do not know of any society', said C. Wright Mills, 'which is altogether democratic', but by acting 'as if we were in a fully democratic society . . . we are attempting to remove the "as if".'[27] In terms of the major changes in the half-century or more from the departures of the 1780s and 1790s, such a definition and discussion reveal some of the most uneven of the developments. The central fact of power, for example, was the expansion of the middle class. We shall discuss the concept of 'class' in later chapters, but it is important to note that in the early nineteenth century those who belonged to the middle class had no difficulty in identifying themselves. The expansion of old industries and the inauguration of new ones led to more widely based industrial and commercial prosperities, to the growth of new clerical and managerial occupations, and of new professions. The profession of architect, to take a single instance, is closely related to the new order. The Industrial Revolution had led to the involvement of industrialists and men of commerce in town government, and the middle class 'was making its voice heard in architectural matters through the medium of the building committees. Theatre shareholders, prison boards, the committees for new public buildings, all became important clients, and their influence on the development of professionalism was considerable.'

Architects now dealt not with patrons but with committees. Their status and interests needed protection. The

Institute of British Architects, founded in 1834, 'rigidly defined the relations of its members not only with other architects but with clients and builders'.[28] The profession of civil engineer, or of solicitor, could also illustrate the scale of growth of the professional wing of the middle class. If the middle class was a reality and wielded industrial power, as well as social power of many kinds, it did not wield power in the obvious political sense, in the first half of the century. Its involvement in the fight up to the 1832 Reform Act was a conscious bid for such power, at least in the negative sense of removing some of the prominent bars to its participation in it. The Act disfranchised some rotten boroughs and created new parliamentary seats (Sheffield and Manchester, for example), gave the vote in the boroughs to owners of property of a value of ten pounds or more, and (to balance the urban increase) increased the number of seats in some counties and extended the county vote. A quarter of a million new, for the most part urban middle-class, voters were admitted. The middle class was closer to the centre of power, but parliament continued to be a landowners' parliament. The old order did not collapse – it fought back, adapted itself, absorbed its challengers. To Cobden or Bright the old landed order was 'feudalism', and neither of them 'disguised their desire to see the whole "feudal order" disappear along with the Corn Laws'. The Corn Laws went in 1846, but in 1863 Cobden was still meditating 'that feudalism is every day more and more in the ascendant in political and social life'.[29]

The central argument of Major Cartwright's reform movements of the 1780s had been that property should qualify for the vote. The central argument of Cobden and Bright and the Manchester School of Liberal politics was that the middle class had the greatest right and the greatest ability to govern. In 1850 they were masters of urban society, but they did not, in the fullest sense, govern.

The way in which power was exercised in early nineteenth-century Britain is bound up with the second part of our discussion of democracy – the right to dissent. Working-class dissent and organization is the most important index of the consciousness of change, not only of *response* to change but of awareness of the need to *control* it. Working-class and popular movements are in this period an extension, through the zigzags of economic growth, of the aspirations formulated in the 1790s. They reach out, not towards the kind of political adjustments sought by the radical associations of the eighteenth century, but towards a complete revision of the terms of social progress. The popular political radicalism which preceded the Reform Act of 1832, and the radicals' sense of betrayal which accompanied and followed it, were of a new scale and passion. With increasing momentum through the early century, in defiance of stamp tax and the law, the popular radical press self-consciously fought to change the framework of democratic discussion. Chartism, as a popular movement for political reform, on a scale and with a basis of organization and propaganda quite new in history, pursued with varying success the right to participate in the nation's affairs, in a major way to 1848, and in a diminishing way beyond. For his *Political Register* William Cobbett fled the country after the Habeas Corpus Act was suspended in 1817; for his publishing and bookselling Richard Carlile went to jail in 1819; for selling O'Brien's *Poor Man's Guardian* scores went to jail in the early 1830s; and for being militant Chartists men went to jail in 1839, and after.

The organized demand for a share in political power was not, however, the only form of popular dissent. The Owenite co-operative movement from the late 1820s looked towards co-operative production and community settlement, in an attempt to turn its back on the chaos of capitalist industrialism. Trade unionism in different phases, after the repeal of the Combination Acts in 1824, looked towards wider forms of self-protection, and even, in some cases, in an Owenite phase in the early 1830s, the by-passing of capitalist forms of production. By 1850 co-operation, in the form that had come out of Rochdale in 1844, was a growing network of consumers' organizations, and trade unionism was about to enter the New Model phase, with a sophisticated form of the organization of such skilled workers as engineers, carpenters and joiners, and iron-founders. If the middle class had not achieved its full share of power, the working class had achieved, in any obvious sense, none of it. Not until 1867 was the urban working man, generally speaking, admitted to the franchise. Not until 1855 were the 'taxes on knowledge' finally removed from the press, although already the trend towards mass communications had given the advantage in reaching the minds of men to the larger, the more efficient, organization (such as the *Daily Telegraph*, selling at one penny after the removal of the final tax in 1855, and at a rate of 141,000 copies a day by 1861).

The discussion of democracy reaches out in all directions, and the third factor – the position of the individual in society – must be left as an implication of the discussion so far. All we have done is to hint at some of the dynamics of a Britain which by 1850 had come to operate within quite different terms of reference, but in which the major processes of political and social change were still far from complete. Implied in the change that we have suggested is the major contrast between Britain as a nation in 1850 and in the late eighteenth century – a contrast between the essentially local, regional or metropolitan activities of society at the earlier point, and the substantially nation-wide ones at the later. Chartism itself, for example, was in every sense a *national* movement, reaching into every corner of Great Britain, including Chartist churches in Scotland and Chartist insurrection in Wales. The *Daily Telegraph* was a *national* newspaper, carried on a nation-wide network of railways. The economy was a *national* one, developing national economic responses, possible with national communications and a single national market (resulting in new forms of standardization, as bricks and foodstuffs, for example, were carried throughout the country). Organization, from trade unions to banks (there were 554 of the latter in 1826 and, by a process of unification, 311 in 1842), was becoming more national in scope. Thomas Cook, on 5 July 1841, took 570 people from Leicester to Loughborough by rail for a temperance convention. The fare was one shilling, and the excursion age had opened. Social tension, poverty and deprivation were still facts, but a belief in a never-ending, ever-widening prosperity was a pervasive mid-century view.

2 *Hardware at the Great Exhibition, 1851*

All of this, and more, was symbolized in the Great Exhibition and, for this reason, 1851 is probably the most useful date to use as the doorway into Modern Britain. The Great Exhibition in Hyde Park was designed to demonstrate the confidence of Britain's manufacturers, the supremacy of British trade, manufacture and finance. It was intended to be, and was, a symbol of British material progress. In itself it was a feat of technology. It contained nearly a million square feet of glass (the window tax had just been lifted), 3,300 iron columns and over 2,000 girders. It showed the produce of 7,381 British and Empire, and 6,556 foreign, exhibitors to over six million visitors, between 1 May and 11 October 1851 (including the thousands brought on excursions by Thomas Cook). Daily tickets ranged in price between one shilling and five shillings; 934,691 bath buns and 870,027 plain buns were sold. Sunday opening was not allowed. Nor were alcohol, smoking or dogs.[30] *Punch* (and not only *Punch*) reminded its readers of the realities of the working conditions in which the exhibits were produced, but the Exhibition went its course as an immense achievement. And workers, to the surprise of many, bought shilling tickets and alcohol-free drinks, and broke no windows.

The concept, the fact, the implications, of industrialization had arrived. Entangled with it were the population, social, political and other changes which are the main themes of this book. The hardware and the household paraphernalia of the Great Exhibition, the excursions and the technology, were symbolic of all of this range of changes – and none more than that of urban growth.

Notes

1 NEIL SMELSER *Social Change in the Industrial Revolution*, Ch. X (London, 1959).

2 PETER LASLETT *The World we have Lost*, Ch. 8 (London, 1965).

3 JOHN FOSTER *Class Struggle and the Industrial Revolution*, p. 41 (London, 1974). See *passim* for a lively discussion of economic and social developments in three English towns.

4 PHYLLIS DEANE *The First Industrial Revolution*, pp. 11–12 (London, 1965).

5 T. S. ASHTON *The Industrial Revolution 1760–1830*, p. 127 (London, 1948; 1964 edition).

6 JOHN CARTWRIGHT *Six Letters to the Marquis of Tavistock on a Reform of the Commons House of Parliament*, p. 23 (London, 1812).

7 *An Appeal to the Nation by the Union for Parliamentary Reform according to the Constitution*, p. 61 (London, 1812).

8 For an account of this world (though with a strong anti-radical bias), see E. C. BLACK *The Association, British Extraparliamentary Political Organisation, 1769–1793* (Cambridge, Mass., 1963). See also GEORGE RUDÉ *The Crowd in History, 1730–1848* (New York, 1964).

9 For a critical dissection of Dicey's assumptions, see J. B. BREBNER 'Laissez-faire and state intervention in nineteenth-century Britain', in E. M. CARUS-WILSON (ed.) *Essays in Economic History*, III (London, 1962).

10 S. E. FINER *The Life and Times of Sir Edwin Chadwick*, pp. 24–5 (London, 1952).

11 G. D. H. COLE 'Ideals and beliefs of the Victorians', *Essays in Social Theory*, p. 196 (London, 1952; 1962 edition).

12 MAX WEBER *The Protestant Ethic and the Spirit of Capitalism* (published in German 1904–5, English 1930). Quotations are from Ch. V, 'Asceticism and the spirit of capitalism'. For an attack on Weber's thesis, see H. R. TREVOR-ROPER *Religion, the Reformation and Social Change* (London, 1967).

13 J. D. CHAMBERS and G. E. MINGAY *The Agricultural Revolution 1750–1880*, pp. 3–5 (London, 1966).

14 MATTHEW ARNOLD *Culture and Anarchy*, p. 12 (London, 1869; 1906 edition).

15 G. D. H. COLE 'Roads, rivers and canals', *Persons and Periods*, p. 98 (Harmondsworth, 1937). See, in general, CHARLES HADFIELD *The Canal Age* (Newton Abbot, 1968).

16 H. L. BEALES *The Industrial Revolution 1750–1850*, p. 13 (London, 1928; 1958 edition).

17 For a survey of attitudes to all these factors, see R. M. HARTWELL 'The causes of the Industrial Revolution', *Economic History Review*, 1966, pp. 164–82. See also FOSTER *Class Struggle and the Industrial Revolution*, Ch. 2, 'Industrialization and society'.

18 The largest compilation of evidence and argument is in D. V. GLASS and D. E. C. EVERSLEY (eds.) *Population in History* (London, 1965). Some relevant material is in MICHAEL DRAKE (ed.) *Population in Industrialization* (London, 1969).

19 See F. A. WRIGLEY (ed.) *An Introduction to English Historical Demography* (London, 1966), and PETER LASLETT (ed.) *Household and Family in Past Time* (Cambridge, 1972), Introduction, 'The history of the family'.

20 WRIGLEY *Introduction to English Historical Demography*, p. 24.

21 See DRAKE *Population in Industrialization*.

22 G. KITSON CLARK *The Making of Victorian England*, pp. 69–70 (London, 1962).

23 ALAN ARMSTRONG *Stability and Change in an English County Town: a social study of York 1801–51*, p. 196 (Cambridge, 1974).

24 See ibid., Ch. 8, for a discussion of the national and international implications.

25 E. P. THOMPSON *The Making of the English Working Class*, pp. 323–4 (London, 1963).

26 Summarized from S. G. CHECKLAND *The Rise of Industrial Society in England 1815–1885*, Ch. 2 (London, 1964).

27 C. WRIGHT MILLS *The Sociological Imagination*, pp. 188–9 (New York, 1959).

28 FRANK JENKINS 'The Victorian architectural profession', in

PETER FERRIDAY (ed.) *Victorian Architecture*, pp. 40–1 (London, 1963).

29 Quoted in ASA BRIGGS 'Cobden and Bright', *History Today*, VII, 8, August 1957, p. 503.

30 G. H. GIBBS-SMITH *The Great Exhibition of 1851* (London, 1950).

2 Towns, people and problems

Urban growth

Neither towns nor urban problems were a product of the nineteenth century. Industrialization, however, generated new energies of urban growth. Industry and transport may produce new towns – as the canals did at Stourport and Goole, the railways at Swindon and at first coal transport and then iron-ore mining at Middlesbrough. More frequently, however, they confirm the status of the larger existing urban centres. Generally speaking, the largest towns in 1801 have remained among the largest.

The processes of urban growth, particularly across the middle of the nineteenth century, highlight changes in social conditions and attitudes to social policy and help to explain some of the patterns of life, relationships and attitudes which were projected into twentieth-century Britain.

Between 1801 and 1891, the population of England and Wales increased by roughly 20 million. The rural population (living in places with fewer than 5,000 people) in this period increased from 6·6 to 9·2 million, and urban population from 2·3 to 19·8 million. Eighty per cent of the total increase went, therefore, to the towns. Not only did urban

Britain increase disproportionately to rural Britain – there were also disparate increases in the rate of growth of the towns themselves. Towns with a population of over 20,000 increased at approximately double that of towns of 5,000 to 20,000. As natural increase (excess of births over deaths) was not larger – and in fact in the early years of the century was considerably smaller – in the towns than in the country-side, the more rapid growth of towns in general and large towns in particular could have been caused only by migration.

The balance of urban to rural population in Britain was roughly equal at mid-century. By 1891 the ratio was roughly 21 million to 8 million for Great Britain as a whole. The highest percentage growth rates of the major cities tended to occur roughly between the 1820s and 1850s. Migration to cities had been common in pre-industrial Britain, but cities had been comparatively small in number, and the high death rate had kept down their actual rate of expansion. The growth of towns in the nineteenth century cannot be attributed automatically to the overall increase in population. The increasing population was a *condition* of such growth, but

> it has not necessarily been a positive cause of their *relatively* rapid growth as compared with the remainder of the population – a cause, that is, of the phenomenon of concentration. Positive forces may exist to drive a larger proportion of people into the rural districts notwithstanding an all-round increase in population . . . the growth of cities must be studied as a part of the question of distribution of population, which is always dependent upon the economic organisation of society.[1]

The factors which induce a redistribution of population in this way are both negative and positive. Men may leave the countryside because there is surplus labour; and in fact they did so. Increased agricultural efficiency, together with a rising population, caused city-ward migration, contributing to a larger growth rate for the cities (though not a depopulation of the countryside in absolute terms).

The positive attraction of urban centres was, of course,

the demand for labour. Machinery and factory organization were central factors in the new patterns of the distribution of the population, although in many cases (particularly in centres with natural communications and trading advantages) industrial developments led to higher densities in existing urban areas. Once a momentum of expansion has been established, the process is self-sustaining:

> When an industry has been established in a region it creates conditions favourable to its own growth; concentration brings advantages and these advantages in turn strengthen the attraction not only of the region but also of the locality in which the industry has started. Thus, regional concentration, due in the first place to natural advantages, fosters local concentration and the growth of large urban areas. But these, in turn, not only offer further advantages to the 'basic' industries but also offer advantages to other industries. Thus the chosen district tends to grow like a snow-ball and become a large conurbation.[2]

When an industry has become established it gives rise to what economists have called 'external economies'. An industry such as the cotton industry produced workers with the appropriate skills, and provided a market for them. Groups of factories, of industries, create 'general' external economies, by evolving a network of industrial and urban services, notably transport, which themselves act as focal points of attraction. This was the basis for the growth of towns with a dominant industry, such as the steel trades in Sheffield and cotton in Manchester. Sheffield, for example, grew from 45·8 thousand in 1800 to 135·3 thousand in 1850 and 324·2 thousand in 1890 (though, in addition to natural increase and migration, the extension of boundaries to incorporate other villages and townships was an important factor). Manchester and Salford between 1800 and 1890 grew from 90·4 thousand to 703·5 thousand. This was the basis also of the growth of towns like Liverpool, Hull, Birmingham and Glasgow, with more 'general external economies'. Glasgow, with 77·1 thousand in 1800, had reached 329·1 thousand in 1850.

The intensity and direction of city-ward migration was not a constant pattern, but was affected by varying factors, such as the revolution in transport caused by the railways from the 1830s, the pull of different regions at different times, with the disparate growth rates of different industries, and the presence of opportunities (including those for immigrant Irish labour) on a new scale in new situations. In the early nineteenth century the largest towns, we have suggested, gained most population; London was no exception. Its expanding population, commerce and 'external economies' were in every sense the result of the economic and social mobilities we have seen projected into the nineteenth century. The 'million-mark cities', commented the Barlow Commission in 1940, had in the past century 'tended to increase their populations at rates at least twice as great as the mean rate of increase for their respective countries, and especially is this characteristic of the capital cities'. In every intercensal period of the nineteenth century the percentage growth in the population of Greater London was substantially greater (at its greatest nearly double) than the national percentage. The population of Great Britain was in 1911 roughly four times what it had been in 1801. In the same period the population of Greater London had grown from 1·1 million to 7·3 million.[3]

Transport

Britain's progress towards urbanization was in many respects most clearly confirmed by the achievement of an unprecedented transport system.

The canals, as we have indicated, had contributed to the efficiency of movement required by early industrialization, to the expansion of industries dependent on efficient transport for marketing (the Staffordshire potteries are an outstanding example), and even to the mushroom growth of certain towns. The canals and railways shared in common the fact that, through their speculative construction, they opened up new areas to industrial expansion, at the same time as they both 'often assisted industries to remain in their traditional centres'.[4]

By mid-century the railways had made it impossible for
social advance to be effectively discussed, as it had often
been in the early decades of the century, in terms of nostal-
gic glances backwards to pre-industrial society. The railways in a sense ultimately helped to make it possible for
Englishmen to remain country-dwellers, or at least seaside
homers, at heart by offering increasingly long-term and
long-distance opportunities for ritual holiday-making. Their
most conspicuous achievement by mid-nineteenth century,
however, was the final unification of the economy through
the cementing of a pattern of inter-urban relationships.
They linked, and confirmed, a network of major regional
centres, each becoming the focus for further transport and
commercial developments.

The fact that the railways were large-scale units was in
itself important. Britain opted for private railway ownership. The sponsorship of railway companies was an elaborate and expensive business, involving a private Act of
Parliament. In the absence of State intervention and ownership, which (unlike, for example, in Belgium) was not seriously advocated in Britain, it became accepted as socially
necessary for the pooled resources of the joint-stock company to be developed. The formation of such companies
was, therefore, one of the main steps along the road to the
large-scale enterprises which became readily possible
throughout the economy after the crucial limited liability
and joint-stock legislation of the 1850s.

The fact that the promotion of a railway company was a
public enterprise, raising share-capital and requiring an Act
of Parliament, was of equal importance. *Laissez-faire* had no
railway policy, and government in the 1830s vacillated,
unwilling to regulate or leave alone.[5] The State, however,
was involved in railway developments in a way in which it
was involved in nothing else. It had to sanction the building
of lines, choose between rival schemes, and be concerned
with problems of competition and co-ordination. Factors
affecting the safety and convenience of the public had to be
borne in mind. A Railway Department was first established
in 1840. In 1844 Parliament legislated for companies to
provide one train each week-day at a speed of not less than

3 *Waiting for the excursion train, 1880*

twelve miles an hour and at a fare of not more than a penny a mile (the 'Parliamentary Trains'). Inspection of track, design of carriages, speed of trains, were accepted as legitimate concerns of a department of government (at a time when the principle of government inspection had also been accepted, in education, for example, from 1839, and in factories from 1833, and at a time when other forms of regulation were beginning to be admitted). The railways, therefore, mark an important step towards the acceptance of the idea of the Responsible State.

The history of railway expansion in Britain has been divided into five periods: (1) the period of experiment, 1820–30; (2) the period of infancy, 1830–45; (3) the period of mania, 1845–8; (4) the period of competition by great

Companies, 1848–59; (5) the period of contractors' lines and Companies' extensions, 1859–65.[6] By the end of the third of these periods the main trunk system was completed or about to be completed, and only the regional networks remained to be filled out. By 1836 London had Euston Station with its once familiar classical portico (celebrating the completion of a railway line from London to Birmingham, 'rightly considered an overwhelming achievement of the human intellect').[7] Trains were running from Paddington to the West Country from 1841. Victoria Station was opened in 1850 and King's Cross was built in 1851–2 (incorporating the clock from the Crystal Palace, which was moved to Sydenham when the Great Exhibition closed).

The establishment of the railways meant doom for the canals, which had in any case by the early decades of the century taken advantage of their monopoly position to raise charges, and had become incapable of carrying the volume of freight efficiently and rapidly. The railways spelled doom also for the increasingly rapid and efficient coaching and posting network, which could not stand up to the competition. Economically the impact of the railways in increasing the speed of delivery (of goods and passengers), in lowering costs and in cementing the nation-wide market, was considerable. When, in addition, are added their effect on a whole complex of related industries (building, iron and steel, engineering, etc.) and the accelerated export of railway track, rolling stock, engineering know-how and experienced labour, there can be no doubt about the impetus given to the second phase of industrialization.

Socially also, the consequences of railway expansion were vast. The railways carried post and newspapers, providing a new and radically different outlet for the book and periodical trade in the station bookstall, which started life as a concession 'to injured employees or their widows, who vended an unappetizing stock of newspapers, magazines, beer, sandwiches and sweets to jaded travelers'.[8] By the end of the 1850s, however, the trade was virtually a monopoly in the hands of W. H. Smith. The railways led to the use of standard Greenwich time (in order to standardize timetables) and provided facilities for expanding the electric telegraph. They also brought new crafts, a renovation of the hotel and inn industry, and new standardizations in goods, architecture and manners.

It is not clear whether it is right to argue 'that of all classes in the community, the railway brought most benefit to the poor'.[9] Certainly the changes wrought in ordinary people's lives by the new transport were immense in the long run. Britain ceased, in senses other than the economic one, to be hollow. Slowly, but inevitably, the age of the tour, the heroic discovery of North Wales, the Lakes or the Scottish lochs, and the elegance of the spa, Brighton and Scarborough, was replaced by the age of public transport and the day-trip. Although cheap fares, from Gladstone's Regulation of Railways Act of 1844 (and later the Cheap Trains Act of 1883) were an incentive to suburban growth, the importance of their impact on working-class housing before the end of the nineteenth century must not be exaggerated. The early railway lines opened in the vicinity of London affected only those strata of the community which could afford to travel and to build homes at a greater distance, or buy those built speculatively. Small margins of extra cost and distance were of crucial importance to people in the lower income groups. This was true even with London's improved transport system (the first underground line was opened in 1863), and a particularly striking example occurred in 1877, when the London Metropolitan Board of Works proposed in a bill to try to accommodate people displaced from the West End (by road and other improvements) in Gray's Inn Road, a mile or so from their previous dwellings. The Board considered this reasonable, given the small distance involved, and the fact that most of the workers concerned were migratory. It was shown in evidence, however, that these allegedly migratory workers often remained 'weekly tenants in one house for ten or twenty years, and in some cases have been known to occupy the same room as weekly tenants for forty or fifty years'. What was more important, however, was that:

> Their employment obliges them to remain stationary. The fashionable shops of Regent Street, Bond Street and St James's do not move, and they require their workmen near at hand. The numerous coach factories are still about Long Acre. The large warehouses of Crosse & Blackwell in Soho Square, where over 1,000 hands are employed – men, women, boys, and girls – are supplied from the neighbouring streets. Covent Garden, with all its dependents of coster-mongers and labourers, who have to begin work at four in the morning, is still flourishing, and therefore these working people now living on the West-End line of improvement must continue to live there, or in many cases they would be thrown out of employment . . .

The extra mile represented 'an hour a day in time lost, to say nothing of the fatigue'. The loss of an hour a day, at a wage rate of 5*d* an hour, meant 2*s* 6*d* a week, 'a tax that would be put on the workmen by removing them to a distance'.[10] Urban 'improvements' of many kinds (what A. S. Wohl called 'the continual dislocation caused by street, commercial, and railway building'[11]) resulted in major occupational and housing difficulties for working-class families. The growth of towns and transport had helped to loosen traditional obstacles to geographical mobility, but had created others.

Housing

There remained in the middle of the century considerable obstacles to the growth of new working-class residential areas, though the middle-class suburban villa now became a reality. The railways transformed the transportation of perishable food: market gardening on the fringe of cities became of critical importance, fish and meat could be transported greater distances inland (becoming of even greater importance in the 1860s and 1870s when the steam trawler and the use of ice for preservation put fish imports on a new footing, and from the 1870s the large-scale trans-oceanic transportation of frozen meat and grain was made possible).[12] Nuisances, similarly, could be removed from town centres, and 'slaughtering, like cow-keeping and other trades dependent on perishable produce, naturally tended to move from the City [of London] as the use of the railways for transporting such produce increased'.[13]

If Goole and Birmingham are rooted in the canal age, towns like Crewe and Swindon, both created in the 1840s to serve railway needs, are more totally products of their age. Given the arrangements for company housing, and the organization or financing of the building of churches and social amenities, the growth of the railways was related to the history of ideas about town planning. More often than not, however, the construction of a railway, and more especially a railway station, meant a further disturbance in an already chaotic urban environment, including the displacement of some of the poorest of the population. Not until well into the twentieth century was the notion of alternative accommodation a serious part of social policy.

The overriding considerations in the field of housing throughout the nineteenth century were those of the sanctity of private property and the need for everything 'to pay'. With few exceptions, housing was an entirely private or speculative affair. The picture one must have in mind is of towns which never really recovered from a profound shock. Eighteenth-century towns contained elegant homes, and squares and wide streets, but also miserable cottages and squalid alleys: nevertheless there was a certain urban decorum, visible still in Britain's Roman and medieval towns. The towns of industrial Britain were faced with a bigger task and registered a greater failure, in attempting to cope with the aggregate of problems. They were less aware of, and less equipped to deal with, their corporate responsibilities.

Even by the 1850s the wealthier home, the elegant

Georgian or Regency house or the newly built terraced or detached house, was relatively primitive so far as its services were concerned. A cold-water tap was still the height of luxury in 1840. Flush toilets were known in the eighteenth century, but did not begin to come into use in even very wealthy homes until after the 1830s. The privy and the cesspit, and water drawn by servants from the stand-pipe and the rain-tank, were still the rule. The fitted bath was not to become common for the wealthy until the 1870s. Planning, for the wealthy, was a question of new self-protective residential areas like Birkenhead or the Regency or early Victorian squares of Belgravia or Bloomsbury, continuing the traditions of the co-ordinated elegance of the Georgian areas of London and the provincial market towns. The work of Thomas Cubitt, for example, who built for expensive tastes from the fashionable districts of West London through to the one he created in Clapham, was 'characterized by broad and airy streets, spacious squares and formal design'. His development schemes, many still surviving, 'contrasted markedly with much higgledy-piggledy development at the same time in other districts catering for less wealthy residents'.[14] By mid-century, with growing middle-class affluence, the scale of wealthy 'higgledy-piggledy' had increased, at the expense of wealthy 'formal design', as is shown by a glance at unrelated, individual house-building in the once-superior streets of mid-century urban development. For the rapidly growing lower middle class also, the large house, perhaps with basement, ground floor and two upper floors, had become common by mid-century. Middle-class housing of all kinds, its scale, design and architecture, proclaims the economic position of the occupiers, the size of the families and the number of the servants (an income of £1,000 a year in 1857 would support at least five servants, from butler to nursery maid, and £500 a year would support three). Such housing was not, however, the Victorian problem (whatever problems it was to cause in many areas in the middle of the twentieth century).

Generally speaking, the unplanned, minimal housing provided by mine and mill owners (and around which towns often mushroomed), was built to the most elementary standards. In existing and expanding towns industrialization and urbanization brought increased population density and the proliferation of overcrowded and slum districts. In the centres of towns, the effects of these processes could be seen in the insoluble problems of areas completely without sanitation. The problems ranged from the cholera epidemic to the homeless sleeping in stairways and to the overstocked graveyard. There were attempts at philanthropic housing, and even working-class self-help in housing, but in the 1850s none of this had yet become of any consequence (and in any important sense it had not yet done so by the end of the century). Edwin Chadwick's *Report on the Sanitary Condition of the Labouring Population* (1842) and Engels's *Condition of the Working Class in England* (1845) were only two of the more famous documents which, in early Victorian England, presented the desperate picture of the housing conditions (and their related mortality) of London and Manchester. Engels describes St Giles's, close to the fashionable West End, with its narrow roads, street-markets 'in which baskets of rotting and virtually uneatable vegetables and fruit are exposed for sale', foul smells and fantastic overcrowding. He describes the narrow alleys and courts, with 'hardly an unbroken windowpane to be seen, the walls are crumbling, the door posts and window frames are loose and rotten . . . piles of refuse and ashes lie all over the place and the slops thrown out into the street collect in pools . . .'[15] Enid Gauldie has pointed graphically to one of the salient features:

> The smell alone must have been nearly intolerable. To a generation which spends thousands of pounds on scents and deodorants to ensure that we are never aware of the odours of other bodies, it is astonishing that the smell of the 1830s could have been (even temporarily) endured. Yet thousands of families lived with years' old accumulations of filth permanently accosting their nostrils.[16]

A description of Manchester in 1805 (equally true of conditions in the 1830s or 1840s) includes this description of the cellar-dwellings:

They consist of two rooms under ground, the front apart-
ment of which is used as a kitchen, and though frequently
noxious by its dampness, and closeness, is generally
preferable to the back room: the latter has only one small
window, which, though on a level with the outer ground,
is near the roof of the cellar, it is often covered with
boards or paper, and in its best state, is so much covered
with mud, as to admit little either of air or light. In this
cell, the beds of the whole family, sometimes consisting of
seven or eight, are placed. The floor of this room is often
unpaved: the beds are fixed on the damp earth . . . I have
seen the sick without bedsteads, lying on rags; they can
seldom afford straw.[17]

These were the conditions which helped to bring about the
cholera epidemics of 1831-2 and 1848-9. Of the 4,000
houses in the Low Town area of North Shields in 1849 only
300 had a piped water supply from the mains. They housed
7,000 people, and contained sixty-two lavatories (mostly in
tradesmen's houses).[18] Water supplies were widely, in some
towns universally, polluted by sewage, and were irregular
and inadequate. The Commission which reported in 1844
on the State of Large Towns found innumerable cases of
contaminated water. In Newcastle the principal supply from
the Tyne and springs was 'impure from the drainage of the
sewers'. In Portsmouth the 'poor beg water of the neighbours'. It was bought widely from hawkers and private
pumps and was polluted in every conceivable manner.[19]

Agricultural workers, it should be remembered, generally
lived in equally insanitary and rudimentary conditions,
often sharing their accommodation with chickens or horses,
without furniture, with earth floors and mud walls. 'Attraction to the towns' was, in Enid Gauldie's view, 'much more
a repulsion from the countryside'.[20]

From mid-century it is possible to trace a higher rate of
involvement by government and municipal authorities in
the problems of urban living. It is not possible, of course, to
separate problems of housing from those of health and of
poverty. The domestic environment of the poor offended
the ideals of the Victorian moralist in relation to the family

4 'A Court for King Cholera', 1852

and morality; it was the despair of the reformer: 'The housing ruins all.'[21]

Working-class housing ranged from the improved dwellings of New Lanark or Saltaire to the cellars of Liverpool
and Manchester, the rural cottage, and the desperate wretch-
edness of St Giles, of the courts of the City of London,
and of those of Sunderland where, in 1831, cholera first set
foot in Britain. The urban environment of the poor was, it
must be remembered, more than a purely physical environment susceptible to various, and necessary, forms of social
engineering. The improvements in conditions of health
which we shall be discussing must not divert attention from
the fact that, for the poor, improvements in health and
hygiene, drainage and refuse disposal, water supply and the
range and purity of food supplies, did not mean any spectacular change in the environment itself, or in their style of

life. It was an environment which throughout the century blocked both escape and the imagination of anything different for enormous numbers of people. Built into it was the inevitability of many of the attendant features of poverty – charity, the Poor Law, the workhouse, dirt, disease, early death and almost total defencelessness against the machinery of society, whatever form it might take. To imagine that improved sanitation, greater attention to the problems of disease and greater national prosperity rapidly or substantially altered the conditions of poverty would be to make the same mistake as the generations at the end of the century made, who were *surprised* at the revelations of the extent and conditions of poverty.

Attempts were made to legislate for housing improvement. The earliest of consequence were in the 1850s and 1860s. With the City of London Sewers Act of 1851, John Simon, the City's Medical Officer of Health, extracted from both the City and parliament 'the first and unequivocal recognition of the right of compulsory clearance of unhealthy housing'. In 1864 Liverpool and Glasgow acquired 'much more elaborate and effective compulsory purchase powers', but 'the City and John Simon deserve the credit for the initial step in controlling a major social evil'.[22] Also in 1851 came the first national housing legislation in the form of Shaftesbury's Labouring Class Lodging Houses Act and Common Lodging Houses Act, the first of which permitted local authorities to build lodging houses, and the second of which made inspection of lodging houses compulsory. Inspection did in fact begin to take place, and to produce improvements, but the other Act was a dead letter. Acts concerned with wider health and sanitary problems, including the great Public Health Act of 1848, were by implication concerned also with housing. The Sanitary Act of 1866, for example, declared overcrowding to be a nuisance and enabled local authorities to take action. Definitions and enabling clauses did not, however, always and everywhere produce results.

The first real housing act, the 1868 Artizans' and Labourers' Dwellings Act (the first of three 'Torrens Acts'), was concerned with the individual insanitary house, enabling local authorities to compel its owner to demolish or repair it at his own expense. The Cross Acts, the first of which was passed in 1875, were concerned with the insanitary *area*, and enabled authorities to make compulsory purchases, for redevelopment schemes, involving the erection of houses for sale. Both sets of acts were permissive, both were aimed at maintaining adequate standards without excessively drastic action. Both were relatively ineffective, in that, although they looked ahead to firmer powers and wider consequences, the only result was demolition and prohibition, as remained substantially true of all such legislation until after the First World War. Even the 1890 Housing of the Working Classes Act (following on a Royal Commission on the Housing of the Poor in 1884–5) achieved little. It gave the newly created councils powers to deal with unhealthy areas, erect new houses and buy land compulsorily, but only the new London County Council made a start with the use of such powers. By-laws were increasingly being introduced and taking effect, in regulating such things as the height of buildings and ceilings, sanitation and the size of rooms. Given the prevalent view of housing as a commodity, however, the public authorities themselves continued to condemn and to demolish, but not to erect.

Local government

The absence of any comprehensive system of local government can be inferred from every aspect of mid-nineteenth-century British society. Urban England inherited as constituents of local government a medley consisting of the ancient city corporations, various *ad hoc* Improvement Commissioners, the parish vestries and local justices. The corporate towns had won their degree of independence as a result of being at some point rich enough to bargain for it or powerful enough to win it. The Municipal Corporations Act of 1835, following a Royal Commission set up by the Reform Parliament, tackled the abuses of a self-perpetuating, corrupt system, altered the composition of 178 incorporated towns, and destroyed or undermined the power of the exclusive groups. Although a wider measure of democracy was introduced in this way into local than existed in national government, it was not to be until well into the twentieth century that a pattern of elected local government was finally cemented. The new corporations, where the middle-class gained considerable power, in self-conscious industrial and commercial towns like Manchester, Leeds and Liverpool, were to find it impossible to adjust their thrift-conscious philosophies to *public* needs. Tempted as they were to respond to the needs of civic dignity and build town halls, urban overcrowding and disease were responded to only under legislative pressure from central government, and then more often than not with reluctance and delay. David Roberts demonstrates this effectively in a discussion of the growth of social policy between 1833 and 1854 by taking the case history of Macclesfield, 'the silk manufacturing capital of England'. All the improvements that took place in local conditions (including, for example, child labour, education and the treatment of criminals and the insane) were, he concludes, 'largely owing to the intervention of central government', and all met with local resistance:

> The mill-owners, the wealthiest and most respected citizens of Macclesfield, had petitioned Parliament in 1844 to allow those 4 to 12 years of age to work ten hours a day in the silk mills . . . The nonconformist *Macclesfield Chronicle*, which called the Factory Act a great abomination and oppression, described the Government's education plan in 1847 as 'hostile to economic and civil freedom'. The same *Chronicle* and Macclesfield's 150 police commissioners, along with the town's two M.P.s and 4,000 ratepayers, protested vigorously in 1851 against the General Board of Health's plans for sanitary improvement, considering them too expensive. Apathy and an antagonism to higher rates led them to tolerate the old lockup and to put pauper lunatics in the workhouse. All this would have continued but for the new acts of Parliament and the new civil servants from London.[23]

Another of the ancestors of modern local government was the system of Improvement Commissioners, appointed as a result of the passing of individual local Improvement Acts, particularly in the late eighteenth century, to take responsibility for such matters as paving and clearing nuisances. Open, like the corporations, to corruption and abuse, the Commissioners were in most of the older towns the only vehicle for attempting to cope with the problems of early industrialization, and very often their powers came to conflict among themselves and with other organs of local government. The parish vestry, in its 'open' form, was an ancient democratic institution, a local assembly with the right to impose taxation and responsible for ensuring the appointment and proper conduct of such local officers as constable, overseer of the poor and surveyor of highways. This, too, had often degenerated over the centuries into a self-perpetuating abuse of the system.

The early years of the nineteenth century had, however, destroyed the logic of these forms of local administration. The towns grew beyond them, in two senses; they grew beyond their ability to cope, and beyond their geographical confines. The problem after the 1830s was to improve and extend the machinery of borough incorporation begun in 1835, and to define authorities for the two precise and most important considerations of health and the poor.

The gradual elimination of contradictory powers, the incorporation of new boroughs and the extension of their machinery, did in fact take place slowly. The role of the justices, traditionally country gentlemen appointed by the Crown, became of diminishing importance. They were normally Tory in politics, and strongly opposed by the radicals and utilitarians who shaped the legislation after 1832. That the justices began to lose many of their powers as a result of it is not only a political fact. They became increasingly unable to handle the growing weight of legislation – relating, for example, to mining and industry – and urban expansion undermined their authority. They continued to supervise the operation of the laws in the country districts, and remained identified with local power and rule until the enfranchisement of the rural labourer and the creation of county councils in the 1880s.

Public health

Questions of health encompassed all these aspects of environment and administration. Even though germ theory was unknown until the late 1860s, it was obvious enough that disease had *something* to do with dirt. It was also clear from the beginning of the 1840s that urban concentration and conditions were more lethal, more liable to epidemic, more productive of disease, than non-urban conditions. Greatly increased population density in York between 1821 and 1851 halted the favourable trend in mortality, and shows 'that where urban growth occurred in that period (with or without industrialization) it brought various apparently inescapable public health problems'.[24] Conditions in Preston resulted in the highest death rate in the country: in the 1840s 47 per cent of children died before their fifth birthday, and 56 per cent before they were 25. Only three out of five of those who were alive at 25 reached the age of 50, and only two reached 60.[25] The areas of greatest poverty coincided with those of the highest mortality. Expectation of life, it was clear at the time, was also directly related to social class. Edwin Chadwick's famous *Report on the Sanitary Condition of the Labouring Population* demonstrated that in 1839 in Bethnal Green, for example, the average age of death could be tabulated as follows:

No. of deaths		Average age of deceased
101	Gentlemen and persons engaged in professions and their families	45 years
273	Tradesmen and their families	26
1,258	Mechanics, servants and labourers and their families	16

Similar demonstrations were made for towns like Leeds and Liverpool.[26] The vast class differential in the infant mortality rate was, and continued to be, a considerable factor.

Suspicion of the general findings of Chadwick's *Report*, based on the work done by a select committee and initiated

by Chadwick from his position as Secretary to the Poor Law
Board, led to the appointment of the Royal Commission
on the State of Large Towns (the Health of Towns
Commission) in 1843. One of the Commissioners appointed
was Lyon Playfair, already an eminent scientist. Playfair was
given the large towns of Lancashire to investigate, and he
later wrote:

> The effects of bad sewerage, defective or intermittent
> instead of constant water supply, overcrowded tenements,
> bad construction of streets, and the abuse of opiates
> among the working-classes, were traced to their sources.
> In 1844 the sanitary condition of the kingdom was de-
> plorable. Lancashire was especially bad. One-tenth of the
> population of Manchester and one-seventh of that of
> Liverpool lived in cellars. In the streets occupied by the
> working-classes two rows of houses were often built back
> to back, so that there could be no efficient ventilation; the
> supply of conveniences was altogether insufficient, and
> their condition and drainage were shocking ... Civic
> powers were split up into a number of discordant and
> often conflicting authorities, constantly overlapping each
> other in their duties ... The mortality was great, and the
> average age of death was low in manufacturing towns.

All the features of urban growth we have discussed come
together in Playfair's recollection. His findings – and those
of the Commission – in fact bore out Chadwick's picture.
Playfair compared the average age at death in different
Lancashire towns in 1844 with that in Kendal,
Westmorland, 'a healthy agricultural town', where it was 36:
at Manchester it was 22, Liverpool 20, Preston 19 and
Ashton 16.[27]

All these factors in ill health and early death were
discussed and in some respects acted upon most strikingly
in the cholera epidemics of 1831–2 and 1848–9. The Public
Health Act of 1848, setting up the General Board of Health,
resulted from the imminent danger of cholera. In the words
of a writer in the *Edinburgh Review* in 1850, 'Cholera is in
truth a Health Inspector who speaks through his inter-
preter, the Registrar General, in a language which reaches

all ears.'[28] The dominant local attitude, at least until new terms of reference were established in the 1870s, continued to be indifference. So far as infant mortality was concerned (more than 57 per cent of working-class children in Manchester, reported Chadwick, died under the age of five) it was not until the twentieth century that any substantial progress was made. Three things were required for headway to be made on health problems: changes in social policy, adequate national and local machinery, and improvements in medical knowledge and care.

Those responsible from the 1830s for shaping changes in social policy spanned the range from the evangelical Tory, Lord Shaftesbury, to the utilitarian Benthamite, Edwin Chadwick. Chadwick was the central figure, and he was concerned exclusively with the environmental factors involved in health reform. His position at the Poor Law Commission enabled him to see the dimensions of the health problem, to have it investigated, and to publicize it. His 1842 *Report* was a product of the processes which brought about the parliamentary reform of 1832, and it is important to note, as Playfair was acutely aware, that Chadwick was entirely committed to national policy and central planning:

> Chadwick . . . is the father of modern sanitary reform. He had the faculty of seizing upon an abuse with the tenacity of a bulldog, and never let it go till the abuse was worried to death. But this self-absorption in a subject carried him into extremes, and he failed to see both sides of a question. Thus, seeing the evils which had arisen in local self-government, he could not recognize its benefits, and magnified the power and capabilities of centralized government.

Playfair urged on him the need to throw greater responsibility on the local authorities and reduce the functions of central government, to which Chadwick replied: 'Sir, the Devil was expelled from heaven because he objected to centralization, and all those who object to centralization oppose it on devilish grounds!'[29] Perhaps the most succinct summary of Chadwick's career was G. M. Young's view that its mainspring 'seems to have been a desire to wash the people of England all over, every day, by administrative order'.[30] Chadwick was unable – and in this differed most emphatically from the more open-minded John Simon – to accept new medical evidence as to the causes and treatment of disease, but the fact that his tenacious views on the atmospheric causes of disease led to an equally tenacious dedication to the improvement of ventilation, sanitation and environmental conditions generally meant that 'he inaugurated the first era of English public health as one concerned more with the physical environment than with the personal health of the individual'.[31] His work altered the framework of discussion of social policy as the mid-nineteenth century approached. The 1848 Public Health Act symbolized the strengths and weaknesses of the new situation. This was a more restricted Act than Chadwick had hoped for, and was surrounded by hostility from many quarters, including many liberals, because of the centralization it entailed. *The Times* was implacably against Chadwick and the Act. Nevertheless the Act did give the General Board of Health real powers, including that of ordering an inquiry in a town if a tenth of the ratepayers petitioned for it, or if the annual mortality in the town exceeded 23 per 1,000. A local Board of Health, however, whether set up voluntarily or not, was exempt from national inspection or control. The General Board of Health lasted, in that form, only until 1854. Alternative approaches to public health were by now taking clearer shape.

The City of London, in gaining exemption from the operation of the 1848 Act, framed the terms for the first really full-scale experiment in effective local health administration. John (later Sir John) Simon, its first Medical Officer of Health, was ultimately more influential than Chadwick partly because the techniques he evolved (again, in the teeth of prolonged opposition from the forces of apathy and vested interest) could be seen to be viable and effective, and partly because British experience clung to the policy of local independence and initiative on which Simon relied. After seven years spent in building the first local health machinery of any importance, Simon became medical adviser to the government's reconstituted Board of Health in 1855, and in 1871 Chief Medical Officer of the newly formed Local Government Board. He was himself an eminent medical figure, and worked towards a conception of public health administration dominated by medical considerations. By 1870 he had made the Privy Council's Medical Department supreme in the formulation and operation of public health policy. It was to the doctor, not the sanitary engineer, that Simon delivered the direction of health policy at the beginning of the 1870s.

The policy that prevailed, therefore, was that of reliance on medical expertise (which made great strides in the 1870s) at national and local level, combined with local machinery for investigation, medical and environmental improvements. It can be seen, then, that of the three factors necessary for change – new policies, administrative machinery and medical knowledge – the first two made visible, though far from spectacular progress between the 1840s and 1870s, and it was after 1870 that the main impact of the changes began to be seen in the mortality statistics. The anaesthetics and free vaccination of the 1840s, sanitary improvements from the 1850s in particular, and the lessons learned from epidemics, all contributed to the developments. And yet during the period 1841–75 the death rate remained almost constant, at just over 22 per thousand. The major killers, such as tuberculosis, scarlet fever, diphtheria and the numerous infectious diseases connected with maternity and childhood, were still far from being conquered.[32]

Poor relief

Although all these questions are closely bound up with that of the poor, influential Victorian Britain preferred not to recognize the presence of poverty as such. New directions in social policy at the turn of the twentieth century were to be very closely connected with the conception of poverty. Public policy for the major part of the nineteenth century was, in the sector of poor relief, based on the concept of pauperism. Poor relief had, since Elizabethan England, been accepted explicitly as a moral responsibility, and two of the

5 *Field Lane Refuge for the Destitute, London, 1859*

elements of local government inherited by the nineteenth century, the vestries and the justices of the peace, were involved in its administration. Parish officers were responsible for raising and distributing the local poor rate, and the justices to one degree or another established the rate and supervised the procedure. They were torn between the relative merits of 'out-relief' and the 'workhouse'. Parishes were responsible for their own poor (the 'settlement', as it had always been called, was to continue to operate to some extent right through the nineteenth century, and, in veiled forms, through to today); a distinction was made between the able-bodied (out-relief) and non-able-bodied (workhouse) recipients of relief. An Act of 1782 (Gilbert's Act) had aimed at the creation of workhouses by unions of parishes. The Speenhamland decision of 1795 to supplement wages on a sliding scale according to size of family and price of bread was the last major Poor Law development of the old dispensation.

The Poor Law Amendment Act of 1834 sought to stop the pauper from obtaining advantages without penalties. It tried to deter him from seeking aid, by insisting that he receive *in* and not *out* relief, at a lower level of comfort than the poorest worker in employment. Benthamite economic orthodoxy held that the right level of wages was the one dictated by the market, and that interference by legislation or combinations of workers or employers distorted the market. Similarly, in a free market situation poverty had nothing to do with the economic system and could not be regulated; there was nothing *in the situation* to prevent the industrious from prospering. Relief of the Speenhamland variety merely discouraged industry. The Act of 1834 went as far as its authors felt they could persuade the public to follow, and they expected by it to be able to bring outdoor relief for the able-bodied to an end sooner or later. Relief from now on was to be minimal – that is, to prevent actual starvation – but the conditions in which it was to be given were to deter people from applying for it. This doctrine of 'less eligibility' was the crux of the Act. The Report of the Commission on which the 1834 Act was based thought it essential that the situation of the person relieved

> shall not be made really or apparently so eligible as the situation of the independent labourer of the lowest class ... in proportion as the condition of any pauper class is elevated above the condition of independent labourers, the condition of the independent class is depressed; their industry is impaired, their employment becomes unsteady, and its remuneration in wages is diminished. Such persons, therefore, are under the strongest inducement to quit the less eligible class of labourers and enter the more eligible class of paupers ... Every penny bestowed that tends to render the condition of the pauper more eligible than that of the independent labourer is a bounty on indolence and vice.[33]

Restrictions on poor relief were the result both of utilitarian philosophy and of cost. The mounting cost of relief can be seen in the case of London, for example, from Lambeth. In the first two decades of the century the population of the parish of Lambeth, in which machinery, earthenware and tiles, for example, were manufactured, more or less doubled.[34] In 1800, 413 people were admitted to Lambeth Workhouse and 347 outdoor relief payments were made. The total cost to the rates was £11,691. By 1818 the numbers had risen to 1,250 workhouses inmates, 1,867 payments, and a rate of £47,870.[35] The new national administration from 1834, with a Central Board of Commissioners (from 1847 the Poor Law Board) supervising the Boards of Guardians, administering 600 to 700 unions (into which the 15,000 parishes of England and Wales were combined), was designed to end the indiscriminate element in relief. Chadwick and the 1832–4 Commission intended that separate workhouse provision should be made by local Boards of Guardians for different categories of pauper, but this did not happen. The general mixed workhouse prevailed. The Commissioners, in recommending separate buildings for children, able-bodied males, able-bodied females and the sick, were in fact trying to combat the concept of the mixed workhouse, and they – and others – were dismayed at its continuance. The Minority Report of the Poor Law Commission in 1909 explained that the intention of 1834 *had been* to follow these emphatic recommendations, but the intention had foundered on the structure of the system itself:

> Parliament had placed the care of all these classes of poor in each Union under a single Local Authority, and had charged that Authority, not with the treatment of any one of these classes, not with the education of the children or the prevention and cure of sickness, but generally, with the relief of the destitution of all of them.

To the local Boards it seemed a waste of money to maintain separate institutions. 'Within a few months we see the attempts given up, and all the classes of poor huddled into a single building.'[36] The reality of workhouse life was, in Longmate's account of it, 'even worse than the Poor Law Commissioners intended'. Inmates were deprived of their own clothing, fed on meagre rations, made to eat with their fingers and prevented from leaving the building, even to

Agricultural labourer's family budget, Lavenham, Suffolk, 1843

Name	Age	Earnings		Expenditure		
		s	d		s	d
Robert Crick	42	9	0	Bread	9	0
				Potatoes	1	0
Wife	40		9	Rent	1	2
				Tea		2
Boy	12	2	0	Sugar		$3\frac{1}{2}$
				Soap		3
ditto	11	1	0	Blue		$\frac{1}{2}$
				Thread etc.		2
ditto	8	1	0	Candles		3
				Salt		$\frac{1}{2}$
Girl	6	—		Coal and wood		9
				Butter		$4\frac{1}{2}$
Boy	4	—		Cheese		3
Total earnings		13s	9d	Total expenditure	13s	9d

'But there are numbers of families who, although in the possession of the same amount of wages shown above, do not dispose of it with such frugality, but appear in the greatest state of destitution; many others, with the same number of children, do not get the wages this man's family have. The family I have given as an example is more to show you that with industry and frugality, their diet consists principally of bread and potatoes. There are, however, some who, when their families are grown up, by putting their earnings together, occasionally get a piece of meat at their supper-time, and their Sunday dinner.'

From: Reports of Special Assistant Poor Law Commissioners on the Employment of Women and Children in Agriculture (1843), quoted in JOHN BURNETT *Plenty and Want*, pp. 26–7 (London, 1966).

attend church.[37] Husbands and wives were separated, and even though in 1847 an Act permitted couples over sixty to occupy a separate bedroom in the workhouse, 'few had the courage, or the knowledge of the regulations, to take advantage of the concession, and it was not until 1885 that it was made obligatory'. Not until 1868 'were Guardians compelled to provide such minor comforts as backs to the benches on which old people sat or little chairs for children's sick-wards ...'[38] Inmates were subjected to every conceivable major and minor tyranny. Paupers in Lambeth Workhouse were not allowed to receive gifts of money, their letters were opened and even their newspapers confiscated.[39] As late as 1895 a Royal Commission on the Aged Poor was urging masters and mistresses of workhouses to abandon uniform times of going to bed and getting up for old people, and again recommending that they should be allowed their separate cubicles, to be allowed (if well behaved and within 'reasonable limits') to go out for walks, visit friends and attend their own places of worship. Some Unions did begin to introduce more humane practices from the 1850s, and to re-introduce out-relief where it had been discontinued. But the severities persisted. The whole system in fact, 'born in 1834 with astonishingly little difficulty, and grown to maturity with remarkable speed, was to be a long time a-dying'.[40] The approach to poverty as a condition to be punished, and to relief as requiring stringent moral and social controls, was to continue as an important element in social attitudes through the rest of the nineteenth and twentieth centuries.

Across the whole field of relief spread the stigma of pauperization. The general mixed workhouse was through-benches on which old people sat or little chairs for chil-every kind of contingency. The Minority Commissioners of 1909 pointed out that the authors of the 1834 Report failed to make a distinction between able-bodied pauperism and able-bodied destitution. The men of 1834 had considered that they were dealing with pauperism only, that is, with a condition about which moral judgements could be made, and over which control needed to be exercised. Benthamite economic orthodoxy blinded them to the fact that whole sections of the population in the 1830s (hand-loom weavers, millwrights and workers deprived of employment by seasonal hazards, for example) were unemployed or under-employed. With such able-bodied destitution 'the Royal Commission of 1832–4 chose not to concern itself. We find in its voluminous proceedings no statistics of Unemployment, no statement as to fluctuations of trade, no account of the destitution produced by the new machines.' The Commissioners, in fact, 'concentrated their whole at-

tention on one plague spot – the demoralization of character
and waste of wealth produced in the agricultural districts by
an hypertrophied Poor Law'.[41] The new Poor Law policy
did not match the reality of forms of poverty which were
now endemic and which – as those who suffered it were able
to realize and made explicit – directly related to the conditions of industrial growth. The authorities struggled to
maintain the purity of the system. The awareness of its
unreality and cruelty drove northern working men in particular to emphatic and even spectacular protest against the
new Poor Law and its representatives when it began to be
implemented in the towns. Out-relief, in fact, did not die.
The Act drove a wedge between the middle-class radicals
who subscribed to utilitarian philosophy and their former
working-class allies, and created, momentarily, an alliance
between a generation of Tory reformers and working-class
radicals, which at one and the same time was aimed against
the mill-owners and for wider rights for working men. The
fight against the Poor Law was of major importance in the
growth of Chartism.

The operation of the Poor Law illustrates vividly the use
of stigma as a form of social control. Different in many ways
from the forms of punishment inflicted on the criminal, the
treatment of paupers was in other ways parallel. The
criminal and the poor were both seen as miscreants, both to
be punished. The workhouse was punishment of another
sort. Poverty or any kind of social disability has retained
many of these elements of stigma. Robert Pinker, discussing
modern public services, emphasizes the element of humiliation often involved in the allocation of resources to the
underprivileged:

> The imposition of stigma is the commonest form of
> violence used in democratic societies. Stigmatization is
> slow, unobtrusive and genteel in its effect . . . It can best
> be compared to those forms of psychological torture in
> which the victim is broken psychically and physically but
> left to all outward appearances unmarked.[42]

The fight against the Poor Law was a fight against a conception of society which drove the poor into exile, a society

6 *Scripture reading in a night shelter, 1871. From a print by Gustave Doré*

which sought to purify itself by 'imprisoning' the poor just as it imprisoned the criminal.

During the middle decades of the nineteenth century the (for the most part unsolved) problems of urban scale and administration, and most of the individual but related urban problems of housing, health and poverty, were explicit and prominent features of social affairs. These were not, of course, the only urban problems, and mid-Victorian society as a whole was not obsessed by them. The philosophy underlying prevailing middle-class attitudes towards social policies remained that of do-nothing. In restricted fields, restricted legislation was seen to be necessary, and a restricted amount of machinery, spending a severely restricted amount of money, was being created. Administrative authority was frequently vested in *ad hoc* bodies (the Poor Law Commissioners, for example) which, it was felt,

might ultimately efficiently organize themselves out of existence. Other authorities (like the Committee of the Privy
Council on Education of 1839) crept awkwardly and uncer-
tainly into existence. A constant fight was waged to keep
down the size and functions of departments of State and
some (the Education Department and the Railways Board,
for example) proved far more formidable and far-reaching
than their creators could have envisaged. The expert was
taking his place: the specialist adviser and administrator, the
inspector of schools or of factories, and the medical officer
of health, for instance, was making his appearance. 'However meagre compared to the responsibilities assumed by
Whitehall today,' these developments are open to interpretation as marking 'the beginning of the welfare state'.[43]

We have looked at only some of the most prominent
features of the environment and policies of mid-Victorian
Britain. Although in later chapters we shall not be concerned in the same way with contemporary developments in
these areas of policy and social administration, it has been
important here to illustrate something of the context from
which modern social development began. We shall not, for
example, be following through the details of developments
in water supply, health or the railways; they have been
intended as illustrations of the processes which governed
people's lives, their social relations, their attitudes to themselves and to society. They point to the forces which helped
to shape a particular society, operating on the basis of particular sets of assumptions. A social situation is the product
not of a sequence of automatically changing contexts, but of
changes in which social attitudes and decisions, tensions and
struggles play an important part. Within the situations we
have described there were constant struggles to understand
and to ignore, to describe and to conceal, to conserve and to
alter. Rival versions of the nature of society and of social
progress were taking shape. In the next two chapters we
shall look at other aspects of the transition to the Britain of
recent years, in terms of the broadening of organization for
action, and attitudes to social change.

Notes

1 ADNA FERRIN WEBER *The Growth of Cities in the Nineteenth Century*, p. 157 (New York, 1899; 1963 edition).

2 ROYAL COMMISSION ON THE DISTRIBUTION OF THE INDUSTRIAL POPULATION (BARLOW COMMISSION) *Report*, p. 29 (London, 1940).

3 Ibid., p. 12 and *Minutes of Evidence*, p. 399.

4 Ibid., *Minutes of Evidence*, p. 182.

5 See HENRY PARRIS *Government and the Railways in Nineteenth-Century Britain*, Ch. 1 (London, 1965).

6 R. DUDLEY BAXTER 'Railway extension and its results', in CARUS-WILSON, *Essays in Economic History*, III, p. 33.

7 NIKOLAUS PEVSNER 'Victorian prolegomena', in FERRIDAY *Victorian Architecture*, p. 27.

8 RICHARD D. ALTICK *The English Common Reader*, p. 301 (Chicago, 1957).

9 JACK SIMMONS *The Railways of Britain*, p. 17 (London, 1961; 1965 Penguin edition).

10 MAUDE STANLEY 'West-End improvements', *The Nineteenth Century*, May 1881, pp. 852–3.

11 A. S. WOHL 'The housing of the working classes in London 1815–1914', in STANLEY D. CHAPMAN (ed.) *The History of Working-Class Housing*, p. 17, (Newton Abbot, 1971).

12 JOHN BURNETT *Plenty and Want*, Ch. 6 (London, 1966).

13 ROYSTON LAMBERT *Sir John Simon 1816–1904*, p. 189 (London, 1963).

14 WILLIAM ASHWORTH *The Genesis of Modern British Town Planning*, p. 38 (London, 1954).

15 F. ENGELS *The Condition of the Working Class in England*, p. 34; trans. W. O. HENDERSON and W. H. CHALONER (Oxford, 1958).

16 ENID GAULDIE *Cruel Habitations: a history of working-class housing 1780–1918*, p. 73 (London, 1974).

17 Quoted from Dr Ferriar in FRANCES COLLIER *The Family Economy of the Working Classes in the Cotton Industry 1784–1833*, pp. 20–1 (Manchester, 1965).

18 NORMAN LONGMATE *King Cholera*, p. 45 (London, 1966).

19 ROYAL COMMISSION ON THE STATE OF LARGE TOWNS AND POPULOUS DISTRICTS *First Report*, 1844, I, pp. xxv–xlvii.

20 GAULDIE *Cruel Habitations*, p. 280.

21 JAMES H. RIGG *National Education in its Social Conditions and Aspects*, p. 33 (London, 1873).

22 LAMBERT *Sir John Simon*, p. 175.

23 DAVID ROBERTS *Victorian Origins of the British Welfare State*, pp. 310–15 (New Haven, 1960).

24 ARMSTRONG *Stability and Change in an English County Town*, p. 196.

25 MICHAEL ANDERSON *Family Structure in Nineteenth Century Lancashire*, p. 34 (Cambridge, 1971).

26 Quoted from E. N. WILLIAMS *A Documentary History of England*, 2, p. 230 (Harmondsworth, 1965).

27 WEMYSS REID *Memoirs and Correspondence of Lyon Playfair*, pp. 65–6 (London, 1899).

28 Quoted in ASA BRIGGS 'Cholera and society in the nineteenth century', *Past and Present*, 1961, p. 85.

29 REID *Memoirs and Correspondence of Lyon Playfair*, p. 64.

30 G. M. YOUNG *Portrait of an Age*, p. 11 (London, 1936; 1960 edition).

31 LAMBERT *Sir John Simon*, p. 61.

32 Playfair points out proudly that the death rate attributable to 'zymotic diseases' (arising from filth) fell from 4·52 per thousand in 1841–50 to 2·71 per thousand in 1880–4, but the major gains were at the latter end of the period.

33 Quoted from the ROYAL COMMISSION ON THE POOR LAWS, *Majority Report*, 1909, I, p. 103.

34 The figures were 27,985 and 57,638 in the 1801 and 1821 censuses respectively. *Victoria History of the County of Surrey*, p. 447 (London, 1912).

35 AILEEN DENISE NASH *Living in Lambeth 1086–1914*, p. 52 (London, n.d.).

36 ROYAL COMMISSION ON THE POOR LAWS, *Minority Report*, III, p. 19.

37 NORMAN LONGMATE *The Workhouse*, pp. 92–5 (London, 1974).

38 MAURICE BRUCE *The Coming of the Welfare State*, p. 99 (London, 1961; 1965 edition).

39 NASH *Living in Lambeth*, p. 54.

40 LONGMATE *The Workhouse*, p. 257.

41 ROYAL COMMISSION ON THE POOR LAWS, *Minority Report*, III, pp. 437–9.

42 ROBERT PINKER *Social Theory and Social Policy*, p. 175 (London, 1971).

43 ROBERTS *Victorian Origins of the British Welfare State*, p. 315.

3 Democracy and
social movements

From Golden Age to Great Depression

It is in the economic, social and political conditions of the
final decades of the nineteenth century that the sources of
discussion of our contemporary institutions most obviously
lie. These were decades of economic anxiety, new political
allegiances and pressures, a growing debate about the role of
the State in relation to the problems of society and of the
individual, a developing machinery of local and national
government, and a mounting commitment to Empire. In
those anxieties, discussions and attempted solutions are to
be seen shapes profoundly familiar in our modern world.

The British economy in the Victorian 'Golden Age' was
susceptible to setback and crisis, but the picture of the third
quarter of the century is still one of astonishing economic
and industrial expansion. Britain's industrial revolution had
established for her a paramount position in the world's
economic development and trade. Britain supplied railways
at home and abroad and British ships carried British consumer and capital goods to overseas customers. Metal and
machinery were of central importance in the developments,
but cotton and – increasingly – woollens played a major part

in exports. By 1851 cotton spinning and weaving had become very largely mechanized mill activities; in the 1860s over 80 per cent of cotton manufacturing output was being exported. Imports of raw cotton almost doubled between 1850 and 1870, and those of wool increased almost fourfold. The 1860s and 1870s saw the consolidation of steam and iron as the basis of shipbuilding, and the amount of merchant shipping powered by steam rose sharply by comparison with sail. In 1851 British yards produced 3·6 million tons of shipping, and in 1871 the figure was 5·7 million. The number of workers employed in shipbuilding, iron and steel more than doubled between the two dates.

The advances which thrust Britain's economy into industrial dominance in the nineteenth century came, as we have seen, from defined industries. Economic developments in the second half of the century were possible only as a result of important changes in the very basis on which industrial firms could establish themselves, and by which the economy could be diversified. These changes were to an important extent connected with developments in limited-liability and joint-stock organization. Before 1844 such organization was virtually prohibited, except by special charter, as in the case of the railways. Partnership was the most common basis of large-scale organization, although even on this basis the large, even the enormous, firm was possible. To form partnerships at New Lanark, in the early years of the century, Robert Owen had had to rely at one stage on family investors and at another on London connections. Acts between 1844 and 1862, making joint-stock organization possible, recruited the funds of the small investor impersonally. The effect on industrial organization was dramatic: in the six years following the 1856 Act, for example, nearly 2,500 companies registered. What was demonstrated was that 'limited liability was needed for local enterprises of a useful kind, financed by numerous passive small investors . . . The great increase under this Act of 1856 . . . shows the popularity of the limited form and clearly demonstrates both the need and usefulness of this form as a factor of enterprise.'[1] The eagerness with which small investors had flocked to invest in railways in the 1830s and 1840s was a demonstration of the availability of savings for investment purposes. The rise in and spread of middle-class domestic standards were rooted in railway, banking and joint-stock developments.

The effect of these changes on the size and structure of industrial firms, and on social relations within them, was considerable. In the small firm of the early phase of industrialization, relations between man and master, however cordial or brutal they may have been, were direct. At one level they were, of course, class-divided, as the ferocities unleashed by trade union activity demonstrate, but at another level they were organic: there was a common destiny that could be felt to be involved in the fate of the smaller firm, and the success of the factory owner depended not only on his ability to market his products, but on his ability directly to handle his men. The expansion of firms led gradually to specialization at the level of management as well as to a finer division of labour among workers. The workers' relationships with management (including hiring, firing and wages) came increasingly to be through the all-powerful foreman. In a South Wales valley the difference was noticed 'when the miner who had had a dispute with the deputy or under-manager could no longer walk across the fields and see the owner at the door of his house, but must deal with a manager who was tied down by instructions from the head office of the combine in Cardiff'. Authority became remote and workers had to deal with 'a poker-faced man whose relation with you was dehumanized and strait-jacketed'.[2] Employers became different types of people, hedged around with considerations of education and class position. Social distance increased. The role of the trade union official began to change, London headquarters and national negotiations assumed greater importance, and the pattern of modern British industrial social relations began to take shape in the conditions of the joint-stock, impersonal financing of industrial development.

By the beginning of the 1870s Britain had for a quarter of a century or so been reaping, as a nation, major benefit from the second phase of her industrial revolution. The advantages of having been the first to industrialize were obviously immense; economically, however, there were to be disadvantages. Other nations were to see more readily than Britain the need to readjust old methods and techniques, to invest in newer forms of capital equipment; British industrialists were reluctant to invest in modernization, so long as old plant and old routines continued to be profitable. Capital for new industries, taking advantage of new materials and inventions, was to be slower to come forward in Britain than in newly industrializing countries. Many of the problems of the decline of the staple industries after the First World War derive from the very fact of their dominance in the late nineteenth century. Similarly, with established industrial techniques and a hitherto successful basis of apprenticeship and practical skills, Britain fell steadily behind other nations in scientific and technical education (and education in general). The tradition of the uneducated inventor of the George Stephenson type died hard. What Peter Mathias calls 'a "sub-culture" of interest in science'[3] existed in the late eighteenth century, though this interest probably had relatively little effect on industrial innovation until after the middle of the century. This had been a successful tradition in the early stages of industrialization, although it is possible that its contribution has been exaggerated in past efforts to assess the role of education and science in the Industrial Revolution. Efforts at technical education did exist, from the early decades of the nineteenth century, largely – in the first place – through the Mechanics' Institutes; they were encouraged by government departments and grants after the Great Exhibition. The results, however, were meagre and the radical reorganization necessary in the approach to the basis of industrial skills did not take place. New competitors were entering the world's markets, on which the British economy – by dominating them – had come to be dependent.

From the early 1870s the British economy entered a phase deceptively described as the Great Depression, a period, through to roughly the end of the century, in which it was widely felt that parts of the economy were running down. Foreign competition and free trade were held by many to be responsible. Lord Randolph Churchill strongly expressed this view in 1884, tracing the depression back a decade:

> Your iron industry is dead, dead as mutton; your coal industries, which depend greatly on the iron industries are languishing. Your silk industry is dead, assassinated by the foreigner. Your wool industry is *in articulo mortis*, gasping, struggling. Your cotton industry is seriously come to a standstill . . . Well, but with this state of British industry what do you find going on? You find foreign iron, foreign wool, foreign silk and cotton pouring into the country, flooding you, drowning you, sinking you . . .

Although such rhetoric on behalf of tariffs in the late nineteenth century could not disturb British confidence in her ultimate supremacy through free trade, it nevertheless reflects the growing uneasiness. Churchill was as sure that free imports were murdering British industry 'as if I found a man standing over a corpse and plunging his knife into it'.[4] A Royal Commission Appointed to Inquire into the Depression of Trade and Industry reported categorically in 1886 that Britain was in all fields of production falling behind Germany. The Commission found that those giving evidence were in general agreement on four points: that trade and industry were 'depressed', that this meant smaller profits and less employment, that it was the value of trade and not its volume that had declined, and that since 1875 the depression had more or less consistently affected trade and industry, and especially agriculture.[5] There were indeed serious realities behind the exaggerations of Churchill and the anxieties of the Commission. It was not only a question of German steels and skills. America was now able to supply herself (and others) with railways. The Paris Exhibition of 1867 was a major shock to British industry, demonstrating that in important fields Britain was falling behind and that entirely new ones, such as electricity and chemicals, were being pioneered by other countries. British products – though not British finance – were no longer indispensable. The search for compensatory markets was seriously engaged: the British Empire was buying 35·4 per cent of Britain's home-produced exports in the period 1909–13, and

almost half by the Second World War. International competition was now a question that involved, among other
things, Africa. It was to mean war.

Britain's economy was from now on to remain permanently vulnerable, as new technologies, new uses of raw
materials, new industries, flourished elsewhere. Although
with a continuing major role in international finance, with
strong industrial traditions and potential, Britain's position
in the world economy was never again to seem as impreg-
nable as it did up to the last quarter of the nineteenth
century. Despite the impression of the passing of the
Golden Age, the period was not in any precise sense one of
depression. Increases in production were offset by falling
international prices. The so-called Great Depression was, in
the formulation of H. L. Beales, 'a period of progress in
circumstances of great difficulty. It might be dubbed a period of "lean years" in contrast with the preceding good
years, if profits were the main criteria of welfare. In no final
sense, however, was that period one of retrogression.' The
fall in prices did, in fact, cause the return on investments to
stagnate or fall, and in many sections of industrial and commercial activity, therefore, the sense of 'being depressed'
was acutely felt. The change in 'business psychology' did
not come until 1896, when prices began again to rise.[6] By
this time, as we shall see, fundamental aspects of British
social life had been affected. In addition the future international dangers for Britain's economy were growing distinct. The decline of British dominance coincides with the
beginning not only of more complex economic relations, but
the increasing internationalization of many aspects of industrial social activity. From the later nineteenth century it
becomes more and more impossible to discuss British social
conditions in isolation from those of other countries.

Accompanying the picture of the 'depression' as a period
of slower speed is one of increasing real incomes. Falling
prices, if production and sales do not adequately compensate for them, mean lower dividends. They also, if no significant changes in employment take place, mean higher
purchasing power for wages. The late 1870s and early
1880s, in fact, mark important changes in the value of

working-class incomes. Agricultural prices fell, largely under the impact of the opening up of North American wheat lands and the ability to transport frozen meat. Frozen lamb from Australia arrived in London for the first time in 1880. In the last quarter of the century 'significant improvements are observable in the general standard of working-class diet'.[7]

Social class

We shall see in a later discussion that the concept of social class is notoriously difficult to use and define. It is important to examine briefly here what was happening to the composition of British society in the economic circumstances of the 1870s and 1880s. We have already assumed a good deal about this composition in our use of terminology, and to clarify the picture it will be necessary to look at class composition, the industrial and occupational classification of the population, its regional distribution and aspects of its age, sex and family composition. Before we approach these in outline, and class composition in particular, two points need to be remembered. The first is that in one crucial respect the examination of problems of class in the nineteenth century remains unaltered today; despite the development in social mobility that has taken place, the element of inheritance in people's social position has not disappeared. The boundaries of class, in T. B. Bottomore's view, may have become blurred and some expansion of opportunities may have taken place, but 'there is no general sense of greater "classlessness", nor of great opportunities for the individual to choose and create his way of life regardless of inherited wealth or social position'.[8] It was certainly true of Victorian society that men did not 'choose and create' their way of life, and were aware that they did not.

The second point is that the very process of mobility reminded men in Victorian Britain of the reality of class. Mobility does not, and people were conscious that it did not, alter the fact of an overall class relationship. Edward Thompson emphasizes that class is a historical phen-

7 *Rotten Row, 1872. From a print by Gustave Doré*

omenon. The concept is meaningful only in terms of the interaction between real people in a real context. We do not start with 'two distinct classes, each with an independent being, and then bring them *into* relationship with each other'. Class happens, he suggests, when 'some men, as a result of common experiences (inherited or shared), feel and articulate the identity of their interests as between themselves, and as against other men whose interests are different from (and usually opposed to) theirs'.[9] Thompson's view is that the attempt of some sociologists to stop this process dead 'at any given moment and anatomize its structure' is impossible: the relationship is too elusive. Late nineteenth-century society illustrates, however, that with Thompson's historical reality in mind such an analysis can, in fact, be made. The attempt to stop history dead and anatomize it fails only if sociology itself is unaware of, or rejects, the reality of historical movement and direction contained within the phenomena it investigates. How sociologists consider this question in terms of contemporary Britain is matter for later discussion. Here the point is that, against the background we have described, men did not fail to see themselves in relation to other men, and to use the terminology of class in so doing.

Behind the complexities of nineteenth-century politics lay a continued concentration of major areas of power in the hands of what Kitson Clark calls the 'nobility and gentry – old style'. The 1832 Reform Act was not a symbolic arrival at the ultimate position of power by the middle class; nor did it mark the decline of the ancient English aristocracy. The eighteenth century 'lingered at the top of society as obstinately and as self-confidently as it did anywhere in the social pattern of Victorian England'. Until the new patterns of power that emerged as a result of political pressures before and after the 1867 Reform Act and the economic situation from the early 1870s, parliament continued to be dominated by the old 'feudalism', the 'landed interest'. Politics was still in the middle of the century 'to a remarkable extent the plaything of the nobility and gentry'.[10] What was true of parliament was also true of other aspects of national life, including the Civil Service, although the introduction of competitive examinations (following the Trevelyan–Northcote Report of 1854) began slowly to make inroads into aristocratic patronage and domination in the Civil Service. Until then it was normal for the top administrative positions to be occupied by the aristocracy – 'patricians', whose rule was 'in general conscientious, honorable and enlightened'. The virtues of the 'patricians' were those 'of the eighteenth-century grandee, or as some of them fancied, of Roman senators'.[11] The subsequent history of power in Britain is to a large degree concerned with the way in which the centres of hereditary power continued relatively unmolested through the first exercise in parliamentary democracy in 1832 and its embodiment in the Act of 1867, and survived the social readjustments of the late century. The position of the gentry was undermined in direct ways – in, for example, the loss of the traditional powers of the country justices, greater taxation and the emergence of modern political parties which cut back the traditional ascendancy of hereditary influence. But the gentry 'old style' intermingled with the 'new gentry' born of industrial and commercial expansion. Influence found new ways to operate, and hereditary positions found new ways to reassert themselves. New strengths were found for the traditional qualities of England's aristocratic 'grandees'.

For a prolonged period, therefore, the new middle class, or middle classes, had the problem of defining themselves in terms of their relationships across both an upper and a lower frontier. The middle-class Liberals of the 1860s were as aware of the 'feudalism' above them as they were of the slippery but important boundary which delimited them from the other nation below. The perpetuation of aristocratic power and the attacks on its positions offer a clue to the agonies of self-definition through which the middle class went in the second half of the century.

If class can only be seen as a relationship, it was one that existed across a wide range of social processes. The most obvious relationship downwards was in terms of employment, the economic basis on which Marx's analysis of class identities and class struggle was primarily (though not exclusively) made. This was the relationship of factory owner and worker, of mistress and servant. The relationship was also apparent, however, in the class differentiation of towns as middle-class suburbia spread, in the differentiation of shopping and consumption, education and religious worship. For example, the Board Schools created by the 1870 Education Act were as categorically working-class as the grammar schools had become middle-class. The complex definition of the concept of middle-class people would have to compound not only the economics of their income and the status evaluation of their occupations, but increasingly their postal district, religious affiliation, schooling and – in the case of new professions and the changing status of older ones – their relationship to inferiors. For those at lower levels of the middle class, in small business and clerical positions, the definition was of poignant importance.

The expansion of the world of commerce and trade is, of course, the central fact of the Victorian middle class. The merchant and the middle class were not created by industrial Britain, but the nature of the nineteenth-century economy meant a sharply widening catchment area of population involved in middle-class economic activities; the expansion of joint-stock enterprises, the increase in the scale of industrial (and public) administration, and the growth of industrial invention and production skills, meant a considerable expansion in the numbers of managers, shopkeepers and industrial entrepreneurs. The ideals of the new middle class were a long way from the Protestant ethic described by Weber as a feature of the origins of industrial society. When *The Times* in 1919 reviewed the difficulties of the middle class it traced its history in miniature:

> ... the plight of the middle classes is undoubtedly partly due to a disposition for the last twenty or thirty years to aim at a standard of living which has been far too high, to seek expensive pleasures, and to neglect the more irksome duties of citizenship. In the Victorian era, which it is now the fashion to despise, the middle classes lived far more simply and frugally. They did not frequent costly restaurants, went to the theatre once a month, travelled comparatively little, rarely sought a continental holiday, and were more interested in domestic life ...

The middle class had initially been driven by 'the gospel of hard work', which, in preaching and organizing for others, they had accepted for themselves: 'the middle classes set the example in work and austerity; the manufacturers led a protesting nation into the factories, preaching that its reward would be in the next world – while reaping a considerable interim dividend for themselves in this'.[12]

New foods, new consumer products, new luxuries, new services, new styles of living, were all part of the breakdown of the old ethic, and the adoption of new suburban

8 *'Boulter's Lock: Sunday Afternoon'*, *1897*

shopping-centred, home-centred, comfort-centred standards. This situation is an example of what Veblen described as rising standards of possessions – 'conspicuous consumption'. Veblen explains how human beings, from primitive society onward, become involved, by virtue of the existence of a leisure class, in processes of social emulation. Position becomes identified not only with leisure, but with the possession of its symbols – most obviously servants. A leisure class develops an 'instinctive repugnance for the vulgar forms of labour' and abstention from labour 'is not only an honorific or meritorious act, but it presently comes to be a requisite of decency'. Leisure and evidence of wealth become 'means of gaining the respect of others'. Conspicuous consumption of valuable goods 'is a means of reputability to the gentleman of leisure'. Veblen's thesis up to this point does not apply directly to the Victorian middle class in general in the first half of the century. It becomes relevant, however, when we remember that the increased scale and changing structure of industrial and commercial organizations made it possible for the middle class in greater numbers to attain the trappings of leisured life. The availability of a widening range of 'conspicuous' domestic goods, including the bric-à-brac stimulated by the Great Exhibition, intensified the process. Veblen goes on to explain how, in the modern urban community in particular, greater involvement in large gatherings (theatres, ballrooms, shops, etc.) places people with leisure in front of 'transient observers', and to impress them 'the signature of one's pecuniary strength should be written in characters which he who runs may read. It is evident, therefore, that the present trend of the development is in the direction of heightening the utility of conspicuous consumption as compared with leisure.' In the second half of the century leisure therefore became subsidiary to the 'struggle to outdo one another'. The city population especially 'push their normal standard of conspicuous consumption to a higher point ... The requirement of conformity to this higher conventional standard becomes mandatory ... this requirement of decent appearance must be lived up to on pain of losing caste.'[13] The commitment of the Victorian middle class to this battle to emulate the class above and differentiate themselves from the class below, is apparent in everything from the changing habits of the Victorian owner and manager, to the crinoline, the architecture of the villa and the clutter of the drawing-room. It was, as we shall see in the next chapter, an important aspect of the crisis of incomes and family size in the last decades of the century.

The complex structure of the middle class changed during the century to incorporate the newly expanding and newly aspiring professional groups necessary to industrial and public administration. The rulers of the old order understood, within limits, the virtues of the new middle-class professionals, although the failure to appoint Chadwick one of the Poor Law Commissioners provides an illustration of the limits. In answer to Chadwick's protests at not being appointed, Lord Althorp told him in 1841 'that your station in society was not such as would have made it fit that you should be appointed one of the commissioners'.[14] It was the middle class, however, which provided the growing mass of administrators. Into it came some of the growing clerical and supervisory occupations. Between 1881 and 1901 the numbers employed in 'general and local government' rose from 97,000 to 172,000. Old and stigmatized occupations, from the apothecary to the dissenting minister, acquired firm middle-class status. The new duties and relationships of some sections of established professions, such as the law and engineering, also achieved the raised status. The position of the relatively new occupation of architect and the element of training or impersonal consultation involved in such occupations as that of the civil engineer gained, as we have seen, both accepted status and the cachet of the professional association. The expansion of the middle class, therefore, rested on the morality of impersonal investment, the growth of the larger production unit and bank, and the need for reliable administrators and experts. It rested also on the rising scale of private consumption and the production and commercial opportunities it offered. On the basis of the 1851 census it has been estimated that rather less than one and a quarter million adult males, about 18 per cent of the labour force, were in middle-class occupations. About half of these were in commercial occupations, about a quarter were farmers, and the remainder 'members of the professional, administrative and employing classes' in commerce or industry. 'Most of the middle class', it is pointed out, in the singular, 'was literate.'[15] Those of the middle class who were not involved in a direct relationship with the working class through the process of production were engaged in a constant comparative relationship in terms of housing and style of life, consumer consumption and educational and cultural values.

Working-class identity was a product of the conditions of early industrialization. In a situation of continuing industrial and political confrontation, as John Foster has demonstrated in the case of Oldham, a move 'from trade union to class consciousness' took place in the 1830s and 1840s.[16] As the century progressed groups of skilled manual workers emerged, able to improve their wages and conditions and achieve – within the working class – a special status. There were, of course, distinctions large and small among groups of workers, based on earnings and other factors:

> There was the pride of the craftsman in 'having a trade', which he regarded as his 'property' and was in contrast to the propertyless labourer. In many cases it was the skilled man who paid the wages of his labourer or helper.

In this sense, the trade union membership of some groups, and the absence of unions for others, sharpened these divisions.[17] In the later part of the century a more and more substantial stratum of semi-skilled machine-minders – especially in the metal and engineering industries, and chemicals – grew up between the highly skilled and the unskilled. The process was to result, as science was applied more widely to methods of production, in a decline in the proportion of workers employed directly on production, and an increase in the proportion of service or 'tertiary' groups of workers. In 1851 just over a million people were employed in domestic service. Machine and boiler making accounted for under 64,000, but 'blacksmiths' for over 112,000 and iron workers 80,000. Some 150,000 were employed in different types of transport. In 1881 the number employed in 'domestic' occupations had risen to over one and a half million. 'Metals, machines, etc.' now absorbed some 813,000, and 'conveyance of men, goods, etc.' approached 800,000.[18] The proportion of workers employed in agriculture steadily declined, from 21·7 per cent of the labour force in 1851 to 8·7 per cent in 1901. While the occupational balance of the population was tilting towards industry, mining, building and transport, the standards of middle-class prosperity also led to a high proportion being constantly employed in the 'domestic and personal services' category (15·3 per cent of the labour force in 1871, and 13·9 per cent in 1911). 'Industrialization or no industrialization,' comments Phyllis Deane, 'the army of domestic servants, the host of housemaids which served the Victorian middle-class home, was still growing faster than the labour force, until towards the end of the nineteenth century it reached its peak.'[19]

The occupational structure of the working class reflected both expanding industries and employment in new ones. The old staple industries continued to expand up to 1914. British coal exports, for example, dominated world markets until the First World War. Although Britain was to pay the penalty of her pioneering status in these industries, the end of the century saw aspects of modernization which were important for future industrial development and indicative of occupation trends. At the close of the century industries such as hosiery, footwear, clothing, flour-milling and brewing were almost completely mechanized.[20] Greater precision was achieved and cheaper machinery available, the small steam-engine was brought into use, and new light industries (for example, large-scale bicycle manufacture – an important prelude to the manufacture of cars) were created. An efficient gas mantle, invented in the 1880s, staved off the doom of gas lighting (which had been universally available since the 1820s) until beyond the end of the century. The electricity industry expanded only slowly in the second half of the century. The first modern power station was opened at Deptford in 1889 and by 1900 the incandescent lamp was unchallengeable. British electrical engineering, however, lagged considerably behind that of the United States and Germany.

These are only indications of the industrial context within which the changes in working-class occupational structure were taking place. In the middle of the century wage differentials between skilled and unskilled workers had increased, and were either steady or increased up to 1914. Eric Hobsbawm describes the wage and status gap between the working-class 'aristocrats' and the rest, and also the important 'transfer of the centre of gravity within the labour aristocracy from the old pre-industrial crafts to the new metal industries'.[21] The real wages of all workers in full employment rose considerably in the second half of the century. Wide differences in the wage rates of skilled and unskilled workers were reduced in the 1890s, but widened again between the turn of the century and the First World War. In 1867 a skilled engineer earned on average approximately twice as much as a labourer; in 1914 he earned perhaps 50 per cent more.

It is difficult to generalize about so complex a phenomenon as the structure of the working class over so long a period. The working class was never homogeneous, although in many senses it tended to become less and in others more so. There were, as we have seen, and as some historians have investigated in detail, differences in methods of work, traditions, levels of income and status.[22] Such differences of economic and social position, of course, point to differences in response to such things as industrial bargaining and disputes, suffrage demands and political representation. Rises in the incomes of some lower groups brought them closer to groups above them, but generally speaking economic differentials were real and acutely felt. This did not, however, preclude a growing sense of working-class identity which accompanied the establishment of specifically working-class institutions, such as the Trades Union Congress (in 1868) and the working men's clubs (most of them combined in the Club and Institute Union, founded in 1862). Trades Councils at one level and the T.U.C. at another were vehicles through which this sense of identity was cemented. Chartism in the 1830s and 1840s and suffrage agitation in the 1860s expressed forms of awareness of identity. The fight for the reform of trade union legislation

9 *Lock-out in South Wales, February 1875. A pawn-office at Merthyr Tydfil*

was another form and 'the successful campaign from 1867 to 1875 gave the movement a new unity, expressed in the establishment of the Trades Union Congress'.[23] The Webbs saw the T.U.C. as 'an outward and visible sign of that persistent sentiment of solidarity which has ... distinguished the working class'.[24]

In many ways, some hazy, some intensely practical, this sense of working-class solidarity was strengthened in these decades. Working-class experience throughout the century developed an approach to society, to social organization and purpose, and to concepts of democracy and community, fundamentally different from that which rested on the individualism of the middle class. Where middle-class values were predominantly those of consumption, emulation and competition, working-class survival and advance depended in general on collective action, on the erection of objects and ideals from the starting point of common experience, shared deprivation. This growing range of working-class institutions, which encompassed trade union and co-operative, political and educational activities, pointed towards many of the critical disputes about politics, culture and society in the twentieth century. Working-class experience and organization in the nineteenth century provided, Raymond Williams suggests, not only a system of 'sectional defence', but a 'steady offering and discovery of ways of living that could be extended to the whole society, which could quite reasonably be organized on a basis of collective democratic institutions and the substitution of co-operative equality for competition as the principle of social and economic policy'. This challenge was, in fact, eroded, under strong pressure for the co-operatives to 'be simply trading organizations, the trade unions simply industrial organizations with no other interests, each union keeping to its own sphere, and the Labour Party simply an alternative government in the present system'.[25]

Power and politics

From social class, therefore, it is a short step to the concept of democracy. Social history is concerned, when it turns its attention to politics, with popular politics, representative movements and the relationship between political change and social assumptions and behaviour. It is concerned with movements not only for the suffrage, but also for industrial legislation and trade union rights, for co-operative organization, a free press and the political, legal and social rights of women.

The prime feature of a social movement is its desire to arouse and sustain public opinion in such a way as to effect change. A diffuse movement like Chartism and a tightly organized movement such as the National Education League both aimed to stimulate public concern and to attain precise targets. Rarely can action and achievement be directly correlated; widespread public concern is matched, however, by corresponding shifts of opinion and response on the part of policy-makers. The 1867 Reform Act and the 1870 Education Act were the product of such changing responses – in these cases over long periods of time. The

important new feature of nineteenth-century social development was precisely, as was shown outstandingly by
Chartism and the Anti-Corn-Law League in one respect
and the popular press in another, a new dimension in the
marshalling and organizing of opinion.

The 1832 Reform Act disfranchised some rotten boroughs, created new boroughs and enfranchised a quarter of
a million new property-owning voters. It deliberately left
the working class outside the structure of power. Working-
class support for the reform movement went unrewarded.
Before the Bill was passed the radical working-class press
made it clear to working men that 'the measure gives nothing to you':

> . . . it is considered that it will be a 'stepping-stone to
> something which will do you good'; now the only ground
> upon which it can possibly be so considered is that the
> 'reformed constitution' will be more favourable to your
> interests than the present, or rather, that £10 house-
> holders or 'middle-men', who will acquire a voice in the
> government, will be more inclined to admit your right to
> Universal Suffrage, &c.: we have already exhausted all
> our argument to prove to you that the 'middle-men' are
> the 'master-men', and that you are the 'serving-men', and
> that the interest of the former is to depress the latter . . .

The Bill would not benefit 'the degraded mob'. It 'may
perhaps benefit a few, but it will still be at the expense of
the many. It will benefit none but the proud and arrogant
"shopocracy".'[26]
. There were already strong traditions of working-class
independence born in the system of Methodist study
classes, trade unionism, political and Luddite agitation, and
Owenite co-operation. The experience of the Chartist
movement, which reached its peaks in 1842 and 1848,
confirmed this sense of a need for independent working-
class political and social action. The working class had
defined its aims in relation to the 'middle-men'. Chartism
aimed formally at annual parliaments, universal male suffrage, equal electoral districts, the removal of property

qualifications for membership of parliament, the secret ballot and payment for members. The middle class in (or holding some of the strings of) power did not feel strong enough to absorb a new democratic development towards the working class and resisted the strong Chartist pressures. Growing national prosperity, the alliance between skilled trade unions and Liberalism, and the internal uncertainties of working-class radical programmes, made it possible for working men to be kept outside the structure of political

Voters as a percentage of the population aged over 20 years

1831	5·0%
After 1832 (First Reform Act)	7·1%
After 1867 (Second Reform Act)	16·4%
After 1884 (Third Reform Act)	28·5%
After 1918	74·0%
After 1928 (Equal Franchise Act)	96·9%

After S. GORDON *Our Parliament*, Cassell (London, 1964).

democracy until the middle class felt capable of containing and indeed benefiting from its further extension. Chartism made universal suffrage ultimately inevitable, projecting important social ideals into the national consciousness, but this, the first major organized political movement of the working class, was unable to dictate the speed and terms on which the political and social concessions were finally to be made.

Reform came in 1867, with an Act which took seats from small boroughs and gave them to large ones, gave the suffrage in boroughs to all householders and to lodgers paying ten pounds a year or more, and added one million voters to the registers. The Act was not an immediate outcome of the Chartist movement, but new pressures had built up between the decline of Chartism and the late 1860s. Trade union pressures especially had been strong in the early 1860s, and even when agitation for reform was not taking place there was a sense of its imminent possibility. In 1866 and 1867 agitation for reform was firm and influential.[27] With the Act of 1867, working men in towns were largely admitted to the franchise. The 1884 Act created another two million voters by putting the vote in the countryside on the same basis as the urban franchise.

The history of parliamentary reform comprises other considerations. It has to answer the question: what difference did these developments make to political life and public opinion? Apart from their reflection of changes in the centres of political power, they also reflect profound changes in the very nature of political awareness. The pressures towards the 1867 Act, for example, and the Act itself, demonstrated the new need to 'capture' the working-class voter. Out of the confused alliances which had hitherto characterized political groupings was emerging the concept of the modern political party, which needed to try to enlist mass support. Before 1867 Gladstone had become leader of a Liberal Party profoundly different from the old Whig and Radical alliances. 1867 marks the appearance of nation-wide leaflet circulation, and for the first time in the late 1870s Gladstone established the practice of making speeches in his constituency during the parliamentary session, and courting press publicity. It was Disraeli and the Conservatives who, after much manœuvring, had promoted what he called the 'leap in the dark' of the 1867 Act. The working-class vote went, however, in the election that followed, to the Liberals. For the next five years Disraeli worked to set up the first efficient centralized English party organization – the National Union of Conservative and Constitutional Associations. It won him seats at by-elections and 'had candidates ready in every constituency which he could conceivably hope to win. The general election of 1874 was the first triumph of the Conservative Central Office.'[28]

The impetus to local organization was given by the need to recruit and retain the popular vote, to dominate local government with its growing powers, and to manipulate the voting system in constituencies with more than one member. The result, in the mid-1870s, was the Birmingham 'caucus'. Joseph Chamberlain, using the experience of the 1868 election and of School Board elections, built a local Liberal organization which was the first effective local

10 *Bloody Sunday, 13 November 1887. The Life Guards hold Trafalgar Square*

political machine of its type. A complex machinery of ward and committee organization was established, combining democratic features with strong central control. Two results ensued: first, Chamberlain's 'caucus' dominated Birmingham local government; secondly, other local Liberal organizations, and then the powerful National Liberal Federation, came into existence, confirming the arrival of the age of mass political organization and appeal.[29] From within the parliamentary parties pressures had been exerted which resulted in the creation of Liberal and Conservative constituency organizations. The Labour Party, at the beginning of the twentieth century, was to work in the reverse direction, with organizations outside parliament seeking to build a parliamentary representation. National and local politics were a two-way process. All major legislation in the field of parliamentary representation was followed by important legislation affecting the structure and operation of local government and affairs. The 1832 Act, as we have seen, was followed by Acts directly affecting factory conditions (1833), school building (1833) and municipal government (1835). The 1867 Act was followed by the reconstruction and expansion of the basis of elementary education (1870) and the machinery of central and local sanitary administration (1871–2). The 1884 Act was followed by the 1888 Local Government Act, bringing the country districts into line with urban administration by the establishment of county councils. In very many cases such legislation followed on the work of Commissions appointed by incoming governments elected on the basis of new franchise conditions.

Working-class efforts to achieve a wider measure of political participation continued through the century to lie uneasily between the necessity to use Liberal machinery to exercise political influence and the necessity for independent action. The rival socialist organizations of the 1880s (including the Social Democratic Federation and the Fabian Society), and the hostility during the 1890s between the old unionism of the skilled workers and the new unionism of the organized unskilled, reflect some of the tensions in the labour movement before the Labour Representation

Committee was – with many hesitations – created in 1900 (changing its name to the Labour Party after the election of 1906).

Throughout the century the thrust towards independent action vacillated between different forms. The working class had its own radical political organizations, its own radical press, a long history of involvement in organized political protest, and experience of various forms of repression. The working-class co-operative movement had begun in the 1820s with the aim of creating communities for production and a better way of life. Co-operative store-keeping grew from the beginnings at Rochdale in 1844 through to the establishment of a nation-wide network of shops offering cheap, unadulterated food, and the creation of the Co-operative Wholesale Society in 1860. The co-operative movement in its first phase was a design for an alternative way of living; in its second phase it was a way for working-class families to participate in some of the benefits of rising material standards.

The trade unions of the 1830s were also involved to a considerable extent with ideals of social reorganization which went far beyond the immediate problems of the trade unionist – though it was frequently the bewilderments of the immediate situation that led to the identification of trade unionism with wider ideals, including those of Owenism. The New Model unions from the 1850s, with high rates of subscription and benefit, aimed explicitly to organize the craft labour aristocracy. The unions of skilled workers played a dominant part in the early history of the Trades Councils, and their officials played a skilful and successful part in pressing for improved legislation affecting the unions. Conciliation and expert political pressure on the one hand could be accompanied by decisive strike action on the other. The New Model, however, in the conditions of the 1880s, had become old unionism. The New Unions, organized for the most part by socialists, covered the unskilled across whole industries, offering low subscriptions and effective militancy as the stimulus to membership. Unionism among the unskilled had been alive in places like the ports of Hull and Liverpool from the 1870s, but the union and strike of the Bryant & May match-girls in 1888, the organization on a larger scale in 1888 and 1889 of unions among the gas workers and dock workers, and the London dock strike of 1889, demonstrated the arrival of general unionism. These developments in trade unionism, though they were not consistent in the 1890s, pointed (as did the foundation of the Independent Labour Party in 1893) towards the future coalescence of working-class organizations into the Labour Party.

Factory legislation

The kind of social and political movements we have been considering both reflected and shaped changes in social consciousness. Many of the settled assumptions of mid-Victorian Britain were crumbling by the final decades of the century, and we have been glancing ahead to some of the new frameworks of discussion and action. Discussions of social problems and even awareness of social realities are conditioned not only by what *is* but by what is *pointed out to be*. By the end of the Golden Age settled assumptions had been assailed by the demonstration of fact and the campaign for change. By the 1870s these changes had begun to take place against a background of at least one set of assumptions in which firm changes had already taken place – that relating to industrial conditions. From the late 1860s trade unionism was not only placed in a new situation of political influence, but also found itself having to adjust to new responsibilities and accommodations with the law and the employers. The nature of the regulation of factory conditions is obviously related to the strength and purpose of the working-class movement, but it is also related to technical and structural changes within industry, to assumptions about social and economic organization, to complementary legislation (on, for example, education and health), and to differing attitudes towards the economic and social roles of male and female, adult and child. We have not traced the earlier history of factory conditions and legislation, and we can do so now only in the barest outline. It is important, however, to establish how far this process had gone, indicative as it is of some of the contradictions in the Victorian scheme of things. There are two important facts about the situation to bear in mind: factory reform throughout the century was concerned almost exclusively with women and children; and the subject of legislation was not wages, but hours of work.

The first Factory Acts of 1802 and 1819 were concerned with pauper apprentices in cotton mills. The first effective Act (that of 1833) limited hours to nine a day for children under thirteen, and twelve a day for young persons between thirteen and eighteen. Pressure for a ten-hour Bill covering adult males had been evaded and, by organizing children in shifts, firms could in fact work adults fifteen hours a day. The Act involved a number of gains: textiles other than cotton were included, schooling was made a requirement for factory children for two hours a day, six days a week (the first form of compulsory schooling in England) and the principle of compulsory holidays for children and young persons was introduced. The appointment of four factory inspectors – not in itself enough to check abuses – was an important departure for the whole development of the structure of public responsibility. The 1842 Mines Act prohibited the employment of women and of children under the age of ten underground (a measure evaded for a long time in some places) and introduced safety restrictions. Other legislation gave mining by the 1870s a basic legislative code (the first national miners' union had been formed in 1858).

Textiles, however, continued to be the area of main legislative attention until the 1870s. An Act of 1844 made a further step towards industrial safety and the protection of children; women and young persons were now classified together, with the maximum working day remaining at twelve hours, and a schooling requirement of fifteen hours a week for children. This 'half-time' system (applauded by Marx, who considered that it provided a proper combination of learning and industrial experience) continued until after the First World War. The direction of the legislation was now clearly to protect workers in general by restricting the work of women and children, on whom – in the textile industries – the operations performed by adult males depended. The Ten Hours Act of 1847 was the culmination of nearly two decades of agitation for such an Act, agitation which had brought together Shaftesbury-type 'social Tories' and ten-hour committees organized by the workers in the northern textile countries. This agitation interlocked with Chartism, trade unionism and other protest movements. The Act set the pattern for subsequent factory legislation. The basic provision was a ten-hour day (and a fifty-eight-hour week) for women and young persons. The manufacturers found a loop-hole by organizing irregular relays, and a compromise Act of 1850, which defeated the relay system, stipulated a twelve-hour period within which the hours had to be worked, but extended the working day by half an hour. Dicey's agonized verdict on these two Acts was that they laid the basis 'for a whole system of governmental inspection and control'. Their success 'gave authority, not only in the world of labour, but in many other spheres of life, to beliefs which, if not exactly socialistic, yet certainly tended towards socialism or collectivism'.[30] This is an exaggeration, but it does locate some of the importance of the Acts, and by the time the 1860s and 1870s arrived the history of factory legislation had become interlinked with the history not only of industrial and economic conditions, but also of the changes in political and social assumptions we have discussed. Legislation from then on widened the range of industries covered and intensified the system of inspection. By the First World War it had taken in wider considerations. Employers' liability and compensation for accidents, the conditions of shop workers and the supervision of dangerous industries had become, albeit in some cases timidly, subjects of legislation and controls. The Coal Mines Regulation Act of 1908 regulated hours for *male* labour, and the 1909 Trade Boards Act represented another new departure in legislation by seeking – as a result of a campaign against 'sweating' – to protect the ill-organized workers in trades such as tailoring (there were fifty-two Trade Boards by 1945, when they became Wages Councils). Joint Industrial Councils (Whitley Councils) came into existence in 1919.

We have looked ahead at this point to some scattered moments of legislation in order to see how, in the special case of industry, a process of broadening social responsibility, covering an increasing range of persons and interests, can be discerned. The process demonstrates how interrelated were factors such as the direction of economic expansion, the strength of popular organization and public opinion, the educational machinery and the economic status of women. It demonstrates how far parliamentary and public involvement was seen to be necessary or inevitable. It illustrates some of the changes taking place in social institutions and social relations, and some that were not, some of the ways in which social assumptions and expectations were being subjected to pressure. It was not only the precedents of previous industrial legislation, but the campaigns to obtain and implement it, that produced responses. Political reform Acts and industrial legislation were surrounded by an awareness that popular organizations, social pressure groups and popular action were now important elements in social change.

Notes

1 H. A. SHANNON 'The coming of general limited liability', in CARUS-WILSON (ed.) *Essays in Economic History*, I, pp. 375–9.

2 E. H. PHELPS BROWN *The Growth of British Industrial Relations*, pp. 105–13 (London, 1959; 1965 edition).

3 PETER MATHIAS 'Who unbound Prometheus? Science and technical change, 1600–1800' in PETER MATHIAS (ed.) *Science and Society 1600–1900*, p. 63 (Cambridge, 1972).

4 Quoted in KEITH HUTCHISON *The Decline and Fall of British Capitalism*, pp. 19–22 (London, 1951).

5 The relevant extract can be found in HERMAN AUSUBEL *The Late Victorians*, p. 106 (New York, 1955).

6 H. L. BEALES 'The "Great Depression" in industry and trade', in CARUS-WILSON (ed.) *Essays in Economic History*, I, pp. 406–15.

7 BURNETT *Plenty and Want*, p. 156. See also HELEN MERRELL LYND *England in the Eighties* (New York, 1945).

8 T. B. BOTTOMORE *Classes in Modern Society*, p. 41 (London, 1965).

9 THOMPSON *The Making of the English Working Class*, p. 9.

10. CLARK *The Making of Victorian England*, pp. 206–14.

11 ROBERTS *Victorian Origins of the British Welfare State*, p. 138.

12 ROY LEWIS and ANGUS MAUDE *The English Middle Classes*, pp. 52–3, 70 (for *The Times* quotation) (London, 1949).

13 THORSTEIN VEBLEN *The Theory of the Leisure Class*, pp. 37–88 (New York, 1899; 1912 edition). See especially Chs. III, 'Conspicuous leisure', and IV, 'Conspicuous consumption'.

14 Quoted in ROBERTS *The Victorian Origins of the British Welfare State*, p. 146.

15 DEANE *The First Industrial Revolution*, pp. 264–5.

16 FOSTER *Class Struggle and the Industrial Revolution*, p. 125. Chs. 4 and 5 are particularly useful in this connection.

17 W. HAMISH FRASER *Trade Unions and Society: the struggle for acceptance 1850–1880*, p. 209 (London, 1974).

18 See J. H. CLAPHAM *An Economic History of Modern Britain, Free Trade and Steel 1850–1886*, p. 24 (Cambridge, 1932; 1963 edition); and DAVID C. MARSH *The Changing Social Structure of England and Wales 1871–1961*, pp. 112–18 (London, 1958; 1965 edition).

19 DEANE *The First Industrial Revolution*, pp. 255–6.

20 See WILLIAM ASHWORTH *An Economic History of England 1870–1939*, Ch. IV (London, 1960), for a discussion of technological changes in the final decades of the century.

21 E. J. HOBSBAWM 'The labour aristocracy in nineteenth-century Britain', *Labouring Men*, p. 284 (London, 1964).

22 See H. A. CLEGG, ALAN FOX and A. F. THOMPSON *A History of British Trade Unions since 1889*, Vol. I, 1889–1910 (Oxford, 1964), particularly the chapter on 'The trade union movement before 1889'.

23 Ibid., p. 48.

24 Quoted in ibid., p. 250.

25 RAYMOND WILLIAMS *The Long Revolution*, p. 302 (London, 1961). See also the conclusion in *Culture and Society 1780–1950* (London, 1958).

26 *The Poor Man's Guardian*, 3 December 1831 and 26 May 1832, pp. 185 and 401.

27 See ROYDEN HARRISON *Before the Socialists* (London, 1965).

28 J. L. HAMMOND and M. R. D. FOOT *Gladstone and Liberalism*, pp. 124–5 (London, 1952).

29 For a brief account of these developments and questions of parliamentary reform in general see H. J. HANHAM's pamphlet

The Reformed Electoral System in Great Britain 1832–1914 (London, 1968).

30 A. V. DICEY *Law and Public Opinion in England*, pp. 239–40 (London, 1905; 1962 edition).

4 New dimensions, new attitudes

Social policy

The Great Depression, as we have seen, amounted to a crisis of confidence. If, by the end of the century, 'Britain's easy leadership among the industrial nations of the world was over',[1] so also were many of the assumptions and social relationships that went with early industrialization. Although the economy of early industrial Britain had had certain acute effects on many people's way of life, on family and class relations, there were, as we have also seen, continuities with pre-industrial Britain. From the 1850s the picture is clearer, and from the 1880s it can be discussed in terms which have a recognizable ring to modern ears. By the 1920s the entire range of discussion of social problems had been reordered.

By the final decades of the nineteenth century the very process of growth, in population and cities, industrial output and the scale of industrial, commercial and social organization, had brought about widespread changes in attitudes towards the problems which these things represented. Growth and scale do not affect our attitudes and emphases alone and unaided: human agency is involved.

People have to learn to recognize facts before they can act in the light of them. It is important to remember how surprised people were in the 1840s by Chadwick's 'revelations', or Simon's of the state of the City of London, and how shocked they were by what Booth revealed at the end of the 1880s. The same was true in Britain after the Second World War, when 'until the mid-1950s ... even the term "poverty" had not been disinterred for the purposes either of popular or scientific discussion of contemporary society'. Only in the 1960s was poverty 'rediscovered', debated, studied and acted upon.[2] Recognition and surprise, as well as the conditions themselves, play a part in the reshaping of social assumptions and social policy.

What men were prepared to believe about the role of human agency in social affairs in the 1840s was something quite different by the 1880s. *Laissez-faire* doctrines, as our discussion has shown, were never applied consistently, even when they were most influential; the dominant *assumption* about human agency in the middle of the century was certainly, however, that it should be allowed to operate unhampered in social matters. It implied the operation of self-help, production for a free market, the absence of interference between employer and employee, and minimal intervention by the collective agencies of society, even in such matters as health. Resistance continued throughout the century to any form of collective action in situations where it was thought that personal or family responsibility should be paramount. Even after 1900, to take one example, when none of the general hospitals had maternity wards, the proposal that St Thomas's in London should introduce one 'was carefully considered with great anxiety, so common at that date, as to whether it might not demoralize those who ought to be able to make provision for the birth of their children at home'.[3]

Where collective agencies did exist and operate successfully, they were generally anxious to keep their activities and expenditure to a minimum. It was a constant and unwelcome surprise to the Victorians to see how relentlessly some of these agencies grew. By the middle of the century a wide range of them had, in fact, been created, including independent commissions in the fields of the Poor Law, charities and the registration of births, deaths and marriages, inspectorates for factories, prisons and mines, Privy Council departments to deal with problems of education and railways, and a variety of more temporary commissions of inquiry. The powers granted to such agencies, however, were intended 'to regulate social and economic matters. Economic freedom was infringed only to correct scandalous evils . . .'[4] Every such development had to overcome resistance. Even in the 1880s the Treasury was asking the Education Department irritably if it foresaw any end to its constant requests for more inspectors. The Department replied that the limit of this demand had 'been very nearly reached'.[5]

Collective self-help, and enthusiasm for it, had developed in many ways, mainly through popular organizations like the co-operative and trade union movements. Victorian Britain preserved, however, an underlying economic and social philosophy which sought to make the concept of individual responsibility paramount. It was Herbert Spencer who expressed this doctrine at its sharpest. A latter-day utilitarian and liberal, Spencer rejected completely the path towards legislative, collective solutions, to which he felt Liberalism and Toryism were both increasingly committing themselves. In *The Man versus the State*, first published in 1884, he catalogued the long and – for him – criminal list of State legislative interference in social processes, interference which meant that the citizen was being gradually 'in the growth of this compulsory legislation deprived of some liberty which he previously had'. The assumption was everywhere being fostered in Spencer's view, that government should step in whenever anything was not going right, a view which took it for granted 'that all suffering ought to be prevented, which is not true: much suffering is curative'. It also took it for granted that all evils could be removed, which, given the existing defects of human nature, was also untrue. It took it for granted, thirdly, that evils of all kinds should be dealt with by the State, ignoring the proper role of other agencies.[6] *The Man versus the State* is typical of Spencer's general appeal for the

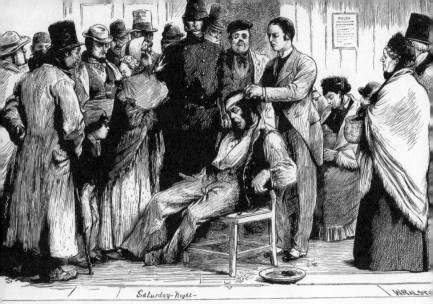

Saturday-night-

11 *Saturday night at a London hospital, 1879*

limitation of the powers of parliament, and for the encouragement of individual effort. The State could not cure, and suffering was a stimulus to effort. For Spencer, therefore, the doctrines which had underlain Victorian prosperity, and which were being eroded, needed to be reaffirmed. His enormous contribution to the literature of education, sociology and popular science embodied this message.

From the 1880s onwards, social problems began to attract attention in a new way – although it is important, when examining end-of-the-century forms of 'collectivist' growth, not to assume too drastic a shift away from earlier attitudes. Those attitudes, indeed, are visible in many aspects of contemporary social policy and the operation of social services. National insurance, it has been pointed out, which 'is still an essential part of our social security system, originated during the 1880s as a proposal for training the feckless poor in thrift through compulsory contribution'.[7] The individual, it was becoming more widely and uncomfortably realized in the late nineteenth century, could not bear full responsibility for his status in society. Was it always possible – it was seriously asked – for the individual, however talented, however industrious, to be the agent of his own success? Was self-help meaningful when it was suspected that there might be structural defects in the economy? How much of what had been interpreted as pauperism was in fact poverty? Was it, after all, undesirable to admit the intervention of collective agencies to set limits on the 'freedom' of the individual, by relieving him of responsibilities which he could not in any case properly bear? Were not housing, health, education, hours of work and the quality of food, for example, already to one extent or another subjects of legislation, and should not the range and scale of this kind of 'interference' be extended? Not everyone in the closing decades of the century asked these questions, and there was certainly no wide measure of agreement even among radicals and liberals on how to answer them. The momentum of change in attitudes had, however, become powerful by the 1890s, to a major extent as a result of pressure from new socialist organizations for policies which would tackle some of the basic causes of poverty. The Poor Law illustrates how, in relation to one of the main structural defects in society, the older attitudes clung tenaciously.

Poor Law arrangements after 1834, as we have seen, were a machinery for the protection of the community against what was assumed to be the irresponsible and feckless nature of pauperism. The workhouse, in order to deter, was self-consciously forbidding. It was what one sociologist has called a 'total institution' – that is, 'a place of residence and work where a large number of like-situated individuals, cut off from the wider society for an appreciable period of time, together lead an enclosed, formally administered round of life'. He explains that 'their encompassing or total character is symbolized by the barrier to social intercourse with the outside and to departure that is often built right into the physical plant, such as locked doors, high walls, barbed wire, cliffs, water, forests, or more'. Those immured tend for the most part to be the incapable and the dangerous, but also those whose work qualifies them (e.g. soldiers) or whose way of life requires it (e.g. monks).[8] Although the indigent appear in the list of candidates, in modern British society indigence is not a qualification. In the nineteenth century it was. Poverty, in the final analysis, required as 'total' a treatment as crime, insanity or military training. Despite relaxations in regulations, the workhouse remained a persistent fact and a symbol of a basic continuity in the dominant forms of social action, at least until after the First World War. George Lansbury, the Labour leader, describes his first visit to a workhouse in the 1890s as follows:

> Going down a narrow lane, ringing the bell, waiting while an official with a not too pleasant face looked through a grating to see who was there, and hearing his unpleasant voice . . . made it easy for me to understand why the poor dreaded and hated these places, and made me in a flash realize how all these prison or bastille sort of surroundings were organized for the purpose of making self-respecting, decent people endure any suffering rather than enter . . . Officials, receiving ward, hard forms, whitewashed walls, keys dangling at the waist of those who spoke to you, huge books for name, history, etc., searching, and then being stripped and bathed in a communal tub, and the final crowning indignity of being dressed in clothes which had been worn by lots of other people, hideous to look at, ill-fitting and coarse – everything possible was done to inflict mental and moral degradation.[9]

Conditions remained arbitrary; cruelty was common. A writer in 1886, pointing to improvements in infirmary nursing, emphasized by contrast the continuing workhouse cruelties, the maltreatment of the mentally and physically sick and the aged, the brutality of the workhouse rulers: 'the days of such tyrants are not yet over, and it is well that we should be reminded of this fact, and aroused from a pleasant dream to the terrible reality'.[10] Only in the 1890s, in fact, did major concessions over conditions (the permission of tobacco and tea, the ending of the segregation of married couples and the withdrawal of other harsh conditions) improve workhouse life significantly and widely.[11]

The late-century development which revealed this general approach as clearly in the field of social action as did Spencer in the field of ideas was the establishment of the Charity Organization Society. The C.O.S., founded in 1869,

New dimensions, new attitudes 99

made important contributions to forms of social work, but its main role was to carry over into the charitable field the philosophy of deterrence. Although it intended to co-ordinate and even to supersede existing charitable organizations which, it believed, handed out charity too indiscriminately, it failed from the start to obtain sufficient co-operation from rival charitable bodies. What it did achieve, however, was a prominence in charity work which made the C.O.S. symbolic of a particular view of poverty and the poor. Its aims included 'the promotion of habits of providence and self-reliance, and of those social and sanitary principles, the observance of which is essential to the well-being of the poor and of the community at large', and also 'the repression of mendicity and imposture, and the correction of the maladministration of charity'.[12] The Society withheld, and tried to persuade others to withhold, charity for purposes which the poor ought themselves to have planned and provided for. Although in emergency, and to restore independent endeavour, it was prepared to help with a sewing machine, a horse or training, it strongly resisted any form of action which might seem to encourage idleness. It fought undeviatingly against old age pensions. In the view of its Secretary, C. S. Loch, 'to supplement low wages is to prevent wages from rising: even a postponed supplementation, old age pensions, will have the same effect by discouraging thrift'.[13] One of the first lady almoners, recommended to St Thomas's Hospital by Loch, was greatly relieved in 1908 when Lambeth failed to implement a proposal to open a subsidized meals centre for mothers (as Chelsea had done). 'Fortunately,' she wrote, 'this scheme was not adopted. Any movements of this kind would be disastrous to the neighbourhood and would undermine much of the present effort to raise people from pauperization.'[14]

What this type of philosophy meant in personal terms was recalled indignantly by George Lansbury. His mother used to do little things for the poor of the neighbourhood, including the sending of a Sunday dinner to an old couple living in an East End slum. His wife's mother also visited the sick and needy, and in both cases they came up against the 'malignant work' of C.O.S. policy and the Board of Guardians:

> On at least two occasions these wretched experts in rate saving actually had the impudence to write and request us not to help certain people, as our assistance prevented the Guardians – the Guardians, mind you – from sending them to the workhouse, which in the judgment of these Christians was the best place for them.[15]

For the C.O.S. and its supporters there were two kinds of pauper: those who could be helped back to independence by properly applied, short-term, conditional remedies; and those who could not be helped. The proper organ of support for this latter residue was the Poor Law Board of Guardians with its workhouse. 'There is a subtle and constant influence,' moaned the Majority Poor Law Commissioners in 1909, 'fostered by the kindly instincts of impulsive humanity, which is ever at work sapping and undermining restrictions upon the grant of public relief.'[16] Such instincts, inside or outside the Poor Law machinery, damaged it. Indiscriminate dinners were a distraction from the process of deterrence, and for the sake of the whole apparatus they must be discouraged!

This view of the stigma of pauperism and of poverty is present in contemporary discussions of the social services. It has underpinned all forms of means testing, and it has often inhibited the use of services and the acceptance of entitlement. Discussing the absence of research into means-test systems, for example, Robert Pinker makes the point that 'stigma, complexity and secrecy are the modern counterpart of the workhouse test, namely processes of exclusion depending on value judgements rather than research into their effects'.[17] Poverty and the Poor Law are major indicators of how the Victorian middle classes defined society, and who was accepted into it, and in what conditions. There were two principal factors in the emergence of organized resistance to social attitudes of this kind, and of alternative policies. The first was the growth of a labour movement better equipped to formulate political and social policies and to take significant action; the second was, partly for this very reason, the elaboration by various social thinkers of alternative policies. An element in social consciousness after the Reform Acts of 1867 and 1884 was the realization that the working man and his movement were to be reckoned with. As a historian of the growth of the social services has put it: 'politicians could see before the turn of the century that something would have to be done about unemployment. No matter what was the cause of the idle man's condition, after 1885 he was a man with a vote.'[18]

Social investigation

Coupled with this consciousness was the elaboration of policies rooted in investigation. Social investigation was not, of course, created in the 1880s by Charles Booth. The collection of social data had already become an important and influential activity. Since 1801 the compilation of census data had been refined. Henry Mayhew (*London Labour and the London Poor* was written between 1849 and 1862) had been preoccupied with data as well as with moral demonstration. We have already looked at Chadwick's efforts to discover and confront the facts. Statistical societies attempted – notably in education – to draw accurate guidelines. Out of the reports of inspectors slowly emerged a realization that social policy and action needed to be based on something more than haphazard information. Industrial reformers understood the role of precise evidence. Engels (in *The Condition of the Working Class in England in 1844*) and Marx (in *Capital*, the first volume of which appeared in German in 1867) understood the value of detailed documentation. The tradition of 'the discovery of fact' made it possible for Booth, in the 1880s, to grasp the importance of extending the scale of discovery. It is difficult, of course, to define a social 'fact', especially when the Victorian organizations which compiled or discussed them saw them through the lens of moral and social 'improvement'. The 'social problems' which the facts were intended to illuminate were defined by the reformers' view of moral and social reform. It was commonly felt, however, that the exposure of problems and the accumulation of data would promote social action and change. This was the dominant tradition of late nineteenth-century social investigation in Britain, typified by the National Association for the Promotion of Social Science. This preoccupation with problems and facts has continued to be distinguishing feature of British sociology, by contrast with its more theoretical counterparts in other countries.

Booth, wealthy shipowner, Liberal, rooted in the C.O.S. tradition, began in the second half of the 1880s to organize a series of surveys, first in Tower Hamlets, then in Hackney, and then on a widening basis to cover what the seventeen volumes of his great work (completed in 1903) described as *The Life and Labour of the People of London*. In 1887, seven months after his inquiry began, he read a paper to the Royal Statistical Society in which the only conclusion he was prepared to offer was that 'an unexpectedly high proportion of the total population (of Tower Hamlets), 35 per cent, had been found to be living "at all times more or less in want".'[19] The word 'unexpectedly' is crucial. His inquiry in Hackney, to his own dismay, confirmed these findings. A second paper to the Society in 1888 expressed the view that about one third of the population of London was 'sinking into want'.

The magnitude of this discovery for Booth and for liberal opinion generally cannot be over-stressed. When his work began to appear its impact was considerable, being the focus of widespread discussion in the press; its 'significance was immediate and immense, and the first edition was quickly exhausted'.[20] Booth had hoped to demonstrate that British social conditions were not as bad as some commentators – particularly the socialists – had claimed them to be. He set in motion machinery, using census material and detailed material collected from School Board Visitors. He ended by changing the whole context of discussion of social realities. The information he collated was in itself dramatic enough: one-quarter to one-third of the population was demonstrated to be living 'in poverty' (including 'the poor' with regular family earnings of eighteen to twenty-one shillings a week, and 'the very poor', earning less). The breakdown of social categories he gave in the second volume of *Life and*

Labour (1891) indicated that 8·4 per cent fell into classes A (lowest) and B (very poor), and 22·3 per cent into C and D (poor); 51·5 per cent were in E and F (working class, comfortable) and 17·8 per cent in G and H (middle class and above).[21] The crisis of opinion which the findings entailed for Booth himself was considerable. He accepted the need for emphatic social action to alleviate distress which, he had become convinced, was on a scale which made individual responsibility no longer an adequate answer. He came to a conclusion which marks a real turning point in social policies, from the world of nineteenth-century reluctant involvement to that of twentieth-century considered action. 'The individualist community on which we build our faith,' he admitted at the critical stage of his dilemma in 1888, 'will find itself obliged for its own sake to take charge of the lives of those who, from whatever cause, are incapable of independent existence up to the required standard . . . and will be fully able to do so.'[22]

If there is a representative text for the new search for directions in social policy this could well be it. Policy was to remain 'individualist', but society was to 'take charge'. Poverty, it was recognized, could result from a variety of causes, and there were definable and 'required' standards. There is a survival of confidence in all this, but also a recognition of deep difficulties. Not least of these was, and remains, the definition of poverty. Booth's calculations on the basis of income were to be refined in relation to subsistence, that is, the maintenance of basic physical efficiency, by Seebohm Rowntree and others. In the twentieth century discussions of the poverty threshold have focused on nutritional standards and definitions of basic subsistence needs – including fuel and clothing, for instance – but absolute definitions of poverty have always been subject to major disagreements. It is in this context, as we shall see, that the concept of 'deprivation', and the application of relative criteria, have come into play.[23]

The need for social intervention was exhibited most clearly in Booth's assessment of the causes of pauperism: old age, he computed in his survey of Stepney, accounted for 32·8 per cent of pauperism, sickness for 26·7 per cent.[24] The

acceptance of social control over extreme poverty was sig-
nalled by Booth's conversion to the idea of old age pensions.
This was one of the battlegrounds for old and new views of
social action. If the conflicts in the Poor Law Commission
of 1905–9 and between its Majority and Minority Reports
are to be understood, and if the measures taken in the field
of pensions, health and unemployment insurance by a
revived Liberalism are to be properly assessed, the
sharpness of the crisis which Booth had precipitated needs
to be borne in mind.[25] British traditions of social analysis
had now resulted in the elaboration of sophisticated new
survey techniques, and an interest in new types of data.
Booth's questions, answers and techniques were reflected in
other inquiries. A Royal Commission on Labour in the early
1890s, for instance, was inciting those who gave evidence to
collate detailed information. Sir Robert Giffen, Permanent
Secretary to the Board of Trade, computed to the Royal
Commission that 23·6 per cent of 'the actual earnings of
adult males engaged in manual labour' in Great Britain and
Ireland in 1885 were twenty shillings a week or less, and
35·4 per cent were between twenty and twenty-five shillings.[26] Seebohm Rowntree's investigation of poverty in
York, begun in the spring of 1899 and published in 1901,
followed directly from the work of Booth – 'the second great
exercise in basic fact finding, a kind of modern social
Domesday Book'.[27] Booth's principal contribution to social
analysis was the sheer pioneering courage of it. Rowntree's
work was important in that it obtained more of its information directly from working-class families, and 'gave new
precision to the concept of poverty. He constructed in
money terms, a quantitative standard of minimum family
needs in respect of food, clothing, fuel and rent.'[28] A family
of five, he calculated, needed 21s 8d if they were not to fall
below the Poverty Line. He found that in York 10 per cent
of the population were not earning enough to meet this
standard of living and were therefore living in what he
called 'primary poverty'. Another 18 per cent failed to
achieve the standard because, although earning this
amount, expenditure on anything from drink to furniture
meant that the minimum necessary for such things as food

and clothes was lacking. These were living in 'secondary poverty'.

The refinements of other investigators marked important advances, but Booth stands out as one of the most important and influential figures in the history of social analysis and policy. The reception given to his statistics and conclusions forced a consideration of broad aspects of social progress, and of specific items of social reform. Old age pensions became for this reason a central feature of intensive social debate, but other items were achieving prominence, and as a result of other activities and processes. The discussion of housing and living conditions, for example, found new terms of reference from the late 1870s. The first Cross Act of 1875, the activities of Joseph Chamberlain in Birmingham, the gradual growth of regulations covering building density and construction, and the Housing of the Working Classes Act of 1890 – all these indicated a changing climate of opinion over housing. The Local Government Act of 1888 and the creation of the London County Council were crucial growth points in the administrative framework and added powers and example to the good intentions of legislation. In housing, as in town planning, Poor Law reform, health and unemployment insurance, achievements by the advent of the new century were sporadic and often minimal, but the climate in which these things were discussed was quite different from what it had been when the C.O.S. was founded. To complete our picture of this overall transition, there are some aspects of nineteenth-century social developments, most notably education, which need to be brought into perspective.

Education

The history of education in the nineteenth century is the history of two distinct systems, consciously shaped to fit the fact of class relationships. Even the system which comprised the endowed grammar schools, the public schools and the Universities of Oxford and Cambridge was diversified along class lines. The major public schools had separated themselves off from the local grammar school system, and had become predominantly old-style gentry preserves; the expanding middle class found it necessary to establish new public schools, embodying similar values, but more readily accessible to their children. By the middle of the century this whole system was being subjected to pressures which made changes and adaptations inevitable. Prolonged criticism of the public schools led to the appointment of the Clarendon Commission in 1861 to inquire 'into the nature of the endowments, funds and revenues' of the major, ancient public schools. Its Report, in 1864, was followed by the appointment of the Schools Inquiry Commission (the Taunton Commission), which reported four years later on the state of the endowed grammar schools generally. What followed was a gradual improvement in the use of available endowments, the reinvigoration of decrepit and inefficient grammar schools, and attempts to modernize curricula. The secondary education of girls was improved. The second half of the century saw, in fact, a considerable extension of the system of middle- and upper-class education based on privately endowed, fee-paying institutions.

It is important to emphasize the class-connotation of this system: the public school headmaster and the grammar school reformers alike defined educational values in terms of class needs. When the Bryce Commission reported on progress in secondary education in 1895 it could find no better way of defining different types of secondary school than by using a classification introduced in the Taunton Report over a quarter of a century earlier. The Taunton Report had distinguished between three 'grades' of secondary school; the Bryce Commission suggested the preservation of the classification, but the relaxing of class frontiers. The 1895 definition of 'first grade' schools, for example, reads:

'First Grade' Schools are those whose special function is the formation of a learned or a literary, and a professional or cultured class. This class comprehends the so-called learned professions, the ministry, law, medicine, teaching of all kinds, and at all stages, literature and the higher sciences, public life, the home and foreign civil service, and such like. This is the class whose school life continues till 18 or 19, and would naturally end in the universities. The more highly organized our civilization becomes, the more imperative grows the need for men so educated and formed, the more generous ought their education to become and the greater the necessity for recruiting their ranks with the best blood and brain from all classes of society.

Higher education should be 'open and accessible to capable and promising minds from every social class', but children of non-middle- or non-upper-class parents could not yet gain access to any of the components of this system. The Bryce Commission was advocating a 'ladder' (as T. H. Huxley had called it in the 1870s) for the middle class, in clear knowledge of the class rigidities of the existing system. Although a ladder, with narrow and widely spaced rungs, was shortly to be constructed for working-class children, in the 1890s it scarcely existed. Under the Technical Instruction Acts of 1889–91 counties and county boroughs were beginning to aid grammar and secondary schools, and some also awarded scholarships (the Bryce Commission discovered that forty-two out of forty-eight counties and fifteen out of sixty-one county boroughs were making scholarship grants, but the sums involved were for the most part very small).[29] A Joint Scholarships Board was set up in 1895 'to frame conditions of examination for the scholarships enabling children to pass from the elementary through secondary schools to the Universities'.[30] The 1902 Act provided the framework within which this aim could be implemented.

This educational system was therefore almost totally separated from the machinery of 'popular' education. The elementary school system of the nineteenth century was consciously designed for the children of the poor. Up to 1870 the system was dependent on private initiative, although from 1833 it was supported to some extent by parliamentary grants, and from 1839 was subject to public inspection. There are, therefore, two main threads to the story of popular education up to 1870, the expansion of the network itself and the nature of public involvement.

The establishment of the system is directly attributable to the new departures in British society we have previously examined in the final decade or so of the eighteenth century. New ideas were abroad, and new concentrations of population involved threats to the very structure of society. Against enormous resistance, day schools for the poor on an extensive scale (supplementing the Sunday Schools founded from the 1780s and the century-old Charity School movement) were being founded by the end of the first decade of the nineteenth century. The largely nonconformist British and Foreign School Society and the National Society for Promoting the Education of the Poor in the Principles of the Established Church were spreading parallel networks of schools based on the use of monitors. One teacher could teach hundreds of children, with a minimum of cost, by the efficient organization of children to teach other children. The intention was to spread rudimentary literacy, for purposes always defined in religious and moral terms. Although there were more generous interpretations of education, the dominant system was a socially protective mechanism. The Report of the National Society in 1844, for example, discussed recent disturbances in mining and manufacturing areas. Inquiry had shown that 'discontent and insubordination were most rife in quarters which least enjoyed the advantages of education under the superintendence of the Church; whose office it is to teach men, even when suffering under the sorest trials, to possess their souls in patience'. So convinced was the Society that agitation could be prevented by 'the benign influence of an education conducted upon the principles of the Established Church', that it had determined to increase its efforts to 'imbue the minds of our manufacturing population more effectually with the principles which result from good early training', and had established a special fund 'for the extension and improvement of education in the manufacturing and mining districts'.[31]

The rivalry between the two Societies, and the inability of legislators to reconcile the positions of Church and Dissent, and of supporters and opponents of State intervention, meant that the main burden of school provision until

12 *Nature class at an elementary school, c. 1908*

1870 fell upon the religious denominations and the educational societies they sponsored. The system was in serious respects inefficient. Even improvements in teacher supply, the gradual replacement of the monitorial system by a pupil-teacher system from the mid-1840s, rising government grants and improved conditions of inspection, meant only imperceptible improvements in the quality of the education provided. The Newcastle Commission in 1858–61 was commanded to investigate the state of popular education in England and suggest measures 'for the extension of sound and cheap elementary instruction to all classes of the people'. The scheme of payment by results which followed was intended to improve the 'soundness' of the basic teaching in schools (as well as cut the mounting cost). The amount of grant was to be dependent upon the results of inspectors' examinations in the three Rs. One of the most critical of modern commentators on the Newcastle

Commission has described it as representing 'the attitude of the landed gentry and the bourgeoisie of the time, not only towards the "independent poor", but also towards the very idea of education whether for rich or poor . . . They understood cheapness, but perhaps they very well represented the England of 1860 in failing to understand soundness as a quality of education.'[32]

The emphasis of the events of 1861–2 is important in indicating the view of the providers about the *content* of education for the poor. Matthew Arnold, as an inspector of schools, understood clearly what payment by results meant. Inspectors had previously been able to judge – and contribute to – the overall cultural and intellectual standards of schools; under the new code they were concerned with the examination of individual children, with the school's income depending upon the results of his tests. 'I know', he said in 1863, 'that the aim and object of the new system of examination is not to develop the higher intellectual life of an elementary school, but to spread and fortify, in its middle and lower portions, the instruction in reading, writing and arithmetic, supposed to be suffering.' If this was being achieved, and it was not at all certain that this was the case, it was at the expense of raising the general intellectual level of teachers and children, of strengthening learning across a wide range, and of efforts to obtain more consistent attendance. For several generations payment by results concentrated attention, in the schools described by the Newcastle Commission as being for 'the independent poor', on the mechanical attainment of certain basic routines. Children needed to be able to read and take dictation from prescribed texts. 'The circle of the children's reading has thus been narrowed and impoverished all the year for the sake of a *result* at the end of it, and the *result* is an illusion.'[33] The history of the content of elementary education in the remaining years of the century is one of a slow evolution away from the restricting concept of rudimentary attainment.

It would be wrong to pretend that the system of popular education before 1870 was inefficient in every sense. The attainment was considerable if we look, not at the content of education, and opportunities missed, but at the *extent* of elementary literacy. In the two decades before 1870, for example, the literacy rate for males had increased by 11·3 percentage points and that for females by 18·4 points, reaching figures of 80·6 and 73·2 per cent literacy respectively by 1871 (it had been 67·3 and 51·1 per cent respectively in 1841).[34] From the middle of the century illiteracy was declining sharply, even in conditions of a rapidly increasing population. The influence of the 1870 Act was strongest in ironing out regional and local differences, and in extending education in areas of poverty likely to have proved most resistant to improvement through other means.[35] The chapbooks of the eighteenth century, the radical press of the early nineteenth century, and the penny fiction of the middle of the nineteenth century are reminders that active literacy was well established before 1870.

Schools and curricula had come to be shaped, therefore, in the nineteenth century, to suit particular interpretations of what was necessary for a Bible-reading, docile, working population. It was a closed system. It provided, with only the rarest exceptions, no route to secondary education or university. The 1870 Act was concerned with the supply of education for working–class children. Its central feature was the declaration that:

> There shall be provided for every school district a sufficient amount of accommodation in public elementary schools . . . available for all the children resident in such district for whose elementary education efficient and suitable provision is not otherwise made . . . Where . . . the deficiency is not supplied . . . a school board shall be formed for such district and shall supply such deficiency . . .[36]

Local School Boards were formed by direct election. The network of voluntary schools was not superseded, but supplemented, and voluntary bodies were given six months to apply for grant aid to build new schools. The religious question was settled by laying down that 'no religious catechism or religious formulary which is distinctive of any particular denomination shall be taught'. Although local powers were made available to provide for compulsory attendance, education was not made compulsory. For the remainder of the century efforts were directed towards securing regular attendance, making schools free and raising the leaving age. The leaving age in 1870 was theoretically thirteen, with a half-time system operating between ten and thirteen, and exemptions based on attendance and performance making the effective leaving age ten. By-laws making education to the age of ten compulsory were made obligatory in 1880, and the age was raised to eleven in 1893 and twelve in 1899. School fees were limited under the 1870 Act to ninepence a week. In 1891 parents were given the right to demand free education, and in 1918 fees for elementary education were abolished.

The fact that the two educational systems of the nineteenth century were parallel and not convergent can be seen most clearly in the events leading up to the second of the outstanding education Acts in England's history – that of 1902. The reforms of the nineteenth century had confirmed the classical-literary emphasis in the grammar school. Science and modern subjects had gained a foothold, but the classical-literary tradition continued to be considered the right kind of intellectual discipline, and the right kind of cultural and moral contribution to the preparation of an educational and social élite. Out of the elementary system, however, the later decades of the century saw the emergence of an alternative pattern of – if not *secondary*, at least *post-primary* – education. 'Higher grade' schools for pupils wishing to remain beyond the statutory leaving age were established under some Boards, especially in northern towns, and served the purpose – as witnesses demonstrated to the Bryce Commission – of providing a completion to the elementary course. 'The pride of the higher grade school', it was pointed out, 'is that it has engrafted a system on the system already in existence in connection with, and in continuation of it.'[37] The relaxations effected in the system of payment by results, the adventurous policies of some Boards, and manifest local needs for a supply of a better-trained technical and clerical labour force, led to these experiments in senior classes and central schools which would cater for the demand. Scientific, technical, commercial and vocational subjects played a large part in the curricula of these classes and schools. The logic of the 1870 Act itself, when a generation of children had gone through the Board schools, led to many of these developments in higher day (and evening) classes. The Boards, in making such a departure, exceeded their mandate, according to the letter of the law. In 1900, Robert Morant, a towering figure in the establishment of the pattern of education in the twentieth century, engineered a court verdict to the effect, and himself chiselled the features of a new education Act in 1902.

The Act had two main purposes. The first was to demolish the School Boards and place all education under the multi-purpose county and borough authorities; in doing so it completed the demolition of the nineteenth-century tradition of *ad hoc* authorities. Balfour, the Conservative, in sponsoring the 1902 Act, was implementing a policy which, through Morant, was urged and shaped by Fabian Socialist Sidney Webb, the enthusiastic advocate of efficient local government. The second purpose was to ensure that, whatever developments in secondary education might occur, it should be within a single system, in which the dominant values would remain those of the grammar school and its curriculum. If there was to be an educational ladder it should lead into the traditional values. The higher grade schools and the grammar schools 'grew steadily closer together sharing not only the same curriculum, but also the pride in an old tradition and common ideals for the future'. The disappearance of the practical curriculum of the higher grade schools was the responsibility both of Morant and of the teachers and administrators who welcomed the Regulations he shaped in 1904 'as a means of reinstating the literary and linguistic elements in the secondary schools'.[38] The Regulations of 1904 appeared to aim at a balanced curriculum, but it is clear that the higher grade innovations were being discarded. The new Regulations, in the words of Eric Eaglesham, 'certainly effectively checked any tendencies to technical or vocational bias in the secondary schools. They made the schools fit only for a selected few. Moreover they proclaimed for all to see the Board's interest in the literary and classical sides of secondary education. For the future the pattern of English culture must not come from Leeds and West Ham but from Eton and Winchester.' Morant and Balfour shared 'similar middle-class educational values, similar doubts about the abilities of the masses'.[39] The definitions and appeals of the Bryce Commission, the activities of Morant, the Act of 1902 and the Free Place system which formally inaugurated the policy of the scholarship 'ladder' to secondary education, all attempted to open out the secondary school frontiers at the same time as preserving 'middle-class values'. They were successful, and from this point begins the story of secondary school selection.

Related to all of this process were other educational departures in the second half of the nineteenth century. From the creation of London University (from the starting point of University College in 1826) to the beginnings of new provincial universities in towns like Manchester, Birmingham, Leeds, Bristol and Sheffield in the latter part of the century, new concepts of university curricula had begun to be formulated and acted upon. Commissions on technical education sat in the 1870s and 1880s. Out of the Mechanics' Institutes grew Technical Colleges. Others, especially in the 1880s and 1890s, were created. Grants to encourage science and art teaching were available from 1853, and rate aid was available for the same purpose from 1889. Oxford and Cambridge reform began in the 1850s, and from the beginning of the 1870s the University Extension movement carried adult education into towns like Derby, Leicester and Nottingham (and out of some of these activities grew universities). Within the schools themselves there were pressures towards the acceptance of new ideas. Ideas of education in social science and health gained some momentum. New movements in infant and nursery education took shape in the second half of the century. It was demonstrated in 1902 that none of this was to be allowed to influence the basic pattern of English secondary education.

These developments should not cloud the fact that nineteenth-century English society (Scottish traditions were different in many crucial respects) was in fact two societies

('two nations' was Disraeli's phrase), which were educated
for different ends, on the basis of different social and cultural assumptions, with different curricula, for different
lengths of time and above all in different schools.

Religion

The strengths of the School Board system lay in the towns,
and the classrooms of the Board schools were demonstrations of the existence of a working class, and of institutions
designed for the working class. The churches were deeply
involved in these recognitions and processes, but *as churches*
they failed to a large extent to grasp the problems of either
towns or class. The churches themselves in the nineteenth
century demonstrated class divisions as visibly as anywhere
in society. There were polarizations within church bodies
into wealthy and poor, autocratic and democratic branches,
as the Wesleyan and Primitive wings of Methodism illustrate. Within church buildings themselves the existence of
subscribed pews and free 'sittings' marked the class
division. In Sheffield in 1841 there were thirteen churches
of the Establishment which could accommodate 15,000
people, but 6,000 places at most were free. Of the 25,000
places in the thirty-seven nonconformist chapels less than
one third were free.[40] The evangelical wing of the
Established Church and the evangelical nonconformist
churches themselves were to one extent or another aware of
the problem of 'reaching' the urban working class, in conditions of the relative breakdown of the unitary function of
the parish – pre-eminently a rural form of church organization. The churches made various attempts to speak distinc-
tively and make appropriate kinds of appeal to the working
class, but the appeal was limited. At the back of it lay what
Edward Miall, one of the prominent nonconformist spokesmen of the century, considered to be a morbid horror of
poverty: 'The service concludes, and the worshippers retire.
Communion with God has not disposed them to communion with each other, beyond the well-defined boundaries of
class.' In his journal, the *Nonconformist*, he invited working
men to write letters on 'The Working Classes and Religious

Institutions', and in response they denounced social distinctions in churches, their worship of respectability and contempt for the poor, the 'almost total want of sympathy manifested by the ministers of religion of every denomination with the privations, wants and wastes of working classes' and the 'aristocratic character of religious institutions'.[41]

A Religious Census in 1851, and a local count in the borough of Sheffield in 1881, both arrived at the rough conclusion that one person in three for whom there were places attended for worship on an average Sunday. In Sheffield between the two dates the population had slightly more than doubled, so that although the ratio remained the same, the absolute number of non-attenders doubled across the period. Since 1881 the population has again almost doubled, but attendances in 1957 were far smaller than in 1881: 'It is almost certain we have near doubled the population, and more than halved actual numbers of attendants, and this is probably true for every denomination except the Roman Catholics . . .'[42] The falling off of church and chapel attendance at the end of the century, however, was from an already narrow basis. A clergyman remarked in 1896: 'It is not that the Church of God has lost the great towns; it has never had them . . .' People moving into towns lost the habit of worship, and working-class people born in towns never acquired it. The strength of Primitive Methodism, the most working-class of the nonconformist bodies, was not in the large towns, and it was not, in any case, as numerous as the more aristocratic and highly conservative Wesleyan Methodists. The nonconformist churches in general were apathetic about the problem of the cities. Some sections of the Established Church moved, often reluctantly and against opposition, towards reorganization and made efforts to win the working class; in some sections of nonconformity, on the other hand, 'scarcely any effort was made before or after 1850 to reach the working classes. The elect were content merely to preserve their own fellowship.'[43] The decline in religious attendance from the 1880s was an important phenomenon in the history of the middle class, and confirmation of the inability of the churches in the nine-

13 *'The Chapel, on the "separate system", in Pentonville Prison'*

teenth century to confront the problems of urban, and later of suburban, life.

Beginnings of town planning

We have seen a range of areas in which piecemeal action was taken to cope with the growth of urban society; there were, of course, inside towns and in experimental settings outside, attempts at answers of different kinds. Small-scale attempts at rehousing inside cities gave rise to broader ideas of planning. The intensification of urban problems gave rise to new initiatives in town planning, particularly as London's suburban transport developed, as new and scattered industries arose, and as prospects of the disappearance of accessible countryside increased. As ideas of social responsibility spread, and as local and country instruments for the organization of community existence became more effective, it is possible to trace a shift towards more widespread ideas of local community planning. Before the end of the nineteenth century, however, examples of such developments were sporadic and self-contained, and it is easy to exaggerate their importance. The continued confusions, lost opportunities and mistakes of the twentieth century show how important it is not to make such an exaggeration.

Early attempts at industrial planning were confined to relatively remote communities, particularly in connection with textile enterprises dependent upon water supply. The most important was New Lanark, during Robert Owen's management between 1800 and 1824, important not only because it was an attempt to improve industrial conditions and provide community services, but because it was a practical experiment which Owen himself, and other prominent social thinkers influenced by him, used as a demonstration of more far-reaching views on community planning. Owen advocated the establishment of self-sufficient communities for the poor, combining an industrial and agricultural economy, and with basic planned communal services. Others pursued and refined the proposals. Some Owenite and other communitarian experiments were made, though with little influence on opinion or practice in the field of planning. Hardly more influential were Titus Salt's model woollen mills and town at Saltaire, built from scratch near Bradford in the 1850s and 1860s. This was an employer's town, benevolently administered.

In less easy-going conditions from the 1870s, 'changes in the environment and location of industry had become at least a topic for occasional discussion. In most of the basic industries profits were not so easily obtained as in the recent past and the urgent importance of efficient and healthy labour was, as a direct result, beginning to be more widely recognized.'[44] In this spirit a beginning was made on the building of Bournville by George Cadbury in 1879, but not until 1895 did the plans really begin to be developed. Port Sunlight was begun by W. H. Lever in 1888, associating a new village with his expanding soap firm, and making the administration of the village an extension of the firm's interest in labour–management relations. The spaciousness and variety of the village still demonstrate, in the proximity of Birkenhead, the boldness of such new approaches to community planning. Joseph Rowntree's interest in planning at his New Earswick development near York broke away from the enlightened philanthropy of the earlier ventures. The aim of Joseph Rowntree (Seebohm's father) was to provide houses 'artistic in appearance, sanitary, well-built, and yet within the means of men earning about twenty-five shillings a week'. But he was not a paternalist. 'I should regret', he wrote, 'if there were anything in the organization of these village communities that should interfere with the growth of the right spirit of citizenship . . . I do not want to establish communities bearing the stamp of charity but rather of rightly ordered and self-governing communities.'[45] The venture was directly influential in that its architect was later to be involved in new-town planning at Letchworth, and Seebohm Rowntree, on the basis of both his investigation of working-class conditions in York and his involvement in the New Earswick scheme, played a prominent part in the war-time planning of housing needs, helping materially to prepare the way for the Housing Act of 1919, the first of any major importance.

It was, however, the publication of Ebenezer Howard's book *To-morrow* (later retitled *Garden Cities of To-morrow*), published in 1898, followed by the establishment of the Garden City Association (1899) and the first Garden City at Letchworth (started in 1904), that projected the discussion of town and environmental planning squarely into the twentieth century. Cecil Harmsworth, as Chairman of the Council of the Garden Cities and Town Planning Association, explained that he had been 'drawn into the movement by the infectious influence of Sir Ebenezer Howard'.[46] The book, Letchworth, and Howard's promotion of Welwyn Garden City in 1920 arose out of his familiarity with the 'grave warnings against the evils of great towns'. The Association summarized what he had stood for as follows:

> . . . the revolt of philanthropists and reformers and a large proportion of ordinary people against the size and

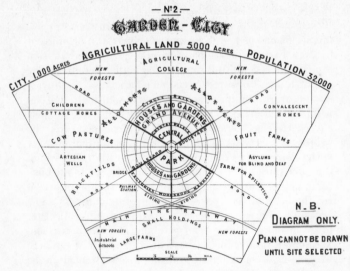

14 *Garden City. From Ebenezer Howard,* Garden Cities of To-morrow

character of the great town had been endemic since the Industrial Revolution, and had been eloquently voiced by Cobbett, Shaftesbury, and many others of great authority... Ebenezer Howard aligned himself with his predecessors in the protest against the squalor and overcrowding inseparable from great towns; but he differed from many of them in accepting whole-heartedly the desirability of the town in itself from the point of view of modern populations ... he discerned that the essential urban advantages ... could be provided in a town of limited size and density; and that in addition many of the amenities of the country ... could be retained in such a town.[47]

Howard's concept was one of 'Town–Country' which would be free of the disadvantages of both. His Garden Cities would be 'Social Cities'. He argued strongly in *To-morrow* that his scheme combined the ideals of individualism ('if by Individualism is meant a state in which there is fuller and

freer opportunity for its members to do and to produce
what they will, and to form free associations, of the most
varied kind') and of socialism ('if by Socialism is meant a
condition of life in which the well-being of the community
is safeguarded, and in which the collective spirit is manifested by a wide extension of the area of municipal effort').
He argued that he had taken a leaf out of the books of Tory
A. J. Balfour on the one hand and Socialist Hyndman and
Blatchford on the other.[48]

Ideas of this kind forcefully raised problems of the kind
of community in which modern urban man was prepared,
and wished, to live. In many respects the garden-city, gar-
den-suburb, new-town thinking of the twentieth century
can be seen as an evasion of fundamental social problems.
In other respects it can be seen as a gesture towards them.

The growing phenomenon of middle-class, and later working-class, suburbanization, and the consequent depopulation of town centres, were accelerated by new developments
in transport. Cheaper rail fares began to be introduced in
the 1870s, and the Cheap Trains Act of 1883 introduced
workmen's fares. The first section of London's underground
railway was opened in 1863, and electric trains date from
1890. The train, however, was largely inter-urban and
metropolitan. For cities in general the new outward impetus
came from the roads. The motor bus and car began slowly
in the late 1890s to replace the horse bus and hansom cab,
but cycling had already made an important contribution to
transport by drawing attention to the state of the roads, and
providing the technological basis on which more advanced
forms of transport were later constructed. The cycling craze
dates from the 1860s (and the 'bone-shaker') and the 1870s
(and the 'penny-farthing'), reaching a peak in the 1880s
with the development of the pneumatic tyre. The creation
of the County Councils in 1888 meant a new dispensation
for the nation's roads. When the Motor Car Act of 1903
required motor vehicles to be licensed, 18,000 were registered in the first year. By 1914 the number had risen to
389,000. Buses and trams, however, made the most decisive
impact on urban life, making it possible for working men
to travel longer distances to work. The early trams were

horsedrawn, and these marked 'a substantial advance in the conveyance of large numbers of people in urban areas at low fares'. Electricity applied to trams at the end of the century provided the real break-through to cheap transport in dense urban areas. By 1909 there were some 2,300 miles of electric tramway.[49] An important feature of tramway transport was that it led to municipal involvement in urban transport.

Towns continued to spread, with industries siting themselves at greater distances from town centres. At the same time as impressive new domestic architecture was appearing in expensive residential districts (such as Bayswater and Hampstead in London), 'by-law housing' was creating the architectural deserts of the speculatively built suburbs within widening transport distance from the centres of every major town. New local government responsibilities led to new surges of public building – town halls, fire stations, public baths, libraries, post offices and – above all – schools, almost all proudly displaying the date of construction. Gaunt and impracticable though many of these buildings now are, many were – and still are – impressive in their scale and ambition.

There had been from the 1840s attempts at philanthropic working-class housing in dense urban conditions. The Improved Industrial Dwellings Co., established in 1863, was the best known of the companies which built at a deliberately restricted rate of interest. Best known of the developments, however, was one which was based on a bequest from the American, George Peabody, and which came to be used for working-class housing.[50] Most of these developments were in London, and in general were available only to the more 'respectable' of the poor. For the housing of the lower strata of the poor, Octavia Hill offered a system of housing management. By raising funds for the purchase of property and recruiting ladies to act as rent collectors, she hoped to establish a system of influence and benevolent incentives to self-improvement and property improvement, a system which has been described as one for 'transmuting improvident savages into solid citizens'.[51] All such schemes accepted the necessity of high urban density, all were reasonably cheap and in one way or another made tenancy contingent upon cleanliness, regular employment and character. None of them made a significant impact on the basic problems of housing and overcrowding.

The family

The population was still increasing, and Britain was, from the middle of the nineteenth century dominantly urban. In the second half of the century the population increased by over 80 per cent, and in the first half of the twentieth century by 34 per cent. The death rate declined steadily in the second half of the nineteenth century (22·5 deaths per thousand of the population in 1861–70; 19·1 in 1881–90; 15·4 in 1901–10). That the population did not increase more spectacularly as a result was due to a parallel decline in birth rate (from over thirty-five per thousand in the 1860s and 1870s, steadily downwards to just over twenty-seven in 1901–10). From the 1870s the rate of population growth began to fall. It is to some of the social realities behind these statistics that we now turn.

Of every hundred women who married in the years 1870–9, there were sixty-one who bore five or more live children; seventeen bore ten or more; only twenty-one of them bore none, one or two. By contrast, of every hundred women who married in the years 1900–9, only twenty-eight bore five or more children; only one in a hundred bore ten or more; the number bearing none, one or two had risen from twenty-one to forty-five.[52] The structure of the family had begun markedly to alter in the last quarter of the century.

In many respects it was the working-class family that was least affected by the new economic and social directions of the nineteenth century. Industrial legislation had, of course, improved the conditions of working women. There were frequent attacks in the nineteenth century on the practice of working-class wives being employed in the mills and factories; such married women, even in the second half of the century, would be away from home from something like 6 a.m. to 6 p.m. The number of married women in industry was, however, considerably exaggerated.[53] The working-class family in the nineteenth century was, in fact, subject

both to severe instabilities, as a result of physical and economic conditions, and to pressures making for an autocratic
family structure. Divorce was not available, the position of
the father was dominant, and the woman in the home was
committed to a life of considerable drudgery. For the
unmarried girl the only escape, for a large part of the century, was into the mill or domestic service. In the twentieth
century, with the removal of intolerable burdens by welfare
provisions, in Ronald Fletcher's opinion, 'the working-class
family has achieved a new condition of stability, well-being,
security and opportunity for the development of its
individual members, which is unprecedented in our history'.[54] Improvements in the nineteenth century, however,
were too slow to impinge on the working-class family to any

15 'Dwellings for the working-
classes, Peabody Square, Shadwell',
1867

significant extent. The woman at work, constant childbirth
and a high rate of infant mortality, the demoralization of
domestic conditions – all these paralleled, with few compen-
sations, life in pre-industrial society. Changes in the administration of poor relief surrounded the poor family with
additional elements of harshness and disunity.

The nineteenth century did, however, see important
changes in the content of middle-class family life. Among
farmers and traders in pre-industrial society 'marriage was
often a business partnership in which husband and wife
worked together in their joint interests'.[55] The cementing of
middle-class affluence, the new patterns of middle-class occupation and the new scale of industrial and commercial
operations broke these elements of partnership and firmly

established the husband as the sole provider. Paid employment for women before the nineteenth century was more widespread than is sometimes imagined. Working-class women had age-old employments in agriculture, textiles, coal and metal mining, straw-plaiting, hat-making, jewellery and fan-making. They worked as 'assistants to masons and bricklayers, as labourers in brickyards and foundries, load carriers to and from markets, as rag sorters and cutters in paper mills, as cinder sifters and collectors of refuse'.[56] Some of the descriptions of women's employment, however, disguise relatively middle-class, entrepreneurial activities. A large number of women's names, for example, appeared in Wren's account books during the building of St Paul's in the late seventeenth century:

> Sarah Freeman undertook some of the plumbing, widow Clare was a joiner, Ann Brooks one of the smiths. It is doubtful how much of the actual work these women did. They may have been contractors employing the actual craftsmen, but the fact that Wren employed them does show that women were running businesses in the City even if they did not work at the trades.[57]

In the early days of the Industrial Revolution, as previously, women – wives, widows and single women – were shopkeepers. English women in the seventeenth century and later managed estates, obtained patents and monopolies, dealt in insurance and supplied clothing to the army and navy. In its early stages 'capitalism enhanced the economic value of middle-class women and brought them into co-operative activity with men; in the succeeding period, women's economic value was again depreciated by developments leading to her isolation from productive activity'.[58] The male head of the household became paramount, and the middle-class (and upper-class) family became more and more strongly home-centred. The wife had no serious occupation inside or outside the home. Her duties 'were limited to supervising, and complaining about, her servants'.[59] By the eighteenth century, among the leisure class 'the triumph of the useless woman was complete', and with the Industrial Revolution 'the practice of female idleness spread through the middle class until work for women became a misfortune and a disgrace'.[60] In domestic structure the large Victorian clergyman's family was little different from that of the industrialist or businessman. The fifteen-member family of Bishop Moberly 'made an immense society with common interests, common tastes and common memories'. A family like this 'was a constitutional body, based on law, and every member had his own place in the social scheme under the father, who was the supreme head of all . . . Something like this existed in all families, but a clergyman had to set a special example in fatherhood as in everything else . . .'[61] Not all middle-class families had the good fortune of the Moberlys to be united in absorbing common interests. Victorian women's writings, and particularly diaries, are full of trivialities of conversation and social relations dominated by boredom. 'A daughter', one of them was still protesting in 1894, 'must arrange the flowers, help with the house-keeping, pay the family calls, entertain the family visitors, always be at hand, well-dressed, cheerful, and smiling . . . she can never undertake any definite work or pursuit . . . She never, in fact, has an hour that she can call absolutely her own.'[62]

Victorian young ladies had time to write enormous diaries; a reconstruction from those of two of them, Ellen and Emily Hall, of the lives of young ladies in early Victorian England, illustrates the situation clearly.[63] West Wickham was a small village, with one public house and one general shop. London, thanks to the railway, was not inaccessible, though in the early trains the girls had to hold 'our handkerchiefs over our noses'; trains were not heated and journeys could be 'unendurably cold'. Distances were not what they are now. Tooting, now an inner suburb of London, was to the girls only 'much nearer London' than Jersey, where they had previously lived. Camberwell was still in countryside which was 'really very pretty'. In their seclusion the girls were busy, busier than they might have been in a city. They drove, rode or walked into Croydon and other neighbouring towns on shopping expeditions. They supervised servants and gardens and rejoiced in the arrangement of flowers. They played music and 'took their fair share in the visits, picnics and the like'. They cultivated guests and read histories, memoirs, sermons and poetry. They enjoyed conversation, and the Church played a large part in their lives. One of them took a part in the Sunday School, made clothes for village children and visited the sick. The same daughter had in 1839 in Jersey helped to dispense soup to the poor, and scolded 'some of the horrid old women who have been telling fibs and getting soup from two boilers at the same time'. The Halls, like the Moberlys, had the advantage of a strong active culture. Like other Victorian middle-class girls, they found the chess games of courtship and marriage going on about them a subject for constant conversation and, like a high percentage of them, they remained unmarried.

It is not difficult, then, to see why importance was attached in mid-Victorian middle-class England to the large family. Like the Villa, the Crinoline and the Servant, the Family – a 'conspicuous' item in affluence – testified to the solidity and permanence of the middle-class way of life. Wealthier families were the first and most to benefit from improved standards of health and environmental conditions – hence the longer fertility of mothers, the better survival chances of children and the greater size of families. The large working-class family – said the middle-class Malthusian – indicated improvidence. The large middle-class family was a symbol of success.

It is from this starting point that we must see the changes in family size, and in the status of women, in the last twenty to thirty years of the century. The decline in family size, in the analysis of J. A. Banks, is related directly to the fact or the possibility of rising material standards. His thesis is briefly as follows.[64] The average family size of couples married in mid-Victorian Britain was between 5·5 and 6 live children, and of those married in 1925–9 it was 2·2. The percentage of women marrying while capable of bearing children, however, remained roughly constant. At some time in the 1860s and 1870s a decline in family size had begun among upper- and middle-class families. The earliest signs of the change in reproductive patterns took place amongst the families of, for example, officers, clergymen, lawyers, doctors, authors, journalists and architects, with not far behind them civil servants and clerks, dentists, teachers and people in scientific pursuits. Commercial men followed. Although some signs of family limitation were early visible among textile workers, not until much later did the decline in family size spread amongst less privileged social groups. Birth control, it becomes clear, was taken up with enthusiasm from the 1870s, and given an impetus by the Bradlaugh–Besant trials in 1877–8. Artificial methods of birth control had, however, been known and available very much earlier. Why had they been spurned, for example, in the 1820s, and adopted in the 1870s? The answer lies in the rising standard of middle-class life and the determination to maintain and secure the higher standards of comfort. It had become prudent to postpone the time of marriage in order to ensure that married life began at the proper level of respectability (and this, it should be mentioned, was one of the factors involved in the dual standard of morality, which involved a high incidence of resort to prostitution inside and outside marriage among Victorian middle-class men).[65] The dominant factor, however, Banks continues, was the maintenance of material standards in marriage. Associated with middle-class status were what he calls 'paraphernalia of gentility' (Veblen's 'conspicuous consumption'), including material objects, servants, holidays and travel. The point at which the cost of any of these basic paraphernalia began to rise (e.g. servants' wages), at which new paraphernalia became desirable (e.g. new types of imported luxury foods), or at which income was in any way lowered or threatened, made a reconsideration of the whole basis of family size imperative. If the threat continued over a long period of time the choice available was to cut back on material standards (or fail to raise them) or to maintain them by reducing expenditure in some other way. A further postponement in the age of marriage was not seriously possible, and the possibility of reducing family size was therefore the most acceptable of the alternatives available. The 'Great Depression' and its attendant psychology, in fact, provoked such a reassessment of the cost of raising children. The decline in the hold, of the Church, the breakdown of old ideas under the impact of new appeals to science and reason, higher rents – these were additional factors helping towards the ultimate acceptance of two-plus-two as the new ideal of family size, with major implications for the status of women in the family and in society.

A certain democratization of family life was, indeed, taking place, and the smaller family intensified the process. The new attitude to family size, spreading downwards through the social classes, had other repercussions. It helped to break down the situation in which solemn standards of marital morality had been combined with resort to prostitution. It made earlier marriages possible. It made it possible for new views of sexual relations and marriage to gain ground. With fewer children, fewer servants and more efficient homes (including gas cookers and water closets) a greater domestic role for suburban middle-class housewives was created. Parallel developments for working-class housewives had to await progress in social reform.

Emancipation of women

The story of the greater emancipation of women involves both the economic and social facts we have traced, and mounting individual and organized pressures. Women over thirty obtained the vote at the same time as it was finally given to all males over twenty-one in 1918, and all women over twenty-one obtained it in 1928, but the story of their political emancipation is one in which neither the pressures of the campaigning, nor the simple facts of economic development and war, can alone claim credit for the final success.

The principal elements in the changing position of women were property, divorce, employment, education and the suffrage.

The existing legal relationship of husband and wife was defined in 1869 by John Stuart Mill, in one of the most famous documents on women in society, as follows:

. . . the absorption of all [women's] rights, all property, as well as all freedom of action, is complete. The two are

called 'one person in law', for the purpose of inferring
that whatever is hers is his, but the parallel inference is
never drawn that whatever is his is hers . . . I am far from
pretending that wives are in general no better treated
than slaves; but no slave is a slave to the same lengths,
and in so full a sense of the word, as a wife is.[66]

At this date the whole of the wife's income, from whatever
source, belonged to her husband. The first of a series of
Property Acts was passed in 1870, and it gave a married
woman the right to possess her earnings, but not any other
property. Millicent Fawcett records how in the 1870s, in the
campaign for another Married Women's Property Bill, she
approached some of the Liberal electors at a meeting at her
father's house in Suffolk with a petition form. 'Am I to
understand you, ma'am,' responded one of the farmers,
'that if this Bill passes, and my wife have a matter of a
hundred pound left to her, I should have to *ask* her for it?'[67]
An Act of 1882 enabled a woman to retain as separate
property whatever she possessed at marriage or acquired
after. A final Act of 1893 removed anomalies and made all
property of a married woman her separate property. From
the 1850s a middle-class women's movement had been
organized, campaigns conducted, signatures collected and
discussion aroused. Hostility to any form of action of this
kind on the part of women was immense (including among
women who saw their femininity undermined), but a beginning had been made and an important shift in status had
been achieved in the Acts of 1870–93.

Since the sixteenth century Scotland had had legal
equality and cheap divorce. A divorce Act of 1857 (a
Matrimonial Causes Act, as it and all subsequent Acts were
named) brought divorce for the first time within reach of
the English middle class, but, in 'making divorce easier for
men than for women, it sanctioned two standards of morality', and the cheaper procedure of the divorce court
'remained so costly that working people were denied the
remedy of divorce for their matrimonial difficulties'.[68] An
Act of 1878, followed by other Acts through to 1902,
gave magistrates powers to grant separation orders with

maintenance to a wife whose husband had been convicted of 'aggravated assault'. Not until 1923, however, could a woman obtain divorce on the simple grounds of adultery, as her husband had been able to do. Not until an Act of 1937 were the grounds for divorce extended to include desertion, cruelty and being incurably of unsound mind. Not until the introduction of legal aid in 1949 did divorce become practicable for the poor.

Again, a minority of articulate women had been involved in exerting – with difficulty – pressure for reform. On the related questions of employment and education the basis of action and the range of achievement were wider. Writing in 1886, Millicent Fawcett forecast what factors would come together to achieve it:

> Women's suffrage will not come, when it does come, as an isolated phenomenon, it will come as a necessary corollary of other changes which have been gradually and steadily modifying during this century the social history of our country. It will be a political change, not of a very great or extensive character in itself, based upon social, educational and economic changes which have already taken place ... the political change will not be a revolution, but a public recognition by the State that the lot of women in England is no longer what it was at the beginning of the century.[69]

This extremely percipient analysis identifies the relationship in this movement between social and political change. Economic change and women themselves had created new attitudes to employment. New occupations were appearing. There were, for working-class and lower-middle-class girls, new opportunities in post offices, commerce and industry. The reformers set up women's employment agencies to try to help middle-class girls. The fight was engaged for access to training and the professions.

In the 1840s women's training colleges and Bedford College, London, were founded, the North London Collegiate School for girls was established in 1850, and the Cheltenham Ladies' College eight years later. The Girls Public Day Schools Company opened thirty-three schools

16 *Members of the W.A.A.C. on motor service*

for girls between 1872 and the end of the century, following
the Endowed Schools Act of 1869, which was described as
'the Magna Carta of girls' education, the first acknowledge-
ment by the State of their claim to a liberal education'.[70]
The Bryce Commission reported in 1895 that since the
Taunton Report of 1868 'there had been more change in the
condition of the Secondary Education of girls than in any
other department of education . . . the idea that a girl, like a
boy, may be fitted by education to earn a livelihood, or, at
any rate, to be a more useful member of society, has become
more widely diffused.'[71] Working-class girls may have
entered voluntary elementary schools or Board Schools after
1870 through a separate gate or doorway from the boys, but
they were being 'fitted' as well, or as badly, as boys for a
livelihood or their place in society. Girton College,
Cambridge, was founded in 1869 (although girls were not
admitted to Cambridge degrees until the 1920s). Bedford

College reached university rank, and university colleges were opening their doors to women. The University Extension movement was reaching a female audience. Women were more widely pressing for occupational opportunities. The sex ratio of the British population in Victorian Britain was tilted towards women; a basic consideration in looking at the position of women was the fact that a quarter of them did not marry.

There was, wrote one cynic in 1860 on the subject of women, 'a great waste and over-production of that feminine article. An unnecessary surplus of half-a-million, say the statistics . . .' The only answer to the problem that this writer could see was that women should be made strictly to choose between the careers of worker or mother:

> If England is to be permanently afflicted with an unavail-
> able margin of women, this surplus must either have the
> courage to make that necessary sacrifice which alone can
> insure its fidelity to its work, or else stifle its discontent,
> and make the best of its unlucky position.[72]

For women in general emancipation within the family and opportunities within society were one and the same thing. The most convenient approach to the story of emancipation, suggests George Dangerfield, is through the wardrobe. The female form, 'as the century progressed towards war, was being released from the distortions and distentions of the Victorian era'.[73] From the crinoline and the bustle and the trappings of uselessness women were to be released by factors ranging from the bicycle to war. Tennis dress (ladies did not *run* after the ball) and swimming costumes would not necessarily have made a great impact on clothing conventions, but the practical and comfortable female cycling costume (and all that cycling itself implied) emphatically did. Edwardian entertainment and the occupations of wartime were for middle-class girls acts of liberation. Poverty, need and the rigours of industry and domestic service still surrounded the working-class girl with considerable obstacles.

We cannot here pursue the outcome of these changes in the shape of the organized fight for the suffrage. It ran from the first recognizable women's suffrage movement organized in 1865, through the half-way manœuvres of the Primrose League and the Women's Liberal Federation of the 1880s, to the Women's Social and Political Union founded by the Pankhursts in 1903 and the militant suffragette movement in the years leading up to the First World War. The role of women during the First World War, in civilian employments of all kinds, on buses, in munitions factories and in service occupations contributed to the post-war political settlement.[74] But the very social and political build-up that Millicent Fawcett had described led to the easy acceptance of women into the war effort. The nation need not have called on or accepted participation by women to the extent that it did: nations do not necessarily do what is best for their survival. Women had, however, improved their status and asserted themselves to the point at which national realities enabled women to drive trams, nurse the wounded, make shells and dig graves. War and the bicycle were the only factors not foreseen in Millicent Fawcett's analysis.

The relationship between the position of women and the content of democracy has been seen to relate to the removal of legislative and other constraints, to education and to employment, and in the case of working-class women, to the achievement of adequate standards of economic security and welfare. All these factors were of central importance in the shifts of attitudes in the quarter of a century or so leading up to the First World War. They were starting points from which a more explicit discussion of the role of women was to develop in the middle of the twentieth century. The attitudes and discussions involved were accompanied by related changes in attitudes towards children – at first in terms of child rearing and early education, and eventually in wider terms of the status and rights of children and young people. The range of such discussion by the mid-twentieth century was to extend to all institutions and processes to which concepts like 'equality' or 'democracy' might be applied. It was in similar terms that the discussions of under-privileged or minority groups were to develop after the 1950s. The position of women, relationships in schools and in industry, the economic and social position of black and other minority racial groups, all became part of an overarching discussion. From these beginnings in the late nineteenth century developed a wide-ranging analysis of the position in society of groups previously little considered or discussed – ultimately an analysis of the meaning of 'society' itself.

In many respects the last two decades of the nineteenth century were an important parting of the ways. By the 1880s the individualist views most fully elaborated by Herbert Spencer were being challenged by alternative philosophies, new concepts of the State and of social responsibility. To the optimist it looked as though society was inevitably becoming more coherent and 'collectivist'. To positivist Frederic Harrison, for example, it appeared that 'the world for the last fifty years has been groping rather towards synthesis, towards social Utopias much more than towards individualist ideals'.[75] The Fabian Society in 1890 was pronouncing the death of Spencer-type individualism: 'the tide of Democratic Collectivism is rolling in upon us . . . There is no resting place for stationary Toryism in the scientific universe. The whole history of the human race cries out against the old-fashioned Individualism.' Four years later it was affirming that since 1880 'an unsystematic and empirical Individualism' had been overthrown: 'the typical young politician, who twenty years ago was a convinced Individualist quoting Mr. Herbert Spencer, is nowadays an empirical Collectivist of a practical kind'.[76] There were, in fact, important and active groups, not merely proclaiming the death of individualism, but also working for it.

Notes

1 BEALES 'The "Great Depression" in industry and trade', in CARUS-WILSON (ed.) *Essays in Economic History*, I, p. 413.

2 PETER TOWNSEND 'Poverty as relative deprivation: resources and styles of living', in DOROTHY WEDDERBURN (ed.) *Poverty, Inequality and Class Structure*, p. 25 (Cambridge, 1974).

3 E. MOBERLY BELL *The Story of Hospital Almoners*, p. 70 (London, 1961).

4 ROBERTS *Victorian Origins of the British Welfare State*, p. 95.

5 P. H. J. H. GOSDEN *The Development of Educational Administration in England and Wales*, p. 27 (Oxford, 1966).

6 HERBERT SPENCER *The Man versus the State*, pp. 16, 34 (London, 1884; 1950 edition).

7 PAT THANE 'The history of social welfare', *New Society*, 29 August 1974, p. 541.

8 ERVING GOFFMAN *Asylums*, pp. 11, 15 (New York, 1961; 1968 edition).

9 GEORGE LANSBURY *My Life*, pp. 135–6 (London, 1928).

10 LOUISA TWINING 'Workhouse cruelties', in MICHAEL GOODWIN (ed.) *Nineteenth Century Opinion*, p. 56 (Harmondsworth, 1951).

11 LONGMATE *The Workhouse*, pp. 145–6.

12 Quoted from the C.O.S. annual report for 1875 in CHARLES LOCH MOWAT *The Charity Organisation Society 1869–1913*, pp. 26–7 (London, 1961).

13 Quoted in ibid., p. 69.

14 Quoted in BELL *The Story of Hospital Almoners*, p. 59.

15 LANSBURY *My Life*, p. 132.

16 ROYAL COMMISSION ON THE POOR LAWS Majority Report, I, p. 100.

17 PINKER *Social Theory and Social Policy*, pp. 137, 189 and *passim* for the assumptions underlying contemporary social policy.

18 BENTLEY B. GILBERT *The Evolution of National Insurance in Great Britain*, p. 233 (London, 1966).

19 T. S. and M. B. SIMEY *Charles Booth, Social Scientist*, p. 90 (London, 1960).

20 Ibid., p. 109.

21 Quoted in ibid., p. 116.

22 Quoted in ibid., p. 95.

23 For fuller discussion, see TOWNSEND 'Poverty as relative deprivation' in WEDDERBURN, *Poverty, Inequality and Class Structure*.

24 Quoted in SIMEY *Charles Booth*, p. 161.

25 For an account of and extracts from Booth's work, see HAROLD W. PFAUTZ *Charles Booth on the City: Physical Pattern and Social Structure* (Chicago, 1968).

26 LYND *England in the Eighteen-eighties*, p. 52.

27 ASA BRIGGS *Social Thought and Social Action: a study of the work of Seebohm Rowntree 1871–1954*, p. 30 (London, 1961).

28 MARK ABRAMS *Social Surveys and Social Action*, pp. 41–2 (London, 1951).

29 SECONDARY EDUCATION COMMISSION *Report*, Vol. I, pp. 34–8, 138.

30 PHILIP MAGNUS *Educational Aims and Efforts 1882–1910*, p. 39 (London, 1910).

31 NATIONAL SOCIETY *Twenty-Third Annual Report*, pp. 1–2 (London, 1844).

32 T. RAYMONT *A History of the Education of Young Children*, p. 212 (London, 1937).

33 F. S. MARVIN (ed.) *Reports on Elementary Schools 1852–1882 by Matthew Arnold*, pp. 93, 126 (London, 1889; 1910 edition).

34 ALTICK *The English Common Reader*, pp. 171–2.

35 See LAWRENCE STONE 'Literacy and education in England 1640–1900', *Past and Present*, 42, 1969.

36 Clauses 5 and 6. The full text is in NATIONAL EDUCATION UNION *A Verbatim Report ... of the Debate in Parliament* (Manchester, 1870).

37 SECONDARY EDUCATION COMMISSION *Report*, p. 143.

38 OLIVE BANKS *Parity and Prestige in English Secondary Education*, pp. 49–50 (London, 1955).

39 E. J. R. EAGLESHAM *The Foundations of Twentieth-Century Education in England*, pp. 39–40, 59 (London, 1967).

40 E. R. WICKHAM *Church and People in an Industrial City*, p. 80 (London, 1957).

41 Quoted in K. S. INGLIS *Churches and the Working Classes in Victorian England*, p. 19 (London, 1963).

42 WICKHAM *Church and People*, pp. 148–9.

43 INGLIS *Churches and the Working Classes*, pp. 3–15. For clerical attitudes to urban society and its problems see R. A. SOLOWAY *Prelates and People: ecclesiastical social thought in England 1783–1852* (London, 1969), especially Ch. VIII, where he expresses the view that 'the Church in the early nineteenth century had barely begun to adjust to the changes of the eighteenth century' (p. 281).

44 ASHWORTH *The Genesis of Modern British Town Planning*, p. 135. For Saltaire and other employers' schemes see the chapter on 'Tied Towns' in COLIN and ROSE BELL *City Fathers: the early history of town planning in Britain* (London, 1969).

45 BRIGGS *Social Thought and Social Action*, pp. 95–6. See also *One Man's Vision: the story of the Joseph Rowntree Village Trust* (London, 1954).

46 BARLOW COMMITTEE *Minutes of Evidence*, p. 626.

47 Ibid., p. 619.

48 *To-morrow: a peaceful path to real reform*, pp. 7, 118–28 (London, 1898).

49 BARLOW COMMITTEE *Minutes of Evidence*, pp. 193–4, Memorandum of Evidence submitted by Ministry of Transport.

50 For these developments, see ' "Philanthropy and five per cent": housing experiments', Ch. XIV in DAVID OWEN *English Philanthropy 1660–1960* (Cambridge, Mass., 1965).

51 Ibid., p. 389.

52 A. M. CARR-SAUNDERS, D. CARADOG JONES and C. A. MOSER *A Survey of Social Conditions in England and Wales*, p. 23 (London, 1958).

53 See MARGARET HEWITT *Wives and Mothers in Victorian Industry* (London, 1958).

54 RONALD FLETCHER *The Family and Marriage*, p. 26 (Harmondsworth, 1962).

55 IVY PINCHBECK *Women Workers and the Industrial Revolution 1750–1850*, p. 1 (London, 1930).

56 Ibid., p. 2. See also HEWITT *Wives and Mothers in Victorian Industry*.

57 GEORGE E. EADES *Historic London*, p. 164 (London, 1966).

58 SYDNEY H. COONTZ *Population Theories and the Economic Interpretation*, pp. 160–1 (London, 1961).

59 O. R. MCGREGOR *Divorce in England*, p. 65 (London, 1957).

60 WANDA F. NEFF *Victorian Working Women*, pp. 186–7 (London, 1929; 1966 edition).

61 EDITH OLIVER *Four Victorian Ladies of Wiltshire*, pp. 27–8 (London, 1945).

62 ALYS W. PEARSALL-SMITH 'A reply from the daughters', in GOODWIN (ed.) *Nineteenth Century Opinion*, p. 89.

63 O. A. SHERRARD *Two Victorian Girls*, pp. 164–7 (London, 1966).

64 See J. A. BANKS *Prosperity and Parenthood* (London, 1954). For an earlier version of the same theme see GRACE G. LEYBOURNE and KENNETH WHITE *Education and the Birth-Rate: a social dilemma*, pp. 57–64 (London, 1940).

65 See PETER T. COMINOS 'Late Victorian sexual responsibility and the social system', *International Review of Social History*, VIII, 1963, No. 18.

66 JOHN STUART MILL *On the Subjection of Women*, pp. 247–8 (London, 1869; Everyman edition, 1929).

67 MILLICENT GARRETT FAWCETT *Women's Suffrage: a short history of a great movement*, p. 23 (New York, n.d.).

68 MCGREGOR *Divorce in England*, p. 19.

69 MILLICENT FAWCETT, 'Women's Suffrage' in GOODWIN (ed.) *Nineteenth Century Opinion*, pp. 84–5.

70 Quoted from Alice Zimmern in JOSEPHINE KAMM *Hope Deferred: Girls' Education in English History*, p. 213 (London, 1965).

71 SECONDARY EDUCATION COMMISSION *Report*, p. 75.

72 MARGARET OLIPHANT in *Blackwood's Magazine*, Vol. 88, December 1860, pp. 711–13.

73 GEORGE DANGERFIELD *The Strange Death of Liberal England 1910–1914*, p. 142 (New York, 1935; 1961 edition).

74 For an account of the role of women in the war see ARTHUR MARWICK *The Deluge*, particularly Ch. 3 (London, 1965).

75 FREDERIC HARRISON in a lecture on Comte and Mill, 1893, reprinted in *On Society*, p. 257 (London, 1918).

76 FABIAN TRACTS (No. 15) *English Progress towards Social Democracy*, p. 3 (London, 1890); FABIAN TRACTS (No. 51) *Socialism: True and False*, pp. 4–6, 8 (London, 1894).

5 Twentieth-century emergencies

Social legislation

After the turn of the century the working-class standard of living remained static or declined, working-class political and industrial organization grew stronger, and the Liberal Party in particular felt an urgent need to identify itself as the popular party, by transforming a heightened social understanding into practical social policy. The pre-war period was what the literary language of one historian calls the 'Indian summer of British capitalism', bringing 'carefree plenty to the well-to-do', but 'for the workers a winter of discontent'. Real wages fell for a large part of the period. If falling prices during the previous decades had obscured economic progress, rising prices now lent to the economy a 'false air of prosperity'.[1] Edwardian developments in social policy arose out of conceptions of communal responsibility, some more altruistic than others. Altruism was, in fact, tempered throughout with a sense of social reality. Behind concern for the unemployed, for example, at the turn of the century lay a new understanding of the causes of poverty, and of the failure and inadequacy of the Poor Law principles of 1834. It was to 'stop this rot in the Poor Law and its administration' that, according to the Webbs, the

Poor Law Commission was set up in 1905 'under the confident assumption that the Commission could not do otherwise than recommend a return to the principles of 1834'.[2]

The Poor Law Commission did not report until 1909. Almost immediately after its creation the reforming Liberal government of 1906 had come to power. Old age pensions were introduced in 1908 (resisted to the last ditch by the C.O.S.) on a non-contributory basis, at a maximum level of five shillings per week. Although the National Insurance Act of 1911 was, unlike the pension scheme, a contributory one, and involved the less magnanimous principle of individual insurance, it was in a sense further removed from nineteenth-century thinking on social legislation. The Act consisted of two parts: Part I concerned health and Part II unemployment. The legislation on health insurance accepted (as legislation on school meals, a school health service and midwives had done in a more limited way already) the welfare of the individual as a matter of primary social concern. Unemployment insurance was necessary because, said Lloyd George, whoever was to blame for the great fluctuations in trade which caused unemployment, 'the workman is the least to blame . . . he is not responsible, although he bears almost all the real privation'.[3] 1911 was, therefore, far removed from the philosophy of, for example, the Public Health Act of 1848. Public opinion in 1906 was prepared to accept, and indeed demanded, State responsibility for much more personal aspects of welfare. The pension scheme called seriously into question, as the C.O.S. clearly understood, the entire basis of the Poor Law. The health insurance of 1911 was more hesitant in its contributory nature but – compulsory as it initially was for everyone earning under £160 a year – it had wider implications for the future shape of the welfare services. The health part of the Act (resisted by the doctors as well as by the Conservative opposition) was operated through approved insurance schemes run by trade unions, insurance companies and others. The unemployment scheme was administered through the new Labour Exchanges. The employee, the employer and the State paid contributions, and the scheme provided sickness and maternity benefits, the services of a doctor and other medical benefits.

Unemployment was made the target of a more limited exercise, providing through insurance a benefit scheme for workers in what Lloyd George called 'precarious trades', that is, those 'liable to very considerable fluctuations', employing roughly one sixth of the industrial population. The coverage of both parts of the Act was gradually extended.

The important consideration here is that by the outbreak of the First World War a serious accumulation of social commitments had been expressed and acted upon, in relation to children, health, unemployment and old age. The process of State and local government intervention and control was being consolidated. The very process of monopoly organization in the private sector of the economy, and of wider public management of services and bureaucratic controls in the national and local government sectors, contributed to a recognition of the collective needs of a complex society. By the early twentieth century local authorities were becoming increasingly involved in, for example, transport, electricity, gas and water services. By 1913, 80 per cent of the consumers of water and of passengers on trams, over 60 per cent of consumers of electricity and 40 per cent of those of gas, were catered for by local authorities. The reason for the growth of municipal involvement was not simply socialist doctrine of the Fabian 'gas and water' kind, but largely 'the need to control natural monopolies, in the hope of relieving the rates, and in a praiseworthy measure of civic pride'.[4]

The period between the mid-1890s and the First World War was also decisive in the process of industrial amalgamation and monopolization (in fields ranging from tobacco to steel). The first Woolworth's was established in 1909. Before the First World War the 'big multiples' in the grocery trade were 'eating up their competitors in every part of the country', though the pace slowed down after 1918.[5] The processes of large-scale production, extensive commercial operations, widespread public controls, impersonal industrial management and public planning, nation-wide industrial bargaining and the national consolidation of trade

17 *London interior, December 1912*

union and employer organizations, were all implanted in the national consciousness by the First World War, though some of them were not finally consolidated until after it. The Federation of British Industries, for example, was born during the war in 1916, and the T.U.C. General Council after it in 1921. Although there had been a national organ-ization of building employers since 1878, it was in 1896 that a full-time general secretary and staff were appointed; in 1901 it adopted its present title of National Federation of Building Trades Employers, and at the end of the First World War it consolidated its local and regional organiza-tion. The 1902 Education Act had already illustrated the transition to more efficient and all-embracing local authority control. Education became *one* of the items in the election manifesto, and in this sense the Act was a retreat from opportunities for popular involvement in educational policy-making, a retreat not to be halted until the widespread interest in education of the 1950s and 1960s.

Between 1902 and the outbreak of war Britain acquired, in fact, a considerable body of legislation and machinery affecting a wide range of social services. The concept of social services other than those provided under the Poor Law was in this period effectively implemented for the first time. Legislation covered not only the provision of education, for example, but also, in 1906, school meals, and in the following year a school health service. The Children Act of 1908 was concerned with wider problems of the protection of children. A Royal Commission report was followed in 1913 by a Mental Deficiency Act. Free school places, Labour Exchanges, town planning – the range of new departures was wide even if their effectiveness was not always great. They illustrate, however, the extent to which awareness of social realities had sharpened since the end of the 1880s.

The Poor Law Commission and after

That the ground had not been totally cleared for the building of a new kind of welfare society can be seen from both the limitations of the legislation itself and the debates about social policy highlighted by the Poor Law Commission Reports of 1909. The analyses and findings of the Commission demonstrate vividly the scale of reference being established for the approach to poverty and social planning for the next half-century. They illustrate the difficulties of matching an awareness of social problems with widely acceptable social philosophies and policies. They highlight different conceptions of what holds a society together, and the difficulty of agreeing on priorities which might remedy its weaknesses.

The two philosophies battling it out in the Poor Law Commission were broadly that of the C.O.S. (the nineteen-member Commission included its Secretary, C. S. Loch, and five other members) and that of the socialists (with Beatrice Webb representing the extremely influential Fabians). The philosophy of the former was based on the retention of the fundamental principles of 1834, however far these might need to be adapted, and on co-operation between the Poor Law authorities, whatever new name might be found for them, and the voluntary organizations. The Fabians were more concerned with efficient local government, specialized social services and the total abolition of the Poor Law and its agencies. The Commission failed to produce an agreed report, and the Minority Report was signed by four members.

The Majority Report was rooted in the explicit awareness that, in spite of moral and material progress and an 'enormous annual expenditure, amounting to nearly sixty millions a year, upon poor relief, education, and public health, we still have a vast army of persons quartered upon us unable to support themselves, and an army which in numbers has recently shown signs of increase rather than decrease'. The Report sought ways of strengthening the machinery of relief. It proposed changing the name of the local Poor Law authorities to Public Assistance Committees – though this was 'not intended to disguise the fact that those who come within the scope of the operations of the new authority are receiving help at the public expense'. It wished to ensure adequate specialization within the system, in order to strengthen the principle of deterrence. An all-purpose workhouse was inefficient, argued the Report. The 'loafer, the in-and-out and the work-shy are influenced as to whether or not they accept the offer of the workhouse by the amount of physical comfort, restraint or inconvenience associated with the particular institution offered them. The more comfortable the house, the less is it a deterrent to this class.' The 'respectable poor', on the other hand, were deterred from accepting the workhouse out of moral considerations, not wishing to 'accept comfort if it involves association with a number of persons of a degraded *status*'. The mixed workhouse, therefore, 'with its higher level of comfort works most unevenly as a deterrent. It attracts the very class it ought to repel, and it may act as a deterrent in the case of the aged and infirm to whom it might legitimately be a refuge.' A streamlined system of classification by institutions would make it easier to provide conditions which could really act as a deterrent to the able-bodied.

The Report demonstrates repeatedly the continued existence of a social philosophy which refused to accept that what was under discussion was the phenomenon of poverty and not the moral stances involved in the concept of pauperism. Its vocabulary makes no effort to disguise the fact. It saw the poor as 'a vast army' which had *intruded* into the social structure; they were 'quartered' upon 'us'. It had a strong sense of poverty as a discrete condition, unrelated to society, outside the society of *us*. The fact that Poor Law institutions had made it easy for paupers to obtain relief on more than one occasion in the year (the 'ins-and-outs') meant that curative treatment was impossible:

> The worst characters may flock into the workhouse to recuperate from the effects of their evil lives, and as soon as they have, at the ratepayers' cost, partially recovered their physical condition, they can leave the workhouse and resume their degenerate careers.

Old persons 'given to drink, or of dirty habits' should not 'be enabled to remove themselves from control either by a pension or by the granting of outdoor relief'. Institutions should have the power to *detain* 'drunkards and persons leading immoral lives . . . after their incapacity to lead a decent life has been proved'. Outdoor medical relief should be conditional upon 'the maintenance of a healthy domicile and good habits'. The Report attacked the school meals Act of 1906 as interfering with the proper processes of relief. The Report argued, as the C.O.S. had argued forty years before, that there were too many agencies dealing indiscriminately with 'a class which is sometimes called able-bodied, sometimes unemployed, regardless of the fact that this class is not really a class at all; but included the honest, the criminal, the unfortunate, the industrious and the loafer, all of whom, 'in the prevailing confusion, are shifting about from one agency to another'. To ensure that they were sifted and classified, and each agency was assigned its appropriate work, the Report urged stronger co-operation between the authorities and the C.O.S.[6]

The vocabulary of the Minority Report is at times not dissimilar in its condescension from that of the Majority. It points out, for example, that destitution authorities rarely bother to ascertain 'how the household is actually being maintained upon the Outdoor Relief ... The result, as we have grave reason to believe, is that a large part of the sum of nearly four millions sterling is a subsidy to insanitary, to disorderly or even to vicious habits of life.' Children were 'actually being brought up at the public expense in drunken and dissolute homes'. Although the Fabian philosophy was as socially manipulative in its way as was the C.O.S., the differences between the underlying social philosophy of this Report and that of the Majority are great. The Minority

18 *Distress in London, July 1912.*
Children waiting outside a hall in
Salmon's Lane for a free dinner

Report is aware of the failures of past analysis and re-
cognizes the processes of social change. Beatrice Webb
had worked with Booth and had been offered marriage
by Joseph Chamberlain. George Lansbury, another
Minority Commissioner, had intimate experience of the
working of relief in the conditions of destitution in Poplar.
They relentlessly carried the Minority Report through
to what must have been intended as the most crucial sen-
tence:

For all sections of the Able-bodied, the Poor Law, alike
in England and Wales, Scotland and Ireland, is, in our
judgment, intellectually bankrupt.

The Majority's recommendations would work, on its own admission, only if compulsory powers of detention were available. This, said the Minority, would make the destitution authorities 'very nearly akin to the Prison Authorities'. The Minority rejected altogether such principles of deterrence. It had become apparent that:

> the condition of the lowest grade of independent labourers is unfortunately one of such inadequacy of food and clothing and such absence of other necessaries of life that it has been found, in practice, impossible to make the conditions of Poor Law relief 'less eligible' without making them such as are demoralizing to the children, physically injurious to the sick, and brutalizing to the aged and infirm.

The Minority Report demanded the complete break-up of the Poor Law machinery, nationally and locally. It considered, in fact, that no residue of pauperism would need to be dealt with through the unspecialized agency of the workhouse or of out-relief, if specialized local authority services were properly organized. The Minority had been horrified by what they had seen, for example, of the typical men's day ward in an urban workhouse, containing:

> one or two hundred wholly unoccupied males of every age between fifteen and ninety – strong and vicious men; men in all stages of recovery from debauch; weedy youths of weak intellect; old men too dirty or disreputable to be given special privileges, and sometimes, when there are no such privileges, even worthy old men; men subject to fits; occasional monstrosities . . . the respectable labourer prematurely invalided; the hardened, sodden loafer, and the temporary unemployed man . . .

This, or any version of this, was for the Minority unacceptable. Britain now had efficient local government; to it, its sub-committees, and its specialists, *all* the functions of the destitution authority should be transferred. Only a Receiving House would be needed 'for the strictly temporary accommodation of non-able-bodied persons found in

need, and not as yet dealt with by the Committees concerned'.[7]

Eventually, in 1929, the Poor Law became Public
Assistance in the hands of the local authorities, nationally
administered by the Unemployment Assistance Board from
1934, and with extended powers and the title of Assistance
Board from 1940. The Poor Law died but a use for its
machinery continued to be found. Neither of the
Commission's Reports proved directly influential. The
Liberal government took no action on the recommendations
of either, and by-passed the problem of the relief of the
indigent poor by pursuing its attempts to combat indigence.
The problem of whether to break up the Poor Law was
simply evaded.

Our analysis of the philosophies embodied in the Reports
has not been intended to suggest that the Reports themselves played a significant part in shaping social institutions
but to illustrate, at their sharpest, alternative approaches to
social policy in the period when the basis of the 'welfare
state' was laid. The Liberal legislation after 1906
represented major achievements in a variety of fields but
accepted collectivist notions only so far as appeared strictly
necessary. Older moral judgements were built in to new
policies. The old age pension was given on condition that
certain criteria were met, including not only age (seventy)
and income (full pension if annual income was below two
pounds per year) but also worthiness – the five shillings a
week would not be paid to those who had habitually failed
to work. National Health Insurance from 1911 provided
benefit for the insured, not their families. It should be noted
that, although the parliamentary Labour Party supported
the 1911 legislation on health and unemployment insurance,
Lansbury, among others, opposed it, because he considered
the contributory principle anti-socialist. The conclusion arrived at by Richard Titmuss about 'the great collectivist
advances at the beginning of the century, with their positive
achievements in social legislation' is that although they were
aimed at the gradual overthrow of the Poor Law, in the
absence of 'new insights into the social phenomena of
human needs and behaviour, the ideas and methods of the

poor law were transplanted to the new social services'. The way in which the new institutions grew, detaching the needs of the individual from those of the family, partly explains 'the *ad hoc* fragmentary growth of the British social services'. The important point Titmuss makes is that the new services catered for certain categories of individual need: 'classes of persons in need and categories of disease were treated; not families and social groups in distress'.[8]

Some redistribution of income was certainly involved (total working-class incomes may have benefited from all the social benefits introduced in 1906–11 by some 6 per cent per year), but the approach was piecemeal and the departures less radical than is sometimes claimed. The notion of 'settlement', of parish responsibility for the poor, for example, continued from Tudor times, through its formalization in the seventeenth century, the changes of 1834, the events of 1906–11, the transition to public assistance in 1929, and beyond. It has remained part of the practice of national assistance and social security. The Minority Report of 1909 revealed that over 12,000 poor persons were still deported annually, under compulsory orders, from one union to another. Although 'settlement' deportations no longer take place in this way, the 'settlement mentality' remains, and Borough X prefers not to have to accept responsibility for the homeless from Borough Y.

The limitations of the collectivist advances with regard to *scope* can be seen most clearly, not only in such fields as family health, but in the failure to tackle adequately such problems as regional industrial decline and housing, both of which affect important aspects of working-class family stability and structure at a fundamental level.

Housing

There is an underlying conflict in all thinking and legislation on housing in Britain. On the one hand is the philosophy of social responsibility, including for the public and perhaps subsidized provision of an adequate standard of housing as of right; on the other hand is the baronial-yeoman-bourgeois concept of the Englishman's private (and

heavily mortgaged) castle. The rage of the suburban bun-
galow-owner against the council tenant has become a major
factor in political argument only since the Second World
War. During approximately the first half of the century the
practice of collective responsibility for the raising of housing
standards was too limited and irregular in its achievement,
and the emergencies in which it was exercised were too
bewildering, for an excessive display of rage.

The housing Acts of the nineteenth century, in so far as
they were effective at all, were concerned with regulating,
not intervening in, the construction of houses. In both town
planning and house building the departures of the early
twentieth century were hesitant or ineffective. The Town
Planning Act of 1909 made it possible for local authorities to
adopt planning schemes, but to all intents and purposes
only for new, that is suburban, developments. The philosophy of suburban planning embodied in this Act coincided with and related to the dilution of Garden City ideas
into the movement towards the Garden Suburb (as it was
called in Hampstead) or the Garden Village (as it was called
in Hull). For existing housing the first move did not come
until wartime. For the first time restrictions on rent
increases were introduced in 1915, with an Act touched off
by an outcry against rising rents in Glasgow. Between the
wars there were, in Marion Bowley's formulation, three
periods of experiment.[9] The first began in 1919 with the
Housing and Town Planning Act, which inaugurated the
principle of Treasury subsidies and made it necessary for
local authorities to survey housing needs, and try to provide
for them. It was widely believed that the Act would need to
be only a temporary measure and that the housing programme would rapidly make up the deficit caused by war,
but the homes for the returning heroes did not materialize.
It was variously estimated that between 300,000 and a million new houses would be needed immediately after the war.
Great hopes were pinned on the 1919 Act, but the result was
derisory. Nowhere 'were suffering and social dislocation more
apparent than in the need for houses . . . The history of the
housing programme is the history of a rout.'[10] By 1921 it was
decided that the subsidy for house building was too expensive.

The second period of experiment runs from 1923 to 1934. Neville Chamberlain's Housing Act of 1923 made subsidies again available, but on a more rigid basis. Local authorities could build houses with them only if they could convince the Minister of Health that it would be better for them than for private enterprise to do so. Again the assumption was that the housing crisis could be quickly overcome. The Wheatley Housing Act of 1924, probably the most important piece of legislation of the short-lived first Labour government, restored the responsibility for working-class housing to the local authorities. Subsidies were increased, but were offered only for houses to be let. The Greenwood Slum Clearance Act of 1930, a product of the second Labour government, was designed to clear and to build under the long-term planning introduced in 1924. The Conservative-dominated National Government of 1931, led by the former Labour Prime Minister, Ramsay MacDonald, ended the Wheatley subsidies in 1933 and defined the terms of the third period of experiment. The new policy launched by the Housing Act of that year was intended to continue slum clearance and attack overcrowding, but urged maximum incentive for competitive private building, to be supplemented where necessary by unsubsidized local authority building.

One thing that this story indicates is that the limits on social policy were now vastly different from those of the nineteenth century. Policy and progress were now features of election manifestos and programmes, and the limits to which they became subjected were those of government mis-estimations and economic stringency. The ethics of the struggle between public programmes and private enterprise were being converted into Treasury considerations. Public responsibility and public planning to some extent overtook all political parties, given the magnitude of the social problems of the 1930s, the magnitude of war efforts and the magnitude of international economic competition.

Not until the mid-1960s was any serious attempt made, within the Conservative Party, for example, to retreat from this commitment to public planning, and not until the 1970s was a Conservative leadership again explicitly committed to strong opposition to public responsibility for important areas of social welfare.

Empire and war

The economic circumstances which, in the first half of the twentieth century, underlay developments in social engineering included both war and the consequences of war, as well as fundamental changes in Britain's trading position. International competition had helped to make the idea of empire widely acceptable in the 1870s, and in the 1880s Britain was involved in the scramble for Africa. The Imperial Idea, for the first time in Britain's history, was strongly justified in terms of tongue, race and destiny. In the 1890s and after the turn of the century – particularly during the Boer War – imperialism became a cause to be fought for, and the relationship between Britain's economic stability and the necessity of empire became a subject for debate. The reluctant political imperialism of Gladstone became the imperialism defended on economic grounds by Joseph Chamberlain, the creation of whose Unionist Party by secession from the Liberal Party in 1886 'may be said to mark the birth of the Imperialism which dominated British politics for twenty years'.[11] Cecil Rhodes, the most forthright of empire builders, contributed to the funds of the Liberal Party, and in 1895 made a sharp defence of empire:

> I was in the East End of London yesterday and attended a meeting of the unemployed. I listened to the wild speeches, which were just a cry for 'bread', 'bread', 'bread', and on my way home I pondered over the scene and I became more than ever convinced of the importance of imperialism . . . in order to save the 40,000,000 inhabitants of the United Kingdom from a bloody civil war, we colonial statesmen must acquire new lands . . . The Empire, as I have always said, is a bread and butter question. If you want to avoid civil war, you must become imperialists . . .[12]

The idea of empire not only captured Chamberlain and inspired Rhodes, but overtook wide sections of the labour movement, and made it popular to believe that 'to us – to us, and not to others, a certain definite duty has been assigned. To carry light and civilization into the dark places of the world; to touch the mind of Asia and of Africa with the ethical ideas of Europe.'[13] The jingoism of the Boer War contributed to the state of mind which made possible the scale of the First World War. Both related to a world in which the internal stability of the great nations depended strongly on raw materials and markets, on success in international competition, and therefore on a new mastery of international relations. Much of the detail of Britain's twentieth-century history is governed, not only by competition and war with Germany, but by the fact that the United States during the First World War replaced Britain as the world's major industrial and financial power, that it was in the empire that Britain found markets to substitute for those lost to the United States and other powers, and that new world economics became bound up with world war.[14]

Not only did Britain lose traditional export relations in the war, to the benefit of the United States, but other competitors (including Japan) were also threatening more urgently. The Soviet Union had come into existence, and more and more spheres of British economic interest (in the Far East, Canada and Latin America, for instance) were weakening – although some lost ground was regained in the 1930s. The war was not, however, the sole, or even the major, cause of many of these and other developments of the 1920s and 1930s.

> Had there been no war the United States would still have become the world's great creditor; industrialization would still have spread in new areas, to the destruction of some British export markets; substitutes for coal would still have grown in importance; the sources and costs of primary commodities would still have changed. Even many of the changes in British society would have come, too. Labour would still have become a stronger and more cohesive political force; women would still have gained the vote and wider social opportunities; there would still have been a larger scale of organization among firms and

trade unions; doubtless, many tastes and consumer demands would have changed in just the same way . . . The war did two things. It accelerated many economic and social changes already in progress . . . And it smashed the delicate framework of international economic and financial organization . . .[15]

World war obviously made fundamental inroads into patterns of social assumptions and consciousness. It produced or heightened a basic spiritual dislocation and malaise, over which attempts were made to plaster the post-war 'business as usual' signs. The politics, the philosophy and the literature of the inter-war decades reflected the experience and the aftermath of the war. It also introduced new factors into the structure of British social organization, in order to meet a new order of emergency. The State became involved in the control of war industries,[16] agricultural production, the running of the railways and the control of a variety of resources and services. Although the end of the war saw the relaxations of these regulations and involvements, extensive State action to meet one sort of emergency meant that it could be called upon to meet another.

Between the wars

British society and economy in the 1920s and 1930s were not what they had been before the war. People's level of expectation was higher, even if the level of achievement was disastrously low. Homes for heroes, full employment, the return to industrial and commercial 'normality' – all of these were slogans which, because they were unfulfilled, helped to set the scene for renewed and intensified social conflict.

Economically, Britain's position after the short post-war boom was one of sharp contrasts. The old staple industries like cotton, coal and shipbuilding were hard hit by competition from better-equipped industries, by over-optimistic estimates of post-war demand, and by the lack of demand from saturated or lost markets. The inflated wartime capacity in shipbuilding, for example (followed by a disastrous decline at the beginning of the 1920s), and the steep drop in coal production at and after the end of the war, were two prominent factors which produced the higher level of regional unemployment, especially in the northern counties of England, in South Wales and industrial Scotland. On the other hand, electrical engineering, road transport, building and artificial silk, for example, made rapid advances. The expansion in electricity consumption and related investments by the State, together with the expansion of the electrical trades, were important examples of growth points; at the moment – in the late 1930s – when the expansion of these and other industries appeared to be past its peak, rearmament stopped any further recession.[17] The annual increase in British industrial output as a whole between the wars was just under 2 per cent: that of electrical goods and motor cars was over 10 per cent, and that of artificial silk over 15 per cent. The structure of the labour force and the relative prosperity of different regions were inevitably being altered.

The Barlow Commission, whose report on the industrial population was completed in 1939, considered some of the factors which, after 1921, had led to a changed pattern of population growth. Between 1921 and 1937 the population of Great Britain had increased by 7·5 per cent (from under 43 to about 46 million). London and the Home Counties had increased by about 18 per cent, the Midland counties by about 11 per cent. The increase in Lancashire, however, was less than 1 per cent, and counties including Glamorgan, Northumberland and Durham registered declines. London, the Home Counties and the Midland counties contained nearly 70 per cent of the population added during the period. Industrial depression, resulting from the contraction of exports, new methods of working, the use of substitutes (such as rayon), and above all the development of industries not dependent on proximity to sources of power, lay behind the new population patterns.[18] Unemployment and slump did not hit the south in the same way as the north and, even within regions, did not hit West Riding wool in the same way as Lancashire cotton or Yorkshire coal. Between 1921 and 1938, although the percentage of the labour force employed in 'manufacture' fluctuated between about 33 and 36

per cent, individual sectors registered considerable variations. The percentage of manufacturing workers employed
in vehicle building rose from 5·75 to 8·85 per cent. The
percentage employed in textiles fell from 21·4 to 16·15.
Large increases took place at the same time in the numbers
of workers employed in the distributive trades, insurance
and banking, and various local government, professional and
other services. There was an increase of 1,246,000 salaried
persons, or 35 per cent, as against an increase of 1,686,000
wage-earners, or 14 per cent, between 1920–2 and 1937–8.[19]

Changes in industrial and occupation structure were also
taking place, affecting, for example, the scale and nature of
female employment; many of the trends did not become
acute, however, until the Second World War. Domestic
service was still, before the First World War and in the
1930s, the largest single category of female employment
(dropping from well over a million in 1931 to under 350,000
in 1951). Women were moving into the distributive trades
and offices to an increasingly rapid extent by the First
World War. It was during and after the Second World War
that factory work passed domestic service in social esteem.

By the end of the First World War national organization,
national planning, national solutions, were a normal dimension of social thought. The national employers' and trade
union organizations, party and ministerial policies, and
national responsibilities in dealing with social problems
which constituted national emergencies – all made this
inevitable. Basic aspects of society were now more than ever
governed or influenced by national decisions, nation-wide
services and government policy. In 1929 government policy
(in the shape of Neville Chamberlain's reforms) altered the
pattern of local government, transferring the powers of the
Poor Law Guardians to the local authorities, and giving the
counties greater powers in public health, welfare, planning
and roads. The Ministry of Health had already been created
in 1919, and from 1929 the new local authority powers were
to extend hospital, maternity and child welfare and other
services. In commerce, combination and the expansion of
multiple grocery and general stores were firm inter-war
trends. So were the increased scale and efficiency of public

administration and services, increased suburban and inter-urban transport, and the greater scale of postal, telephone, news and distributive services. The B.B.C. was created in 1922. The 1930s saw both a rapid expansion in the purchase of radio sets, and acute competition among the large-circulation newspapers for readership. This was a period of expansion above all of the national dailies, offering free sets of the novels of Dickens or other rewards for the regular reader. In transport, too, the trends were clear: a Ministry of Transport was created in 1919, a Railway Act of 1921 compulsorily combined the 120 railway companies into four, ensuring a unified service and system of charges. An amal-gamation of rail, tram and bus services in the London area produced the London Passenger Transport Board in 1933. In 1922 there were some 315,000 private cars in Great Britain. In 1930 there were over a million. More local auth-orities ran their own, and larger, bus services. The first unsuccessful experiments in internal air services took place in 1930. Five years later there were nineteen companies operating services.

Industrial conflict

'There can have been few times', says Ashworth, 'when the lot of the very poor was more miserable than in the early years of the twentieth century.'[20] Real wages fell between the turn of the century and the First World War. They rose again on average in the 1920s and 1930s, in spite of heavy unemployment, as a result principally of a fall in the cost-of-living index, but also increased productivity and an increase in the proportion of higher-paid, salaried em-ployees. Averages, however, are deceptive. The distribution of increased national income was uneven, and although the families of men in employment experienced improvements of one kind or another (including shorter working hours and paid holidays), the incidence of unemployment and its at-tendant suffering makes it difficult to dwell on averages.

Between 1921 and 1938 the percentage of unemployed never fell below 9·6, and at its peak – in 1932 – it reached almost 22 per cent. Unemployment data before the 1920s

19 *Unemployment in Wigan, 11 November 1939*

are not accurate, and have had to be deduced from trade
union records of payments to their members when out of
work. It is likely, however, that between 1856 and the First
World War unemployment fluctuated between 2 and 10 per
cent. Between 1921 and 1938 in only one year was the figure
less than 10 per cent. Even allowing for the widest margin of
error, Lord Beveridge came to the conclusion that unemployment after the First World War was 'most probably
nearly two and a half times as severe as before the war'.[21]
The two facts of declining real wages before the First World
War and mass unemployment in the 1920s and 1930s form
the main background to the presence of social conflict in
Britain up to the Second World War, and the industrial and
social policies and legislation aimed at relief and conciliation. Neither, of course, entirely explains continuing industrial militancy or social tension. Other factors, such as
industrial rationalization and eventually automation, social
problems relating to housing and a growing percentage of
old people in the population, inadequate hospital facilities,
responses to international situations, and the problems of

particular industries – all contributed to tension and conflict.

At the back of conflict lay also the fact of political and industrial organization. A critical moment for the future history of trade union organization had been the new unionism of the late 1880s, which not only widened the basis of trade unionism, but also demonstrated the potential of organized militancy. George Howell, writing in 1891, complained mournfully that the distinguishing trait in the conduct of the militant 'new leaders' was 'their persistent, cowardly, and calumnious attacks upon the old leaders, upon men who have borne the brunt of labour's battles . . . Some of the new leaders have openly proclaimed that their mission is to preach the gospel of discontent . . . In so far as discontent leads to emulation, to vigorous effort to better the condition of the workers, it is healthful . . . But there is discontent of another kind, which aims at lawlessness and licence.'[22] Within the working-class trade union and political movements (both becoming increasingly organized) the dispute over forms of industrial action, and over the relationship between industrial and political action, had now become sharp and portentous.

We cannot here trace the forms of working-class action or the place that the Labour Party came to occupy in British politics.[23] Nor is it necessary to pursue the economic arguments about the reasons for the difficulties of these years. Industrial and economic factors we have mentioned, together with new aspects of working-class political disillusion and militancy, produced a wave of industrial struggles, which a historian of the London Trades Council describes as deriving from 'a sense of power, the will to take charge of working-class destiny'.[24]

Miners, railwaymen, cotton spinners, boilermakers, seamen, dockers and workers in a variety of other trades were involved in intense and prolonged struggles – and those involved were not always the groups who were worst off or with the strongest traditions of militancy. Syndicalism, a form of unionism aiming at industrial control through strike action, provided some of the sense of 'working-class destiny'. Economic hardship or the sense of deprivation fostered by the conspicuous affluence of the wealthy provided some of the incentive. The importance of the Great Unrest to the story of modern British society lies in the fact that it contained the combination of factors which was to be present in future industrial struggles: militancy, sensitive relations with Labour parliamentary politics, local, regional and national levels of strike action, attempts at industrial arbitration, and objectives not always easy to define in terms of money or conditions. It is not only the scale of the strikes and demonstrations, but their implications for future working-class attitudes and action, that make the period important.[25]

Conflict and attempts at industrial conciliation ran in parallel between the wars. In the nineteenth century, industrial relations, in the sense of long-term agreement between owners and workers for the achievement of optimal working conditions, were virtually non-existent. Employers, guided by principles of *laissez-faire* and with their effective power little damaged by industrial legislation, controlled wages, prices and profits. By the early twentieth century, however, a new industrial ethic was taking root. Linked to the scientific management movement in the 1920s, and to research in 'human relations' carried out in the 1930s, the aim of this new ideology was co-operation – albeit more in the interests of greater managerial efficiency than out of any particular respect for the workers' own interests. The activities of the new industrial consultants and managers were directed primarily towards developing the morale and effectiveness of working groups.

As unemployment, wage cuts in declining industries (notably mining) and industrial disputes built up towards the General Strike of 1926, doctrines of social harmony urgently took shape. Stanley Baldwin, Conservative Prime Minister from 1924 to 1929, spent his early months in office propounding a simple vision of service to the country, of the ordinary loyalties of ordinary folk. In a speech early in 1925, with one in ten of the working population unemployed, but with some faint hope of an economic revival, Baldwin watched the signs of an industrial storm gathering. It was inevitable, he considered, that large-scale production should be accompanied by 'great consolidations of capital managed by small concentrated groups, and by great organizations of Labour led by experienced and responsible leaders'. It was suspicion between the two that needed to be eradicated:

> I am whole-heartedly with those men who talk about disarmament on the Continent, peace on the Continent, and the removal of suspicion on the Continent, but far more do I plead for disarmament at home, and for the removal of that suspicion at home that tends to poison the relations of man and man, the removal of which alone can lead us to stability for our struggling industry . . .

He pleaded for peace and harmony:

> I want to plead for a truce. In the Middle Ages when the whole of Europe was in conflict, one part with another and one fragment with another, men of goodwill strove in vain to get what they called a truce of God . . . I want a truce of God in this country . . .[26]

Fourteen months later the breakdown of negotiations between Baldwin and the General Council of the T.U.C. heralded the General Strike.

Conciliation machinery within industry itself had developed in a miniature way late in the nineteenth century. A Conciliation Act of 1896, for example, had made the services of the Board of Trade available for industrial arbitration. The Trade Boards of 1909 and the Joint Industrial Councils of 1919 had more recently lent authority to the process of negotiation on wages and conditions, even though the Councils themselves, and the conciliation powers given to the Ministry of Labour in 1919, were not particularly successful. The Mond–Turner talks between employers and trade union leaders in 1928-9 sought – in the wake of the General Strike – to find approaches to industrial cooperation. 'Mondism', together with the study of management and industrial relations and renewed appeals for a 'truce of God' in the country or in industry, did not, however, remove the reality of unemployment and unrest. They did not remove memories of pre-war struggles, those in which the shop steward movement was born in the First

World War, the Clydeside clashes of 1919, and the consequent strengthening of socialist organization and programmes. For all the failures of the General Strike of May
1926, the search for harmony could not break fundamental
suspicions, even though the collapse of the strike deepened
the divisions within the labour movement between the
advocates of industrial action and the advocates of negotiation and parliamentary pressure. Whatever else the General
Strike did, it left among the workers, as Mowat puts it, 'a
compound of bitterness and pride: pride in the unselfishness
of it, in the skill in organization which their people had
shown'. The strike initially weakened the labour movement,
but helped to strengthen 'the working man's loyalty to his
own movement and his own party'. For the leaders, 'it
confirmed and strengthened all the conservative, rightward
tendencies which were manifest before it'.[27] The election of
a Labour government in 1929, the economic crisis of 1931
and Ramsay MacDonald's defection to lead a National
government, the election success of the Labour Party in
1945 – and constant struggles within the Party over the definition of socialist policy – mark some of the movement's
internal tensions, successes and failures in reconciling them,
and the changing forms and motives of organized action by
the labour movement.

The Labour Party and the trade unions did not, of
course, in the 1920s and 1930s, hold a monopoly of involvement in political and social conflict. The developments we
have mentioned related most directly to questions of wages,
rights or redundancy. Through these, however, they related
also to wider considerations of social relationships, of social
expectations. The 1930s were dominated, in fact, by an
urgent search for ways of mending, quickly, a broken
society, one which had only recently, in the plans and
promises of wartime, seemed to be capable of rapid renovation. The First World War had faced Britain with an emergency of a new kind and quickened the awareness of and
responses to social change. The problems of the inter-war
years, arising from some of these profound economic and
social changes, and from the new international contexts,
faced British society with an emergency of another kind.

The sense of urgency was intensified by the greater sensitivity to world events, to the excitements of the creation of the Soviet Union, the disappointments of its development, and the relentless threat of Fascism, Nazism and war. Alongside the story of industrial action, and closely interwoven with it, is the story of social protest, of hunger marches, of anti-fascist demonstrations, the literature of commitment and protest, the Left Book Club and death in Spain.

Health and living standards

Alongside such real and prominent phenomena as mass unemployment and organized protest we must remember changes that were taking place in vital fields of welfare. This is not only to bring our previous discussion up to date, but also because of the importance of such developments for our later analysis of the age structure of the population, the size and functions of the family, and the whole pattern of marriage, parenthood, employment and length of life.

The Beveridge Report of 1942 summarized the findings of social investigators (including a second survey of York by Rowntree in 1936) about changes in working-class standards of living since the end of the nineteenth century. The York Survey of 1936 and a *New Survey of London Life and Labour* conducted in 1929 gave proof of 'large and general progress':

> ... the average workman in London could buy a third more of articles of consumption in return for labour of an hour's less duration per day than he could buy forty years before at the time of Charles Booth's original survey. The standard of living available to the workpeople of York in 1936 may be put over-all at about 30 per cent higher than it was in 1899 ... In London, the crude death rate fell from 18·6 per thousand in 1900 to 11·4 in 1935 and the infant mortality rate fell from 159 to 58 per thousand ... What has been shown for these towns in detail applies to the country generally ...

Increased real incomes, Beveridge pointed out, were even more marked in the case of people whose earnings were interrupted by sickness, accident or unemployment, or ended by old age.[28] Want had been diminished at least far enough to have a serious influence on mortality statistics.

Between 1911 and 1940 the birth rate dropped sharply and consistently (from 21·8 live births per thousand to 14·8 in England and Wales). The death rate in England and Wales, after falling slowly to 12·1 deaths per thousand in 1921–30, then fluctuated only very slightly. The natural increase in the population in England and Wales in the 1930s was the lowest recorded (2·5 per thousand, compared with, for example, 14·0 in the 1870s). The average annual rate of increase in the 1930s and 1940s was about a third of what it had been a century before. With the possibility of Britain's population beginning to decline, a Royal Commission on Population was appointed, reporting in 1949. With various fluctuations, however, the birth rate rose after the war, and again after 1955. For the United Kingdom as a whole the figure was 16 per thousand in 1951, 18 per thousand in 1961 and 16 per thousand in 1971 (falling to 13 per thousand in 1974).

The most significant improvement in the early decades of the twentieth century was in infant mortality figures. Improvements in housing, diet, welfare and medical services had a considerable impact on the figures, which had lagged behind those of other improvements in the late nineteenth century. What is equally significant, however, is that the infant mortality figures indicated continued – and in some cases *increased* – class differentials. We have seen, in Chadwick's analyses, for example, the earlier class differential in mortality statistics. We have seen also how, in his and Playfair's reports, the same causes produced differentials between industrial and rural or middle-class residential areas. The differentials continued into the twentieth century. In 1912 the average infant mortality for London was ninety-one per thousand. In wealthy Hampstead it was sixty-two; in congested Shoreditch it was 123. Children's weight, as tabulated in an inquiry in Surrey, varied almost exactly in proportion to the average weekly wages of the father. The infant mortality rate among families in L.C.C. housing was less than half that for London as a whole.[29]

For the country as a whole, infant mortality in the Registrar General's Social Class I (Upper and Middle) fell, between 1911 and 1930–2, from seventy-six to thirty-three per thousand legitimate live births. The drop for Social Class V (Unskilled Labour) was from 153 to seventy-seven. The percentage differential had increased. The differential in the same period between towns like Bournemouth, Great Yarmouth and Eastbourne, and towns like South Shields and Newcastle, was also preserved or widened. Evidence submitted to the Barlow Commission showed that infant mortality figures also related directly to the number of persons per room. High density per room almost uniformly meant high infant mortality.[30] It is not always easy to judge from the figures what improvements took place in the death rate for different diseases. In some cases there were enormous regional differences, governed by the state of medical inspection and facilities as well as by housing, diet and sanitation. Actual *increases* in some figures (for diphtheria in the 1930s, for instance) may indicate, not increases in the incidence of a disease, but improvements in the system of notification and diagnosis. Between the mid-1920s and the mid-1930s, however, it is clear that there was a substantial fall (of a quarter to a third in many large cities) in the death rate from tuberculosis, and even more dramatically in the case of deaths from measles, whooping cough and scarlet fever.[31]

The underlying trends in population and family size in the inter-war period were a product of all of these and related factors. A war-time analysis of them pointed to poverty, social and international uncertainties, as root causes of what it described as a parents' revolt. The population decline was 'the most formidable and the most fundamental indictment of our present order of things. Parents are in revolt; they are refusing to bring into the world their own kind.' The people of Britain, the authors concluded, 'have shown in an unmistakable way by their refusal to reproduce that the existing social and economic order just will not do'.[32]

The social services and the protection afforded at moments of crisis by unemployment and health insurance were indications of how far the relationship between the individual (particularly the underprivileged individual) and government had been taken even by 1914. The attack on unemployment in particular, suggests Bentley Gilbert, brought the government for the first time into the life of the 'ordinary, adult, male, able-bodied workman'. For such a man, 'who did not pay income tax, who stayed off the poor law, who did not serve in the army, who rarely used the Post Office, His Majesty's Government was a far-off, olympian thing'. Now, however, 'finally, visibly and intimately, the government was truly his servant. A precedent had been set.' It was one which took the State 'beyond the area of social welfare and into the area of social service'.[33] It would be impossible, henceforward, to consider problems of the individual in modern Britain without close regard to the evolution of a complete, finely organized network of responsible public authorities. Government was from now on in one sense the individual's servant, but in another sense his master. Discussions of the nature of a democratic society, and the details of political programmes, were to become increasingly concerned with the extent and strength of public powers, with the balance between paternal authorities and individual freedom. The spokesmen for nationalization, increased social welfare services and a high degree of public planning, on the one hand, and the spokesmen for private enterprise, individual choice and freedom from controls, on the other, were all to assert that they did so in the name of democracy.

In one important respect the commitment by the State to the principle of unemployment insurance was more than what Gilbert calls a 'precedent'. It was a turning point in that the principle involved was one of insurance, with benefit by right in return for contributions – a principle extended in 1920 to cover all workers. By 1921, however, the magnitude of the unemployment problem had shattered the basis of the principle. For hundreds of thousands, and then millions, of men the benefit entitlement was rapidly exhausted, and the government had to commit itself to 'transitional' or 'uncovenanted' benefits – the dole. More than any other action this response to unemployment interred the principles of 1834. A 'dole' had been paid to unemployed, demobilized servicemen for a period after 1918. In 1921 the principle behind the previous short-term measure was made an inescapable feature of social policy. Unemployment benefit was now paid without regard to contributions, as a right, and at a level which made nonsense of the notion of 'less eligibility'. More than the transfer of the Poor Law machinery to the local authorities in 1929, it marks the turning away from the view of pauperism which dominated the nineteenth century. Subsequent attempts in the 1930s to return to the pure principle of insurance failed; insurance was retained, certainly, as a basic feature of the 1948 Welfare State provisions, but it had by then become *social* insurance, entailing a fundamental right to social protection.

Against the background of considerable unemployment and the poverty, undernourishment and ill-health associated with it, it is possible to detect the pattern of advance. In addition to those we have mentioned, there were such important measures as the Maternity and Child Welfare Act of 1918, which developed services for expectant and nursing mothers and the under-fives. Contributory pensions from 1925 made available a higher rate of retirement benefit. None of this implies that the real definition of the 1930s is in terms of a dedicated movement towards a welfare society. The slum clearance Act of 1930 did not mean the end of slums, or unemployment benefits the end of unemployment hardship. Acute national and international dilemmas perpetuated and deepened old and bitter problems. Whatever the motives – whether humanitarian or, by papering over the ugliness, to preserve the basic structure of capitalism – people's lives and the structure of society were, however, beginning to be affected at many levels by the new concern with welfare. This concern was heightened by the very grimness of poverty in the old industrial areas. Beveridge describes how Britain, after 1918, entered the period of mass unemployment, and yet:

> ... across this waste period of destruction and dislocation, the permanent forces making for material progress –

technical advance and the capacity of human society to
adjust itself to new conditions – continued to operate; the
real wealth per head in a Britain of shrunken oversea
investments and lost export markets, counting in all her
unemployed, was materially higher in 1938 than in
1913.[34]

This is a summary which touches on all the major ambiguities of the period.

Leisure

An interesting specific illustration of these ambiguities lies
in the fact that the decades of heaviest unemployment and
distress in some regions and industries also saw the most
important break-through in the field of holidays with pay.
The widening of facilities for organized leisure had, of
course, been a Victorian and largely middle-class phenomenon. Between the 1860s and the 1890s various sports –
including tennis, cricket and golf – gained their modern
codes of rules, and a new popularity. The urban middle-
class, as we have previously seen, already had its characteristic forms of social intercourse and cultural activity – its
'conspicuous leisure'. For some there were visits to the
resorts, mostly with eighteenth-century or Regency
origins – such as Brighton, Torquay and Bournemouth in
the south, and Scarborough in the north. There were occasional crazes like roller-skating for girls in the 1880s.

Leisure, and facilities for leisure, were obviously of a
different order for the Victorian poor. The urban worker
was cut off from traditional country pursuits, including the
sports which were still popular in country areas well into the
nineteenth century. Sports common in the Pickering area of
Yorkshire in the early nineteenth century included 'fox-
hunting, badger-drawing, duck hunting with dogs and
sometimes duck and owl diving, cock-fighting, cock-
throwing at Eastertide, bull baiting and sometimes ass baiting, squirrel-hunting, rat-worrying'.[35] Cock fighting, for
example, took place in the beautiful Norman crypt of
Lastingham Church. In considering the urban replacements

for these pursuits, we can take a description written in 1870 of one pleasure resort available to the London lower classes:

> That which made this part of Battersea Fields so notorious was the gaming, sporting, and pleasure-grounds at the Red House and Balloon public-houses, and Sunday fairs, held throughout the summer months. These have been the resort of hundreds and thousands, from royalty and nobility down to the poorest pauper and the meanest beggar. And surely if ever there was a place out of hell that surpassed Sodom and Gomorrah in ungodliness and abomination, this was it . . . I have gone to this sad spot on the afternoon and evening of the Lord's day, when there have been from 60 to 120 horses and donkeys racing, foot-racing, walking matches, flying boats, flying horses, roundabouts, theatres, comic actors, shameless dancers, conjurers, fortune-tellers, gamblers of every de-

20 *Late Victorian seaside*

scription, drinking-booths, stalls, hawkers, and vendors of all kinds of articles.

These were 'the unmentionable doings of this pandemonium on earth'.[36] The pleasures of the gin palace and then the pub (ubiquitous, spacious and class-divided into public and saloon bars, from about 1890), of the music hall, Battersea Fields, the trip to Margate or Ramsgate, or on some Cook's excursion, grew alongside the legislation which produced shorter hours, the certainty of a free Christmas Day, Good Friday and Bank Holidays. With many industrial workers enjoying free Saturday afternoons from the 1850s, football had become the dominant sport of the working man in the winter months by the 1870s.[37]

The first instance of paid holidays for manual workers came in 1884, when Brunner-Mond gave some of their employees an annual week's holiday with pay. Progress was made, to begin with, largely in public and semi-public

[margin notes: ① reason for inc in holidays — access to sea.]

enterprises (including the railways and the police); the railways, cycling and other developments made it possible to take greater advantage of available leisure. By 1900 the older seaside resorts were being caught up or outstripped by resorts like Southport and Blackpool, Weston-super-Mare and Southend, which were within reach of large urban centres.

J. A. R. Pimlott points out that the question of holidays with pay was not in the forefront of the programmes of the Trades Union Congress or individual unions until the 1930s. It was under collective bargaining that the main advances had slowly taken place. By 1925, and throughout the 1930s, some 1½ million workers were entitled to paid holidays under collective agreements; by 1937 the number was about 4 million (earning under £250 a year, plus another 1 million from higher income groups). With or without pay, about half the workpeople in London took holidays away from home in 1934. The total number of holidaymakers away from home for a week or more in 1937 was about 15 million. Plans for legislation on holidays with pay were pursued between 1925 and 1938, when a Holidays with Pay Act gave the Ministry of Labour responsibility for helping to bring about voluntary schemes. There was a big response to the appeal for voluntary action:

[margin note: Holiday stats]

> By November 1938, the number of workpeople with £250 a year or less entitled to holidays with pay had risen to about 9 millions, including nearly 4½ millions covered by collective agreements. By June 1939, the total was over 11 millions ... there was no corresponding increase in the number of actual holidaymakers ... One reason may have been the international crisis, and others were the beginnings of a slump in some industries and the high pressure in those engaged in rearmament.[38]

Apart from this spread of holidays, the use of leisure in general was moving rapidly in the inter-war years towards the enjoyment of mass-produced or collective forms of activity, ranging from rambling, hiking and jazz to the crossword puzzle – first introduced into Britain in 1924. The mass newspaper, the popular magazine, the twice-a-week visit to the cinema (Chaplin happened in 1915, and sound came in 1928) – all went further towards undermining long-established Protestant ideas, not only about the sanctity of the Sabbath, but also about 'wasting' time. Football (the first Wembley Cup Final was in 1923) and football pools in the 1930s, together with legalized racecourse betting, also further undermined traditional teaching about gambling. The association of sport and leisure with betting is only a late reminder of the extent to which some of the popular pursuits in urban society – gin drinking, outings, gambling, fantasy literature, theatrical melodrama, the cinema, radio and television – are all in different ways to some extent responses to the need for escape. There are, of course, other ways in which men in society defeat the pressures of routine or ugliness or poverty; and descriptions of forms of 'escape' do not necessarily imply judgements against them.

All these aspects of leisure and holidays relate to other aspects of society. The seaside holiday and the picnic, for example, indicate major changes in the family structure. This use of leisure and holidays was a factor in mental and physical health. The ability to take advantage of holidays, to possess a radio set or to go frequently to the cinema became, in the 1930s, a factor in estimating relative affluence or deprivation. It provided a major stimulus to developments in various consumer goods industries, electronics and transport. These developments point to an increase (in cinemas, light industry, hotels and restaurants, for example) in the number of jobs available to women, and the increased incentive for married women to take employment, in order to provide the additional income, not only to improve standards of accommodation and diet, but also for holidays and family treats. The question of the use of leisure pin-points one of the basic dilemmas in discussing social progress and democracy – the fact that the individual in this period gained greater freedom, greater opportunity creatively to construct his own style of life, and at the same time became more vulnerable to methods of mass persuasion, less active and involved in the processes of entertainment and leisure. The story of leisure, therefore, like the story of economic and industrial growth, urban conditions and social policy, points towards basic features of the complex of problems with which we are concerned: man in modern society.

The Second World War and after

The historical developments we have chosen have been intended to illustrate some of the influences which have shaped our views of the individual and of society. The Second World War and many of the developments which followed it – most prominently in industrial organization and welfare – were obviously momentous contributions to this shaping process. Some of them will become apparent in later chapters, but here we can do no more than emphasize two features of this critical period of change – the commitment to planning, and the principles expressed in the work of Lord Beveridge.

From the inter-war years Britain had inherited strong pressures to prevent any repetition of the social disasters associated with *laissez-faire* or private enterprise attitudes. Apart from socialist pressures there were others which accepted the need for greater collective involvement in vital areas of social life. A representative, and increasingly influential, voice in this tradition between the wars had been the economist John Maynard Keynes. Keynes had seen a need to bury old attitudes based on conceptions of free competition and of a society best composed of free individuals in a state of 'natural liberty'. It was not correct to deduce from economics, Keynes argued, that 'enlightened self-interest always operates in the public interest'. Experience had not shown that individuals together in a social unit were 'less clear-sighted than when they act separately'. The aim, therefore, should be what he called 'improvements in the technique of modern Capitalism by the agency of collective action ... Capitalism, wisely managed'.[39]

Clearly wartime experience could only confirm such a move towards more effective social and economic planning. The anticipation of war, and then war itself, involved the planning and execution of evacuation and rationing, controls on raw materials and production, the direction of manpower and greater involvement by public authorities of all kinds in questions of, for example, transport and health, catering and the information media. A much higher degree of direct civilian involvement made this, more than the First World War, a mass war, in which planning came increasingly to be associated not only with victory but with living in the post-war world. While there were old values to be preserved, there were new perspectives to be established. One wartime writer on town planning summarized this popular view:

> In the long run even the worst democratic muddle is preferable to a dictator's dream ... But the English muddle is nevertheless a matter for shame. We shall never get rid of its shamefulness unless we plan our activities. And plan we must – not for the sake of our physical environment only, but to save and fulfil democracy itself.[40]

It was in such a spirit that wartime controls, rationing and restrictions were widely interpreted.

Post-war commitments to a more planned society can, therefore, be seen to have roots in pre-war experience, in wartime acceptance of the need for certain kinds of social and economic management and centralization, and in varieties of socialist and Keynesian theories. The acceptance of wartime economic planning and of wartime planning for health and welfare were strongly to influence post-war politics. Planning, and even nationalization, were in certain forms acceptable across the political spectrum. Post-war opposition to nationalization was often extremely muted amongst the Conservative leadership, for example, and some forms of nationalization (of the Bank of England, for instance) were supported by Conservative politicians.[41] There was, of course, opposition during and after the war to excessive controls and planning, even to economic planning as such. A widely discussed book by F. A. Hayek, *The Road to Serfdom*, argued in 1944, for example, that British centralized planning, as advocated primarily by the socialists, and as practised in wartime, was no different from that in totalitarian Germany. Economic control was 'not merely control of a sector of human life which can be separated

from the rest; it is the control of the means for all our ends.
And whoever has sole control of the means must also determine which ends are to be served ... what men should
believe and strive for'.[42] Post-war socialism and economic
planning would, therefore, mean the abandonment of liberty. Writing in the same tradition after the war, John
Jewkes traced the origins of centralized economic planning
to the First World War, and ascribed 'the melancholy decline of Great Britain ... progressive restrictions on
individual liberties ... destruction of respect for law, the
steady sapping of our instinct for tolerance and compromise,
the sharpening of class distinctions, our growing incapacity
to play a rightful part in world affairs' to the fallacy that 'the
best way of ordering economic affairs is to place the responsibility for all crucial decisions in the hands of the State'.[43]

The role of the State in ordering social affairs was to re-
emerge in Conservative debate largely through the views of
Enoch Powell in the 1960s. During the war and until that
point a sense of the rightness or the inevitability of economic
and social planning to one degree or another permeated
Conservative as well as Labour thinking: 'an economic history could present a coherent picture of Government policy
before and after 1951 without mentioning the change of
government ... If what Labour was doing at the end of its
term of office was "planning", the Conservatives also
"planned" in office.'[44] The collectivist ideas of the last two
decades of the nineteenth century were most widely accepted and most fully applied in the quarter-century from
the beginning of the Second World War.

These are essential explanations for an understanding of
the role given to the State by the Labour Party in post-war
economic and financial policy, in nationalization particularly. They are also essential explanations of the
Beveridge Report, of all wartime welfare and educational
planning for the post-war world, and the measures taken
after 1945 to constitute the welfare state. Beveridge himself
was acutely aware of the social inequalities and suffering of
the inter-war years (and of many inequalities sharpened in
the war years – 'indefensible and dangerous inequalities that
have resulted between civilians and the members of the

fighting forces, between different civilians, and between different businesses . . .'[45]). Evacuation had brought home to many people in the receiving areas that poverty, ill-health, under-nourishment and all that went with them were still more prominent features of British life than they had been aware, and the health, social background and behaviour of poor evacuees were a subject of much wartime controversy.[46] Women's war work, the role of works canteens and publicly provided British Restaurants, food rationing, and the health hazards of civilian and service life, thrust other aspects of social policy and organization into greater prominence. New beginnings looked possible. 'Now,' said Beveridge, 'when the war is abolishing landmarks of every kind, is the opportunity for using experience in a clear field. A revolutionary moment in the world's history is a time for revolutions, not for patching.'[47]

The Beveridge *Report on Social Insurance and Allied Services* in 1942 is important here not for its role in the evolution of particular social services, but as the major expression of a newly dominant outlook on the relationship between the State and individuals, and on the responsibilities of a society to its own members. What the report aimed to achieve was the promotion of a Plan for Social Security 'to win freedom from want by maintaining incomes' – the certainty that no one would be allowed to fall below a subsistence minimum. The Plan rested on three principles, the statement of which is worth quoting at length, offering as it does a comparison with the previous definitions of 1834 and 1909. The report, which became one of the twentieth century's best-sellers, set out three guiding principles:

The first principle is that any proposals for the future, while they should use to the full the experience gathered in the past, should not be restricted by consideration of sectional interests established in the obtaining of that experience . . .

The second principle is that organization of social insurance should be treated as one part only of a comprehensive policy of social progress. Social insurance fully developed may provide income security; it is an attack upon Want. But Want is one only of five giants on the road of reconstruction and in some ways the easiest to attack. The others are Disease, Ignorance, Squalor and Idleness.

The third principle is that social security must be achieved by co-operation between the State and the individual. The State should offer security for service and contribution. The State in organizing security should not stifle incentive, opportunity, responsibility; in establishing a national minimum, it should leave room and encouragement for voluntary action . . .

The Plan used experience but was 'not tied by experience'. It was a contribution towards a 'wider social policy'. It was 'first and foremost, a plan of insurance – of giving in return for contributions benefits up to subsistence level, as of right and without means test, so that individuals may build freely upon it'.[48]

When Beveridge, in 1944, turned to the problem of unemployment, he was acutely conscious of the implications of social engineering of any kind. In this report on *Full Employment in a Free Society* he was anxious to achieve the one without undermining his conception of the other. Protection of basic freedoms meant excluding 'the totalitarian solution of full employment in a society completely planned and regimented by an irremovable dictator'. His proposals 'preserve absolutely all the essential liberties which are more precious than full employment itself'.[49] The 1942 Plan, Beveridge felt, was consistent with his belief in active democracy. There were people, he knew, 'to whom pursuit of security appears to be . . . something inconsistent with initiative, adventure, personal responsibility.' That was not his view. The plan was 'not one for giving to everybody something for nothing and without trouble, or something that will free the recipients for ever thereafter from personal responsibilities. The plan is one to secure income for subsistence on condition of service and contribution . . .' It could be carried through 'only by a concentrated determination of the British democracy to free itself once and for all of the scandal of physical want for which there is no economic or moral justification'. To those who thought the Report did not go far enough Beveridge pointed out that his Plan was intended only as one prong of an attack on the five giant evils.[50]

The Beveridge analyses, therefore, produced definitions of acceptable minima, allied with 'service and contribution'. The welfare state that was constructed after the war sought to achieve these minima along the lines Beveridge had proposed – through social insurance (which guaranteed the right to a minimum income in important contingencies), through social assistance of various kinds, and through basic services in such fields as education, hospitals and medical care. The Beveridge Plan and the welfare state provisions demonstrated that British society was prepared to accept the implications of precedent in establishing a comprehensive system. In doing so it also accepted the limitations of precedent. Areas of welfare either remained untackled (an antiquated medical and hospital system, for example) or inadequately so. Most conspicuous among the latter were the problems relating to old age, which, the Rowntree–Lavers survey of 1950 showed, was the 'greatest contemporary cause of poverty and accounted for 68·1% of all the poverty in York in 1950'.[51] Beveridge appealed for a unity which could override the interests of 'class or section' – a wartime reminder of the continued awareness of classes and sections.[52]

The post-war problem, as the planners saw it, was to make radical readjustments in the social framework so as to set the seal on a doctrine of social community. The point in history had been reached, said E. H. Carr in 1951, when 'the process of transition from the nineteenth-century *laissez-faire* capitalist order offers us no alternative, short of annihilation in war, to a social and economic order which we can call the "welfare-state", the "social service state", or simply "socialism" '.[53] We are not concerned, in future chapters, to follow through the implications of these approaches to planning. We are concerned, however, to relate notions of democracy to those of, for example, the various roles individuals are called upon to play in society. We have in past chapters followed the growth of some institutions and policies which will play little apparent part in our discussion of contemporary society. It has been important, however, to see, towering behind any such discussion, the ways in which human understanding of the nature and responsibilities of 'society' and 'government' have changed, and the points of social development around which the battles of concept and interpretation have taken place. We have so far traced, primarily, the path of modern economic, urban growth, and its attendant re-adjustments in fields of social thought. This pattern of change in attitudes to social organization has been built up by selecting focal points around which nineteenth- and twentieth-century Britain has crystallized its notions about society. In looking at contemporary England we do not need to select the same focal points. Whatever institutions or ideas we discuss in today's society, however, we are viewing them in the pattern of urban, industrial and political change that we have traced.

Notes

1 HUTCHISON *The Decline and Fall of British Capitalism*, pp. 86–7.
2 SIDNEY and BEATRICE WEBB *The Decay of Capitalist Civilisation*, p. 130 (London, 1923).
3 DAVID LLOYD GEORGE *The People's Insurance*, p. 28 (London, 1912).
4 SIDNEY POLLARD *The Development of the British Economy 1914–1950*, pp. 75–6 (London, 1962).
5 DOROTHY DAVIS *A History of Shopping*, p. 283 (London, 1966).
6 ROYAL COMMISSION ON THE POOR LAWS *Majority Report*, I, pp. 78, 145, 182, 185–6, 232, 260, 281–2.
7 Ibid., *Minority Report*, III, pp. 69, 382, 386, 389, 431, 468, 529.
8 RICHARD TITMUSS *Essays on 'The Welfare State'*, pp. 18–22 (London, 1958).
9 MARION BOWLEY *Housing and the State 1919–1944* (London, 1945).
10 PHILIP ABRAMS 'The failure of social reform: 1918–1920', *Past and Present*, 24 April 1963, p. 44.
11 G. P. GOOCH *History of our Time 1885–1914*, p. 5 (London, 1911; 1946 edition).

12 Quoted in BERNARD SEMMEL *Imperialism and Social Reform*, p. 16 (London, 1960). A classic study of this period is ELIE HALÉVY *A History of the English People*, Epilogue (1895–1905), I, *Imperialism*, 1926.

13 H. F. WYATT 'The ethics of empire', in GOODWIN (ed.) *Nineteenth Century Opinion*, p. 267.

14 For the history and current state of the concept of imperialism see D. K. FIELDHOUSE *The Theory of Capitalist Imperialism* (London, 1967).

15 ASHWORTH *An Economic History of England*, p. 301.

16 The Webbs considered that capitalist industry was 'virtually superseded as a system during the war' (*The Decay of Capitalist Civilisation*, p. 131).

17 See MAURICE DOBB *Studies in the Development of Capitalism*, pp. 339–41 (London, 1946; 1963 edition).

18 See BARLOW COMMISSION *Report*, Ch. IV.

19 POLLARD *The Development of the British Economy*, pp. 287–8.

20 ASHWORTH *An Economic History of England*, p. 252.

21 WILLIAM H. BEVERIDGE *Full Employment in a Free Society*, pp. 40–7, 72 (London, 1944; 1953 edition).

22 GEORGE HOWELL *Trade Unionism New and Old*, pp. 133–5 (London, 1891; 1894 edition).

23 In addition to HENRY PELLING's *Short History of the Labour Party* (London, 1961), RALPH MILIBAND's *Parliamentary Socialism* (London, 1961) is important for the story of the tussle between policies of parliamentarianism and direct action.

24 GEORGE TATE *London Trades Council 1860–1950*, pp. 96–7 (London, 1950).

25 For an account of this 'Workers' Rebellion', see DANGERFIELD *The Strange Death of Liberal England*, Pt II, Ch. IV.

26 STANLEY BALDWIN *On England*, pp. 40–2 (London, 1926; 1937 Penguin edition).

27 CHARLES LOCH MOWAT *Britain between the Wars 1918–1940*, pp. 330–1 (London, 1955; 1962 edition).

28 WILLIAM BEVERIDGE *Social Insurance and Allied Services*, p. 166 (London, 1942).

29 GRACE M. PATON *The Child and the Nation*, pp. 38–9 (London, 1915).

30 See BARLOW COMMISSION *Minutes of Evidence*, pp. 966–7.

31 See ibid., pp. 968–71.

32 RICHARD and KATHLEEN TITMUSS *Parents Revolt: a study of the declining birth-rate in acquisitive societies*, p. 123 (London, 1942).

33 GILBERT *The Evolution of National Insurance*, pp. 287–8.

34 BEVERIDGE *Social Insurance and Allied Services*, p. 166.

35 GORDON HOME *The Evolution of an English Town*, p. 221 (London, 1915).

36 Quoted from the *London City Mission Magazine* in STEEN EILER RASMUSSEN *London: the unique city*, p. 234 (London, 1934; 1961 Penguin edition).

37 JAMES WALVIN *The People's Game: a social history of British football*, pp. 53–4 (London, 1975).

38 J. A. R. PIMLOTT *The Englishman's Holiday: a social history*, p. 221 (London, 1947). Much of the above material is drawn from this source.

39 JOHN MAYNARD KEYNES *The End of Laissez-Faire*, pp. 39–40, 50–3 (London, 1926).

40 THOMAS SHARP *Town Planning*, p. 118 (Harmondsworth, 1940; 1942 edition).

41 See, for example, BERTRAND DE JOUVENEL *Problems of Socialist England*, Ch. 5 (London, 1949); CHRISTOPHER HOLLIS *The Rise and Fall of the Ex-Socialist Government*, p. 38 (London, 1947).

42 F. A. HAYEK *The Road to Serfdom*, p. 68 (London, 1944).

43 JOHN JEWKES *Ordeal by Planning*, pp. vii, 2 (London, 1948; 1949 edition).

44 NIGEL HARRIS *Competition and the Corporate State: British Conservatives, the state and industry 1945–1964*, p. 135 (London, 1972).

45 WILLIAM H. BEVERIDGE *The Pillars of Security and other War-time Essays and Addresses*, p. 22 (London, 1943).

46 See, for example, SUSAN ISAACS (ed.) *The Cambridge Evacuation Survey* (London, 1941); MASS OBSERVATION *War Begins at Home*, Ch. 12 (London, 1940); WOMEN'S GROUP ON PUBLIC WELFARE *Our Towns: a close-up* (London, 1943).

47 BEVERIDGE *Social Insurance and Allied Services*, p. 6.

48 Ibid., pp. 6–7, 153.

49 BEVERIDGE *Full Employment in a Free Society*, pp. 21, 36.

50 BEVERIDGE *Social Insurance and Allied Services*, p. 170.

51 B. SEEBOHM ROWNTREE and G. R. LAVERS *Poverty and the Welfare State*, p. 60 (London, 1951).

52 BEVERIDGE *Social Insurance and Allied Services*, p. 172.

53 EDWARD HALLETT CARR *The New Society*, pp. 38–9 (London, 1951).

Part 2 English society since the Second World War

The following chapters continue to trace some major aspects of social change. They also take up some case studies of contemporary social structure, policy and theory pinpointed by these developments. Each chapter therefore discusses some general themes which go beyond its chronological framework.

6 Planning: towns, work and welfare

Attitudes to planning

The view that prevailed at the end of the war, and influenced the massive Labour victory in 1945, was that social planning was desirable and urgent. The search for planned, fair solutions to fundamental problems turned into 'socialist' legislation. The sense of collective responsibility strengthened in the war began to take tangible forms.

The 1944 Education Act was a decisive expression of the will to intervene for the collective and the individual good, and was popularly seen as such. It was the responsibility of a Conservative President of the Board of Education and a Labour Parliamentary Secretary in a wartime coalition government. Local education authorities were to provide primary and secondary education in a structure that would end the nineteenth-century doctrine of separate routes for different social classes. The most famous passage of the Act declared that each local authority area should have schools

> sufficient in number, character, and equipment to afford for all pupils opportunities for education offering such variety of instruction and training as may be desirable in view of their different ages, abilities, and aptitudes.[1]

Secondary education for all was no longer a slogan. A Labour spokesman confidently told the Party conference in 1944 that 'with these reforms we must have equality of opportunity'.[2] The London County Council, in its 1947 plan to implement the Act, spoke of the 'duty of authorities to establish equality of opportunity for all children'.[3]

The same acceptance of a greater measure of public responsibility was embodied in wide areas of post-war planning. The Children Act of 1948, for example, provided for the care of boys and girls without parents 'or when their parents are unfit or unable to take care of them'.[4] The 1946 National Insurance Act laid down that everyone over school age and under pensionable age 'shall become insured under this Act and thereafter continue throughout his life to be so insured'.[5] The National Health Service Act of 1946 was to establish 'a comprehensive health service designed to secure improvement in the physical and mental health of the people'.[6] Even a Royal Commission on population reported in 1949 that it was 'impossible for policy to be "neutral" ' on the effects of changes in the birth rate, and made recommendations accordingly.[7] The state and public authorities were being given more comprehensive functions, at the expense of *ad hoc* and Poor Law approaches. The 1944 Education Act was seen as a precedent for providing 'the means of fulfilment of other reform movements'.[8] By 1948 Beveridge could describe the Act as 'immensely enlarging the scope of public responsibility'.[9]

The cautious optimism of reconstruction mingled with irritation at post-war difficulties and austerities. The cold war and prospects of atomic warfare took time significantly to affect the national consciousness. In 1945 J. B. Priestley ended an appeal to returning servicemen to play a vigilant part in reconstruction with the words: 'P.S. Stop Press – the atomic bomb has arrived. So I repeat – *There isn't much time.*'[10] For most people the bomb did not mean an immediate sense of threat, though that meaning was increasingly clear in the international tensions of the late 1940s.

The post-war experience of the majority of the population was one of shortages and austerity. Britain's economy and finances proved to be disastrous, and major crises in

Britain and Europe, particularly in 1947, thrust both into
greater dependence on the United States. The crises was to
make life in Britain 'more austere (bombing apart) than at
any time during the war'.[11] Throughout the late 1940s
rationing was a central fact of British life and constituted
what visitors saw as 'an astonishing amount of purely
mechanical detail to learn before one can settle down to the
business of routine daily life'.[12] Shortages of every sort
were constantly being discussed in Parliament and in the
nation at large.

Wartime experience had led to a heightened tolerance of
controls of all kinds. Although these were relaxed as the
situation permitted, reconstruction and economic stringency
required the maintenance of many of them, in the name of
fair distribution and prices. The 'paraphernalia of controls
and rationing and taxation', said E. H. Carr, was 'necessary
to the organization of freedom from want for all ... The
price of some liberty for all is restriction of the greater
liberty of some'.[13] Wartime planning had produced not only
the Beveridge Report and the 1944 Education Act, but also,
for example, schemes for town and country planning and
land usage, and government white papers on a national
health service and employment policy. The post-war
government had 'the advantage ... of having a pattern of
war-time controls already in existence, ready to be taken
over and adapted'.[14] Other virtues seen in the post-war
carry-over of controls and planning included those of
rationing – which for many people had come to mean more
regular access to staple foods, improved diets, increased
consumption of milk, and a decline in infant and maternal
mortality. Wartime planning for nutrition and health, as
well as for supplementary pensions and other aspects of
social policy, laid the ground for wide acceptance of the
principles of welfare state legislation. For some, like Hayek,
as we have seen, controls and planning were reminiscent of
Fascism, but for most people the concept of a planned
democracy displaced such fears. Stephen Spender wrote in
1946 that the Fascists had left 'a sinister inheritance ...
the curse of a necessity which hangs over everyone and
everything, justifying conscription, economies, censorship,

21 *Queueing for meat, London 1946*

discipline . . .'. But the disasters left by Fascism had 'made the total organization of society really necessary. The difference is between necessity as an excuse, and necessity as a reality.' [15]

Policies and politics

The areas of action most identified with the Labour governments of 1945–51 are those of welfare and nationalization. An impressive range of legislation covered national health services and insurance, town and country planning, criminal justice, monopolies and restrictive practices, youth employment, national parks and new towns. Nationalization included the Bank of England, Cable and Wireless, the coal, gas and electricity industries, and iron and steel. When, in February 1946, the Minister of National Insurance moved the second reading of his Bill, the M.P. for Saffron Walden welcomed it in the following terms:

> We regard this plan as part of the mosaic or the pattern of the new society ... This Bill forms part of a series of Bills, starting with the Education Bill, which ... foresaw the pattern of the new society long before this Parliament was ever thought of ... we look forward to a society of which the more unfortunate members are free from the direst dread of penury and want.

The M.P. was Mr R. A. Butler, spokesman for the Conservative opposition.[16] The Labour government's measures for welfare and social planning had crystallized out of wartime advances, and had been embodied in the Party's programme. There were Conservatives during the war who were hesitant about the planned reforms – including Churchill. Beveridge said of such hesitations that he had not understood the diverse responses to his report 'by the British people and the world at large, and by the Government of Mr Churchill'.[17] The needs of post-war planning overcame many such hesitations, however, and Butler's references in 1946 to the 'mosaic' of the 'new society' indicated how far support stretched for the enhanced role of the State in social organization. In 1949 the Conservative Party was welcoming the welfare legislation as 'a cooperative system of mutual aid and self-help provided by the whole nation'.[18] The Labour Party chairman in 1945 offered the diagnosis that 'leading Conservatives recognizing the leftward drift of public opinion, have been talking the language of social reform'.[19]

Opposition to an articulated welfare state was small. When a former Dean of St Paul's called family allowances 'mischievous' and a 'regime of mass bribery and reckless expenditure'[20] he was expressing a manifestly minority view. The prevailing sense was of a new welfare pattern which provided security and to some extent redistributed wealth. Rowntree and Lavers published their survey of York in 1950, and found that the percentage of the working-class population living in poverty had been reduced from 31·1 in 1936 to 2·77. They estimated that 'it would have been reduced to 22·18 per cent if welfare legislation had remained unaltered'.[21] Welfare legislation was accepted as keeping faith with wartime promises.

Nationalization was a more contentious political issue, but again the war had blunted opposition to Labour measures. In wartime, industry had been virtually under State control. In 1943 Aneurin Bevan warned that if the basic industries were not made national property during the war 'they will not be made national property after the war without a very bloody revolution'. Even Beveridge called at the same time for 'a national plan for the use of our resources after this war to meet our needs'.[22] Only over the steel industry was Conservative opposition to nationalization really serious. The Conservative leaders 'had always expected socialism's hour to strike, and when it struck, they submitted'.[23] In 1951 they took over operation of a machinery to whose creation they had often put up only token resistance. The same underlying acceptance of a choice between planned democratic advance and disaster was at work. The bloody revolution forecast by Bevan never loomed near. Economic difficulties, especially from 1947, were a constant national concern. The Soviet blockade of Berlin in 1948–9, the mounting cold war, the creation of NATO in 1949, and the outbreak of war in Korea in June 1950, were pointers to an increasingly disturbing international context. When Mr Attlee, as Prime Minister, went to Washington in December 1950 to argue against the use of the atomic bomb by the Americans in Korea, Priestley's warning that 'there isn't much time' was finally being heard. The threat of destruction was now much more prominent in the nation's consciousness.

Inevitably, post-war realities dissipated much of the social idealism that was strong in the mid-1940s. Plans for the rebuilding of bombed London or Coventry or Hull were exciting, and for a while tangible ideals. The whole Beveridge experience was 'electrifying' – to use his wife's word.[24] The Labour government's programme for social democratic planning was seen as 'a great experiment, which will be an education for the whole of Europe'.[25] The concern for a new, just society also had implications for the

Empire, and with the first steps towards Indian independence there began the process by which the colonies in general were to be given, or to take, their independence. If some of this idealism wore thin, and if wartime experience of collaborative endeavour in suffering and planning gave way to new tensions, there were nevertheless new commitments that were not lost. Concepts such as social justice had become more central to social discourse.

Industry and urban conditions were two prominent areas of such discussion. It is worth turning to both as case studies of social debate and social change since the Second World War.

Industry and employment

As in other fields, wartime experience helped to shape postwar developments. The war had produced 'the biggest industrial transformation in Britain since the Industrial Revolution', with 60 per cent of economic and industrial activity being devoted to war purposes.[26] Planning for full employment was widely urged, as was greater industrial democracy. In 1942 the Archbishop of Canterbury, for example, argued that labour should share 'in some form . . . at least equally with capital in the control of industry'.[27] Beveridge described the birth of his inquiry and report as due to 'the driving force of the Trades Union Congress', and the war confirmed the trade union movement 'as a recognized and essential instrument of government'.[28]

Britain's industries were comparatively antiquated and inefficient, and its traditional markets and trade had been disrupted. Old attitudes died hard, and almost as soon as production for civilian consumption resumed governments tried, often against great resistance, to persuade firms to seek export markets.[29] Attitudes to work often provoked public debate. In mining particularly, after initial enthusiasm for nationalization, responses to National Coal Board and government pressure for increased production were sometimes similar to those under private ownership. Absenteeism and disillusionment with the new administration were common. With a shortage of commodities to buy, the miners 'bought leisure – by absenteeism'.[30]

Wide areas of industrial and social conflict remained unsolved. Nationalization and the involvement of the unions in government planning bodies (the unions were represented on twelve government committees in 1939, and sixty in 1948–9)[31] did not prevent strikes. The number of working days lost in strikes in the immediate post-war years was relatively small, but major strikes began to occur in key sectors of nationalized industry, including the docks.

The main features of industrial organization in this period have remained sharp issues since the 1940s. We have seen that an important feature of industrial organization from the second half of the nineteenth century was the expansion in scale of many manufacturing and commercial enterprises, affecting the production and distribution sides of industry, and the nature of working-class organizations. In the 1870s firms employing more than 200 people were well above average in most industries. According to the 1968 *Report on the Census of Production*, however, while 64 per cent of manufacturing firms (59,000) still had fewer than 25 employees each and accounted for only 7 per cent of the total employment, 21 per cent of jobs were in the hands of the 409 leading firms, each of which had over 2,000 employees. These large firms are especially common in the engineering and electronics industries and vehicle-building.

Developments in technology and the rapid growth of white-collar and service occupations since the war have resulted in a major redistribution of skills within industry. As we saw in earlier chapters, the most important occupational trend in the last century was the decline in agricultural labour and the parallel growth in the numbers employed in factories, offices and shops in the cities. The main upward trend between 1931 and 1951 was in the metal-using trades, the number in the central occupational grade (fitter, mechanic or mill-wright) rising from 400,000 to 511,000. At the same time, the number of coal hewers fell by more than a half, from 495,000 to 226,000. The number of domestic servants fell sharply, while the number of char-women and office cleaners increased. The number of nurses almost doubled, and the number of laboratory technicians rose from 11,000 to 69,000 – a rise of over 500 per cent.[32] In manufacturing industries generally well over a quarter of employees fell into the category 'administrative, technical and clerical' by the early 1970s. The revolution in industrial techniques, new modes of capital accumulation and corporate finance, and the development of new markets, which have been responsible for these changes in the structure of industries and occupations, have also had important consequences for the internal structure of industrial organizations – as did the growth of multi-national companies, and then inflation, the decline in international trade, and unemployment, in the economic setbacks of the mid-1970s.

Over the last century there have been major changes in all elements of industrial organization. Machines, for example, 'have extensively replaced crude manpower, and one machine increasingly instructs other machines in the process we call automation'.[33] Questions of scale have become paramount – what Aldous Huxley in 1947 called 'giganticism and centralization', to which trade unions as well as industries were subject.[34] Questions of ownership and control were thrust into prominence by the events of the 1930s, by the war and by nationalization, and have provoked continuing discussion of industrial relations.

We have earlier referred to the relative absence of formal 'industrial relations' and the concentration of exclusive power in the hands of the employers in the nineteenth century. We have also described the growth of 'human relations' policies and industrial conciliation machinery in the twentieth century.[35] Since 1945 increased government intervention in the labour market, research in such new fields as ergonomics, and responses to management and organizational developments in other countries (such as Sweden and Yugoslavia) have resulted in some changes in industrial relations. The prevailing ideology has become more democratic and egalitarian than it was at the beginning of the century, as is reflected for example in more refined conciliation procedures. In some sectors of industry workers' participation in management and in company profit-sharing schemes has increased. However, in most firms where experiments in 'industrial democracy' have been introduced there is very little real sharing of power. Industrial democracy has very often meant paternalism: 'management, it is assumed, knows what is in the best interests of all the Partners'.[36] Work-ins and workers' co-operatives in the 1970s were to show a strong sense among workers in some industries that they could make a different contribution to policy and management than schemes for industrial democracy had traditionally envisaged.

The serious study of management was a product of the immediate post-war world, with the British Institute of Management, for instance, being created in 1947, partly supported by government funds. The trade union movement, however, was suspicious of management study techniques, and both during and after the war there was controversy in the unions about participation in management, including that of nationalized industries.[37] There has never been an easy passage for the efforts of work study engineers, economists, organization and methods consultants, personnel managers and industrial psychologists, whose work has been identified with the interests of the employers. By viewing the factory 'as a family rather than as a power struggle among groups with some conflicting values and interests as well as some shared ones, and by seeing it as a major source of human satisfaction rather than alienation', the human relations view sees worker dissatisfaction 'as indicative of lack of understanding of the situation rather than as symptomatic of any underlying real conflict of interests'.[38]

New management ideologies have been paralleled by modifications in the conduct of the trade union movement, which, particularly in the Second World War, began to acquire a niche in the edifice of public decision-making. Trade union responsibilities have come to overlap with those of government, gradually sharpening discussion about the power of the trade unions. The State and public authorities employ one in four of the country's labour force. The State has become more directly involved in industrial conflicts since the late 1960s, in the interest of national economic stability. The role of the T.U.C. has reinforced this position, for its General Council normally attempts to restrain strikes so as to avoid embarrassing the government – particularly when a Labour government is in office. This 'institutionalization of industrial conflict'[39] partly explains why, despite the massive increase in trade union membership (from 4·6 million in 1931 to 10·9 million in 1971, of whom 2·7 million were women), active participation in union affairs is at a minimum. In the modern welfare state the unions are often seen as service agencies, with most of their work being done by a handful of 'union bureaucrats'. Union amalgamation has also added to the distance between the leadership and the workers. In 1931 there were over 1,000 separate unions, but by 1973 under half this number (495) remained, with the six largest unions accounting for over half of the total membership. If some of the objectives and procedures of the trade union movement have changed since 1939, however, its aims remain substantially the same.

Questions of ownership and control have been debated sharply since the 1930s. Since the latter part of the nineteenth century the most typical form of ownership in England has been the joint-stock corporation. However, the establishment of public corporations like the B.B.C. and the Post Office and of nationalized industries altered the overall pattern. The concentration of shareholding in private hands has declined, although in one third of Britain's largest industrial companies' share distribution in the 1960s still permitted ownership control.[40] Over one third of all company assets were at the same time in the hands of public corporations, and around 50 per cent of new investments were financed by public – including local – authorities. The role of the State and of public authorities is not limited, therefore, simply to the operation of nationalized industries. They are involved in wage legislation and consumer protection, control of restrictive practices, taxation, regional policies and a host of other activities.

What these and related developments have highlighted since the mid-twentieth century has been the nature of the bureaucracy that accompanies all such large-scale institutions, and especially the role of the manager. The seminal analysis of bureaucracy was that of Max Weber, who suggested the following main characteristics of a bureaucratic structure. There is a clear-cut division of labour, and a fairly rigidly defined administrative hierarchy. Operations are regulated by a uniform system of rules and standards in a spirit of 'formalistic impersonality'. Employment constitutes a career and there is a recognized system of promotion. Finally, the bureaucratic organization is capable of attaining the highest degree of efficiency. It 'compares with other organizations as does the machine with non-mechanical modes of production'.[41] Weber's analysis focuses on many of the central goals of modern industrial and administrative organization, but it tends to give a misleading impression of the degree of stability and integration of which they are capable. Recent research reveals the administrative inefficiency of an over-rigid adherence to organizational rules, secrecy and red tape. It also points to certain 'dysfunctions' – that is, activities which contribute to the disturbance (as opposed to the survival) of the social activities of the bureaucratic system, from the point of view of individual workers or employers.[42] Competing personal loyalties, or 'role incongruence' as some sociologists call this, may be seen in such cases as that of the industrial scientist, torn between the pursuit of knowledge and the need to develop marketable products. The ruling management ideology in big organizations often impedes new industrial methods, since it does not allow for the degree of flexibility which is necessary to cope with modern technological developments.[43]

A particular interest was shown in the 1940s in the implications of such developments for society as a whole. The question of scale suggested that traditional discussion of private and public property 'obscures from us the fact that the mammoth enterprises of our time, be they public or private, are very much the same thing'.[44] This was seen as particularly true when, after the war, many people identified the new shape of society as 'partly managerial, partly socialistic'.[45] This also suggested that Marxist descriptions of class conflict were no longer appropriate, as interests and power were more evenly spread throughout industry and society. E. F. M. Durbin, a right-wing socialist, described the disappearance of the 'early type of the bourgeois entrepreneur who was owner, director, and manager of an enterprise all in one', and the emergence of a new class 'of professional employed managers – that is so greatly neglected in the Marxist discussion of the development of the upper bourgeoisie'. At the same time the position, and indeed the nature, of the working class, had changed:

> The definition of the proletariat given by Marx is made with special reference to the possession of property. The proletariat is the great class of industrial workers who own *nothing* but their labour . . . It is the literal and sober truth to affirm that a class so defined is rapidly disappearing. In Great Britain it is disappearing. In America it has disappeared.[46]

The most famous expression of such a view of 'managerial society' was in James Burnham's *The Managerial Revolution*, first published in the U.S.A. in 1941. Burnham's view was that capitalism must disappear, indeed had already 'entered its final years'. However, he rejected Marx's view that it would be replaced by socialism, and suggested that Western society was already in a transitional stage 'to a type of society which we shall call *managerial*'. Burnham offered a picture of the inevitable dominance of the managers, already prefigured in industrial and social change. The book and its arguments had an enormous impact on political and social debate in the late 1940s, and fed into a continuing discussion about the validity of old definitions of industrial conflict and class society.[47]

Urban policies

'Interventionist' policies were strongly developed during and after the war in relation to the planning of whole social units – communities, towns, regions – and they have influenced discussion and practice in social planning ever since.

A central planning authority for the control of land use and town and country planning was urged in one form or another by three major bodies which reported in wartime –

the Barlow Commission on the distribution of the industrial population, the Uthwatt Committee on land use and values, and the Scott Committee on land use in rural areas. Between 1943 and 1945 a number of Acts began to regulate, for example, the distribution of industry and the preservation of the countryside, and a Ministry of Town and Country Planning was created in 1943. At the same time an impetus towards post-war planning was developed, associated primarily with Professor Patrick Abercrombie. Of the various plans for town reconstruction with which he was connected, the *Greater London Plan 1944* was the most influential, drawing on aspects of earlier garden city and town planning movements. He divided London into rings, and proposed that much of the inner ring should be decentralized. Within the third ring, the Green Belt, any expansion of existing communities was to be limited, and no new centres were to be created. The outer ring was to be the 'chief reception area' for overcrowded London:

> The need for decentralisation arises from the twofold desire to improve housing conditions in those areas which are overcrowded, and to reduce the concentration of industry in the London area which has caused an expansion of the metropolis to a size which has become quite unmanageable, and one which has made of Londoners a race of straphangers.[48]

Abercrombie's decentralization principle therefore led straight to the new town concept, both of which were accepted by the post-war government. War itself had shown the desirability of reducing population density in the cities, and it was perhaps felt that the difficulty of moving people and industry had been lessened by the war, which 'made migration a familiar habit'.[49] Sociologists were to reveal in the 1950s and 1960s how extensive were the human repercussions of the planners' strategies.

The 1947 Town and Country Planning Act has been described as 'the great set piece' and as a 'revolutionary statute'.[50] It gave planning powers to the counties and county boroughs, and instructed them to establish development plans for their areas. Directly from the Abercrombie principles came the New Towns Act of 1946, followed by the designation of the new towns themselves (fourteen were founded between 1946 and 1950). The Minister of Town and Country Planning saw Stevenage, the first to be designated, as an augury of how Britain was 'building for the new way of life'.[51] The principles for planning the new towns were precise: the New Towns Committee set up in 1946 was asked to suggest how the new towns could be 'established and developed as self-contained and balanced communities for work and living'.[52] The concept of balance was central. Each generation of new towns would from this point provide an arena of sociological discussion, and would draw – with varying degrees of success – upon sociological views of the nature of social balance, of community, of neighbourhood. The new towns, wrote Norman Mackenzie in 1955, 'put to the test of practice so many of the theories and the assumptions of social democracy'.[53] They were to be faced, however, with profound social difficulties, including those created by the untypical age-structure of the population (predominantly young and middle-aged) and the consequent pressures on schools, colleges, recreational facilities, commercial entertainment and jobs.[54]

Post-war planning was concerned, of course, not only with new towns, but also with expanded towns, reconstructed town centres and suburbs, new shopping precincts, the curtailment of office building (notably in the South East) and the encouragement of industry in areas needing economic growth and diversification. In all such developments could be found competing theories of urban structure and growth.

Urbanism, as we saw in earlier chapters, produced new patterns of social organization, and disrupted the relative stability of pre-industrial communities. Sociologists employ a variety of theoretical concepts to describe these two different modes of social organization. Durkheim, for instance, contrasted societies which are characterized by 'mechanical solidarity' (for example, feudal societies) and those whose structure, like that of contemporary industrial societies, is 'organic'. Herbert Spencer distinguished between the 'indefinite, incoherent homogeneity' of pre-industrial societies and the 'definite, coherent heterogeneity' of the modern urban-industrial State. Perhaps the most useful model of pre- and post-industrial forms of social organization is that provided by Ferdinand Tönnies's contrast between *Gemeinschaft* (community) and *Gesellschaft* (association). Tönnies himself studied several instances of *Gemeinschaft*: the family, the neighbourhood (in village and town), and friendship groups, while the city and the State (he might equally have selected a large firm) were chosen for his study of the characteristics of *Gesellschaften*.[55]

Since 1930 in particular there has been a great increase in comparative investigations in urban sociology.[56] Some have focused on whole towns or on particular urban or rural neighbourhoods in countries like Britain and the United States. There has also been a great deal of research into the processes of urban and industrial growth (and into its consequences) in the newly developing nations. Whether mainly theoretical or mainly empirical in approach, the essential contrast referred to in all of these studies is the same, based on a comparison of the degree of complexity of the different institutional structures found in the two main types of social system. One, the traditional rural system (*Gemeinschaft*), is relatively simple and based on intimate primary contacts; the other, the urban–industrial system (*Gesellschaft*), is infinitely complex and based to a much greater degree on secondary contacts between people. It is true that at the extremes the distinctions between city and village life persist (although even in most villages today – especially in the Midlands and South of England – agriculture is a minority occupation). Neighbourhoods within the city often maintain many of the characteristics of more simple communities.[57] There are also many extremely different social environments within the city, making it misleading to treat as unities for the purpose of comparison the less homogeneous and the more homogeneous. And while most rural communities differ considerably from one another, each one exerts a greater common influence on its inhabitants than does the city.[58] For most purposes it is useful to think in terms of a continuum between the patterns of social organization which characterize the extremes.

Attempts to classify towns have included a scheme produced by Moser and Scott, based on the criteria of size, region, population structure and social class. They feature three main types of urban system, each having subdivisions:

A   *Mainly resorts, administrative and commercial towns*
    (1 seaside resorts; 2 spas, professional and administrative centres; 3 commercial centres with some industry)
B   *Mainly industrial towns*
    (4 traditional railway centres; 5 larger ports; 6 textile centres of Yorkshire and Lancashire; 7 towns of the North-Eastern seaboard and mining towns of Wales; 8 more recent metal-manufacturing towns)
C   *Suburbs and suburban-type towns*
    (9 'exclusive' residential suburbs; 10 older mixed suburbs; 11 newer mixed residential suburbs; 12 light-industry suburbs and towns within the sphere of influence of large conurbations; 13 older working-class and industrial suburbs; 14 newer industrial suburbs)

A residual category contains London (the area covered by the former London County Council). Such urban groupings reflect differences in the economic structure of different kinds of community, but also differences in demographic trends, housing, education and social class. The most persistent differences are regional ones – the most striking contrast being between the older heavy-industry towns of the North and those in the South where light engineering and administrative and professional activities are more common. Even here, though, there are outstanding exceptions – such as Harrogate, where conditions approximate to those of southern towns, and areas of London like West Ham which are similar in many ways to northern industrial cities. Moser and Scott summarize North–South differences in terms of *population size and structure* (the southern regions having, for example, an older population than the northern); *households and housing* (the North having a high proportion of small dwellings and more overcrowding); *social class* (with southern towns having higher proportions in the upper categories); *health indices* (infant mortality being considerably higher in the North); *education* (the extent of education being higher in the South). They found that social class was the most important variable between the different types of towns and between the main geographical regions. This is perhaps not surprising considering how closely class is connected with all of the other indices.[59]

Such typologies indicate the complex realities with which urban and regional planning has had to deal since the legislation of the 1940s. They indicate the context within which decisions about urban renewal and population dispersal have been made. Choices have had to be made between expanding towns and renewing dead city centres and 'twilight zones', between houses and flats (between 1945–51 and the late 1950s the percentage of new dwellings being built as houses fell from 88 to 60). Decisions have had to be made about competing forms of public transport, and about facilities for the private motorist. Neither housing estates nor new towns have met with the success the planners hoped. Attempts to replicate older spatial arrangements on new estates, for example, have not resulted in the same kinds of neighbourliness and social mixing as in the areas cleared. Josephine Klein comments that all that has happened is that 'relationships, instead of being face-to-face, become window-to-window'.[60] Many of the town planning ideals that were dominant in the 1940s and 1950s have been categorized as having a 'utopian' and 'anti-urban' bias, one that Osborn and Whittick made quite explicit:

> Of all the expedients of man in pursuit of satisfactions and power over things, towns have been the least amenable to considered and intelligent human organization. Much of their past record has been indescribably shocking … And we have to consider whether, in view of the recent evolution of means of communication, physical and mental, close spatial groupings of large numbers of people is any longer necessary or conducive to the further advance of civilization and culture.[61]

Against the anti-urban view other writers have argued in favour of quite different policies – mainly the regeneration

22 *Flats for families, London 1969*

of existing city neighbourhoods rather than the dispersal of urban populations. Some London boroughs, for example, have experimented on the basis of such principles, and some new towns, like Cumbernauld, have relied on much higher densities in the city centre than was the case with the early new towns.

The most important issue in all of these respects, in the period of post-war recovery and ever since, has been housing. When Labour came to office in 1945

> Housing towered above all other domestic problems facing the country. For six years there had been virtually no house-building, dilapidation had thrived unchecked ... The crude hand of war had dashed to the ground many of the slums that had befouled our cities, but half a million condemned slums still awaited demolition. More than four million dwellings were over 80 years old ... Half the houses in the country were without baths.

Aneurin Bevan, as Housing Minister, 'started from the premise that the housing problem for the middle classes had been roughly solved before the war, but for the lower income groups it had not been solved since the industrial revolution'.[62] A local, northern example of this national picture was that of Middlesbrough:

> Hardly any houses in the northern neighbourhoods have baths, and many have only cold water laid on. Soot and dirt continually cover clothes and furniture ... Dirt diseases, such as scabies, impetigo and vermin infestation occur ... the chief cause of continued ill-health on the new estates, as reflected, for instance, by high infant mortality rates, is the poverty of the people ... Every house in the town is now provided with a separate water-closet, but at least half of these are still outside ... About 2,000 old dwellings in the north still have no indoor water taps ...[63]

This is the context in which discussions of housing began in many areas in the mid-1940s, and the problems of housing, if changed, have remained acute. Despite improvements, there are still marked regional and social class variations.

For example, whereas in 1972 34 per cent of employers and managers owned their homes outright and 42 per cent owned them with a mortgage, only 20 per cent of unskilled workers were owners. The majority of the unskilled group in fact were renting their homes from a local authority or new town (56 per cent compared to 10 per cent of employers and managers). A further 20 per cent of the unskilled were living in private rented accommodation, compared to only 6 per cent of owners and managers.[64] The proportion of households sharing or lacking basic amenities decreased substantially in the 1950s and 1960s, but in 1972 8·3 per cent of all households had no fixed bath or shower (and an additional 3 per cent shared these amenities). 12 per cent of all households either had access only to an outside W.C. or had to share a W.C. Overcrowding, homelessness, excessively high private rents, and housing for the old and the disabled have remained intractable problems.

At the level of policy-making the central issues have been those of the provision of adequate housing, home ownership and council housing, transport, and the planning of estates and blocks of flats. At a human level all of these have been seen to lead into questions of how as well as where to live, questions of loneliness and adaptation, the special problems of the young and the old, the very texture of everyday life.

The urban way of life

There have been gains and losses resulting from urban growth in the nineteenth and twentieth centuries. Health and housing standards have improved for the majority, and the urban–industrial way of life has liberated individual citizens to an unprecedented degree. More choices are available in respect of jobs, education, marriage, moral and religious codes, and more people are now in a position to choose not only where they want to live, but also how they want to spend their working lives. The urban community provides a sufficient cross-section of people for everyone to know the kind of people they *want* to know. It also provides an unrivalled range of cultural, educational, recreational and civic amenities. On the other hand, it is also true that the city imposes regulations and uniformities. It may create considerable strains in terms of traffic conditions, noise and lack of adequate recreational space. By the mid-1970s there were some 13 million private cars on the road in England and Wales, a situation of critical importance to every aspect of urban and rural life, and to planning policies of all kinds.

The discussion of living conditions has increasingly involved detailed attention to questions of the quality of social experience, including the leisure activities provided for and by communities and groups within them. There has been protracted discussion since the 1940s of sports facilities and libraries, youth culture and holidays, playing areas for children in blocks of flats, the relationship between boredom and vandalism, and many other related issues.

From 1939, for example, a serious effort was made to raise youth work to a level equivalent to other educational services, and in the 1940s and 1950s in particular there was constant analysis of 'attached' and 'unattached' youth – those who did and did not belong to youth clubs and organizations. After the war there were studies which showed how difficult was the work of the clubs and how limited their success.[65] Memories of the young unemployed in many industrial areas in the 1930s with nowhere to go but the street lent an urgency to the discussion of facilities for young people. In addition

> The public was shocked in the early 1940s by the much-proclaimed fact that after leaving school, between 60–70 per cent of the adolescent population remained thereafter untouched by membership of any socializing influence including membership of a library or a Sunday school.[66]

In Nottingham at the end of the war only about a third of adolescents were members of any youth organization (though the great majority had belonged to some organization under the age of fourteen).[67] Alongside this kind of information were frequently placed survey figures for attendance at cinemas and dance halls. A study of adolescents in Birmingham, for example, found that out of 500 'attached' and 'unattached' boys interviewed, 32 per cent went danc-

23 *1930s Regal Cinema*

ing once a week or more, 34 per cent went to the cinema once a week and 45 per cent went more than once a week.[68]

Nationally, after the war, three out of every four people aged sixteen to twenty-four went to the cinema at least once a week, two out of four at least twice a week. Adult leisure habits (including those relating to gambling) began to be subjected to detailed analysis. Dog tracks had some one and a quarter million admissions weekly in the late 1940s, and half of the men in Britain were filling in football coupons: 'the football coupon is a form of terrifying appearance ruled into innumerable small spaces, but the British public have been trained to form-filling by years of war and controls'.[69] Holidays and the holiday industry began to attract analysis, since some 15 million out of a population of 46 million were taking holidays away from home immediately before the war, and since new classes of holiday-maker entered the picture in 1945 – 'those $18\frac{1}{2}$ million workpeople earning less than £250 per annum and recently granted holidays with pay'.[70] In 1949 slightly over half the population over sixteen had a holiday away from home, though of these a quarter went away for two or more holidays, and of those who had no holiday over half went on day trips of some sort.[71] The future discussion of many of these aspects of leisure was to be affected, for example, by the spread of television, the contraction of the railway network and the increased use of the motor car, and the growth of overseas holidays. Other changes, such as those in teenage economics and culture from the mid-1950s were to influence profoundly the pattern of leisure activity, as well as the focus of social investigation.[72]

The early 1950s

The beginning of the 1950s was in some respects a period of reaction against constraints and controls, and a reassertion of the individual against the State, reflected in an increase in the Conservative share of the vote at the general election of 1950, and the beginning of thirteen years of Conservative government in 1951. Continued economic difficulties and crises, and attendant austerity measures, had moved some public opinion towards the possibility of greater prosperity and 'normality' through Conservative policies.

The social realities of the early 1950s are illustrated in two passages by Labour politicians, written after their defeat in 1951. Attlee, former Prime Minister, looked back at the 'great levelling-up of conditions' that had taken place since the war: 'The great mass of abject poverty has disappeared. Full employment and the development of the social services are, of course, the principal factors in this, but there are many others'. Aneurin Bevan, chief architect of Labour's welfare programme, was profoundly aware of:

the general consciousness of unnecessary deprivation, which is the normal state of millions of people in modern industrial society, accompanied by a deep sense of frustration and dissatisfaction with the existing state of social affairs. It is no answer to say that things are better than they were. People live in the present, not in the past . . .

There is a universal and justifiable conviction that the lot of ordinary man and woman is much worse than it need be.[73]

By the early 1950s there was this strong dual sense of what had been accomplished, and what was undone. Middle-class England was also aware of unpopular Labour austerity budgets (especially that of Stafford Cripps in 1949), and restrictions on private enterprise. Churchill's 1951 government and subsequent Conservative governments did not scrap national controls and planning, the social services and nationalization:

They altered the pattern a little. They ended food subsidies, for example, but increased the rate of house building with a new emphasis on private as opposed to municipal building. Conservative governments had more room for manoeuvre than the Labour governments had found. As the war receded, and the shortages which followed its end became less, successive governments were able to spend more of the growing national income on housing, hospitals, roads, and similar services.[74]

The important feature of the early 1950s from the point of view of the changing shape of British society, however, was not so much domestic political change as responses to international tensions. As early as 1946 the 'cold war' was heralded, when Winston Churchill, an influential figure even out of government, made a speech at Fulton in the U.S.A., calling for an Anglo-American military alliance specifically to meet the challenge of the Soviet Union. By the 1950s and the Korean war the world was effectively divided by an 'iron curtain'. By 1952 it was 'practically all over the world, an era of insecurity and confusion'.[75] In such a situation the atomic bomb had brought people 'to live in expectation of catastrophe on the same universal scale as the day of judgment'.[76]

Only gradually did the social impact of the use of the atomic bomb in 1945 become apparent. The sense of moral shock did indeed find expression, including in the spirit of Edith Sitwell's poem 'The Shadow of Cain':

> We did not heed the Cloud in the Heavens shaped like the hand
> Of Man . . . But there came a roar as if the Sun and Earth had come together –
> The Sun descending and the Earth ascending
> To take its place above . . . the Primal Matter
> Was broken, the womb from which all life began.
> Then to the murdered Sun a totem pole of dust arose in memory of Man.[77]

Looking back from the social conflicts of the late 1960s, Jeff Nuttall saw this event not just as an evil, but as one 'we had espoused'. The bomb was used on Japan, after victory in Europe had been secured: 'VE Night took place in one world and VJ Night in another'. The genesis of many later social attitudes, in Britain and the whole western world, was to be found here:

> What way we made in 1945 and in the following years depended largely on our age, for right at that point, at the point of the dropping of the bombs on Hiroshima and Nagasaki, the generations became divided in a very crucial way.

Here, it was suggested, lay the roots of political and inter-generational conflicts in the 1960s: 'The people who had passed puberty at the time of the bomb found that they were incapable of conceiving of life *without* a future . . . The people who had not yet reached puberty at the time of the bomb were incapable of conceiving of life *with* a future.' The younger generation reacted with 'formalized stoicism', and adopted a popular culture to wear like a protective shell. It was

> the culture of the jitterbug, of the snap-brim trilby and the double-breasted, wasp-waisted, wide-trousered pin-stripe suit, of the hand-painted silk tie and the Boston haircut, of camiknickers and bright red lipstick, of the bombshell blonde and the streamlined bustline, of gilded

pin-tables and lime-green ice-cream, of two-inch crepe
soles and black-market nylons, of Betty Grable and
Veronica Lake; of Humphrey Bogart and Alan Ladd, of
Peter Cheyney and James Hadley Chase.[78]

As Bertrand Russell put it in 1949: 'the young have so much
doubt as to their own survival that many of them feel it
useless to live seriously, while others are driven to an
evasion of painful realities by various kinds of pleasant fantasy.'[79] The bomb generation went on to fashion its own
forms of culture and protest, and to change the content and
style of political and social comment. 1951 saw the Festival
of Britain, intended as an act of confidence. 1952 saw the H-
bomb. Uncertainties and divisions were deepening.
   The extent of the cultural changes beginning to take
shape was to become most dramatically clear in 1956, but
change was already in the air. Sexual and ethical boundaries
were being redrawn. A popular version of the famous
Kinsey Report on male sexual behaviour in the U.S.A. told
its readers in 1949 that the report might end 'an era of
Hush-and-Pretend'. The Kinsey Report 'had done for sex
what Columbus did for geography'.[80] The immense
popularity of James Hadley Chase's *No Orchids for Miss
Blandish* on both sides of the Atlantic had already announced a new dimension in popular literature in 1939.
George Orwell prefaced his discussion of the book with:
'Now for a header into the cesspool', but suggested that the
popularity of its brand of sex and violence would not be
lasting: 'it is possible that it is an isolated phenomenon,
brought about by the mingled boredom and brutality of war'.
If such books became 'acclimatized' in England, 'instead of
being merely a half-understood import from America, there
would be good grounds for dismay'. The book was a 'day-
dream appropriate to a totalitarian age'.[81] But the book and
its successors did become acclimatized, and by the early
1950s Mickey Spillane was a dominant name in the mass-
selling market. Even in 1947 the 'purposeless parade of
violence for its own sake' on the screen was being attacked.[82]
Orwell was wrong on another score. In 1947 he wrote that
'the general weakening of sex morals that has happened

during the past twenty or thirty years ... is probably a temporary thing'.[83] What Orwell viewed as a 'weakening' was not temporary. In life, in high culture and in popular culture, basic and lasting changes in this and other respects were taking place. Between 1950 and 1955 the 'teddy boys' made their appearance, as did *Lolita* in the United States and *Waiting for Godot* on the London stage. *The Blackboard Jungle* brought the first strains of rock music, Johnnie Ray set the scene that Elvis Presley was to occupy, and screen spectaculars like *Quo Vadis* and *The Robe* fought the cinema's fight against television. In 1956 James Dean was to appear in *Rebel without a Cause*, neither the only rebel nor the only new cause to appear in that year.

Of central importance to all these developments was scientific and technical advance. War had cemented confidence in the ability of science and technology to solve social problems as well as to win wars – only the political will was needed. If atomic power threatened destruction, it also had positive potential. In recent generations, said the cynic, science and technology had 'equipped the political bosses who control the various national states with unprecedentedly efficient instruments of coercion'. Tyrants could 'dragoon larger numbers of people more indiscriminately'.[84] Since science had helped to win the war, said the optimistic politician, the government wished it to 'play its part in the constructive tasks of peace and of economic development'.[85] Between the Beveridge Report and the inauguration of the health service, medical discoveries included antibiotics, the means of treating thrombosis with anti-coagulants, cortisone and the medical application of nuclear physics.[86] The early 1950s was the beginning of the plastics era. The demand for household equipment soared into the age of affluence. Not everyone benefited or agreed. Village life was changed, but not at the same rate as in the towns. The ability to benefit from technological progress remained a function of social class and income. But the television set spread relentlessly.

Society was not becoming homogeneous. Basic social distinctions and differences of outlook were in many respects being strengthened. The search for material goods, for comfort, was in competition with profound insecurities, anxieties and the inability to 'live seriously'. Increased leisure and technological growth account for the presence of the concept of 'privatization' in modern sociological discussion. Jules Henry describes American workers (though the concept can be applied to other sections of the community) as having little or no involvement in the institutions where they work, and the latter therefore become '*de*socializing' agencies: 'what finally relates the average person to life, space and people is his own personal, intimate economy: family, house and car. He has labelled his occupational world "not involved", and turned inward upon his little world of family, hobbies and living standard.'[87] His work is depersonalized; he is 'alienated'. If leisure and home-centredness have become important features of contemporary life, in Britain as well as in the U.S.A., this is not simply a result of people's having more spare time; it is the generally unsatisfactory character of work itself, for most people, that gives leisure its significance. Despite progressive reductions in the agreed working week, and despite longer holidays with pay, with overtime many still work more than forty-eight hours a week. Although 'normal' working hours had been reduced to just over forty by the end of the 1960s, average hours actually worked were fifty or more. The retreat into home-centredness need not imply a total withdrawal from the social world beyond the family, or the lack of a positive attraction to better home surroundings. Doing-It-Yourself is a complex outcome of a combination of technological, social and cultural changes accelerated in the early 1950s.[88]

What the decade after the end of the war witnessed above all was a new sense of flux in social relations – between classes and generations, in the family and in the factory, between the individual and public authorities. The reconstructed and the new town, demolition of old housing and the construction of new flats and estates, nationalization and strike action, the use of increased leisure and reactions to major economic and international dangers – all implied a rapidly changing society, and new difficulties in grasping the interpretation of 'society'. T. H. Marshall argued in this period

that economic inequalities were being eroded by 'the enrich-
ment of the status of citizenship' – the impact of new rights
as citizens on the structure of old inequalities.[89] Such an
interpretation, grounded in the confidence engendered by
immediate post-war changes, was becoming difficult to
sustain by the early 1950s, and was to be lost amid the
ideological battles of the 1960s.

Notes

1 *Education Act, 1944*, pp. 4–5.

2 LABOUR PARTY *Report of the Forty-third Annual Conference*,
p. 128 (London, 1944). The speaker was Alice Bacon.

3 LONDON COUNTY COUNCIL *London School Plan*, p. 7
(London, 1947). Ruth Glass, writing about Middlesbrough,
described equal opportunity in education as 'no longer a plan-
ner's dream, it is now the duty of every local education authority', *Social Background of a Plan*, p. 83 (London, 1948).

4 *Children Act, 1948*, p. 1. This Act followed the report of the
Care of Children (Curtis) Committee, 1946.

5 *National Insurance Act, 1946*, p. 1.

6 *National Health Service Act, 1946*, p. 1.

7 ROYAL COMMISSION ON POPULATION *Report*, p. 136
(London, 1949).

8 OLIVE A. WHEELER *The Adventure of Youth*, p. 7 (London,
1945).

9 LORD BEVERIDGE *Voluntary Action*, p. 225 (London, 1948).

10 J. B. PRIESTLEY *Letter to a Returning Serviceman*, p. 32
(London, 1945).

11 FRANCIS BOYD *British Politics in Transition 1945–1963*,
pp. 123–4 (London, 1964).

12 HERBERT and NANCIE MATTHEWS *The Britain We Saw*,
p. 43 (London, 1950).

13 CARR *The New Society*, p. 109.

14 HERMAN FINER 'Planning and nationalisation in Great
Britain', I, *International Labour Review*, Vol. LVII (3), 1948,
p. 158.

15 STEPHEN SPENDER 'Writers in the world of necessity',
reprinted from *Polemic* in DENYS VAL BAKER (ed.) *Little
Reviews Anthology 1946*, p. 103 (London, 1946).

16 *Hansard*, Vol. 418 (76), cols. 1767–8, 1946.

17 LORD BEVERIDGE *Power and Influence*, p. 331 (London,
1953).

18 CONSERVATIVE PARTY *The Right Road for Britain* (1949), quoted in ASA BRIGGS, 'The Welfare State in historical perspective', *European Journal of Sociology*, Vol. II (2), 1961, p. 227.

19 LABOUR PARTY *Report of the Forty-fourth Annual Conference*, p. 79 (London, 1945). The chairman was Ellen Wilkinson.

20 WILLIAM RALPH INGE *The End of an Age*, pp. 245, 287 (London, 1948).

21 ROWNTREE and LAVERS *Poverty and the Welfare State*, p. 40.

22 ANEURIN BEVAN 'Plan for work' and SIR WILLIAM BEVERIDGE 'Freedom from idleness' in G. D. H. COLE *et al. Plan for Britain: a collection of essays prepared for the Fabian Society*, pp. 39, 90 (London, 1943).

23 DE JOUVENEL *Problems of Socialist England*, p. 23.

24 JANET BEVERIDGE *Beveridge and his Plan*, p. 114 (London, 1954).

25 DE JOUVENEL *Problems of Socialist England*, p. 158.

26 JIM GRIFFITHS 'Plan for the key industries' in COLE *et al. Plan for Britain*, p. 53.

27 WILLIAM TEMPLE *Christianity and the Social Order*, pp. 64–5 (Harmondsworth, 1942).

28 BEVERIDGE *Power and Influence*, p. 317; POLITICAL AND ECONOMIC PLANNING, *British Trade Unionism*, p. 114 (London, 1948).

29 WILLIAM PLOWDEN *The Motor Car and Politics in Britain*, pp. 321–5 (London, 1971; 1973 Penguin edition).

30 JAMES LANSDALE HODSON *The Way Things Are*, p. 25 (London, 1947). For a full discussion, see F. ZWEIG *Men in the Pits* (London, 1949), particularly Ch. XXXII, 'Nationalisation and the reaction of the miners'.

31 V. L. ALLEN *Trade Unions and the Government*, p. 34 (London, 1960). See also Graham Wootton, *Workers, Unions and the State* (London, 1966).

32 GUY ROUTH *Occupations and Pay in Great Britain 1906–60*, pp. 17, 29, 37–8 (Cambridge, 1965). For changes in income and differentials see pp. 123–5, and also DUDLEY SEERS *The Levelling of Incomes since 1938*, pp. 57–69 (Oxford, 1951).

33 G. K. GALBRAITH *The New Industrial State*, p. 1 (London, 1967).

34 ALDOUS HUXLEY *Science, Liberty and Peace*, p. 15 (London, 1947).

35 See further ALAN FOX 'Managerial ideology and labour relations', *British Journal of Industrial Relations*, Vol. IV (3), 1966.

36 ALLAN FLANDERS *et al. Experiment in Industrial Democracy: Study of the John Lewis partnership*, p. 193 (London, 1968).

37 A. A. ROGOW *The Labour Government and British Industry 1945–1951*, especially pp. 103–11 (Oxford, 1955).

38 AMITAI ETZIONI *Modern Organizations*, p. 42 (New Jersey, 1964).

39 See RALF DAHRENDORF *Class and Class Conflict in Industrial Society*, Ch. VII (London, 1959).

40 See P. SARGANT FLORENCE *Ownership, Control and Success of Large Companies* (London, 1961).

41 HANS GERTH and C. WRIGHT MILLS (eds.) *From Max Weber*, p. 214 (London, 1948). For a fuller discussion of the characteristics of bureaucracies see PETER BLAU *Bureaucracy in Modern Society*, pp. 28–32 (New York, 1956), and MARTIN ALBROW, *Bureaucracy* (London, 1970).

42 See, for example, A. W. GOULDNER *Patterns of Industrial Bureaucracy* (New York, 1954) and C. ARGYRIS *Integrating the Individual and the Organization* (New York, 1964).

43 See TOM BURNS and G. STALKER *The Management of Innovation* (London, 1961).

44 DE JOUVENEL *Problems of Socialist England*, p. 212.

45 SPENDER 'Writers in the world of necessity', p. 110.

46 E. F. M. DURBIN *The Politics of Democratic Socialism*, pp. 113, 128–9 (London, 1940).

47 JAMES BURNHAM *The Managerial Revolution*, especially pp. 28, 35, 37, 52, 63, 67 (U.S.A., 1941; 1945 Penguin edition).

48 PATRICK ABERCROMBIE *Greater London Plan 1944*, pp. 7–8, 30 (London, 1945).

49 FREDERIC OSBORN and ARNOLD WHITTICK *The New Towns. The Answer to Megalopolis*, p. 79 (London, 1963).

50 COLIN BUCHANAN *The State of Britain*, p. 23 (London, 1972); JAMES W. R. ADAMS *Modern Town and Country Planning*, p. 67 (London, 1952).

51 Lewis Silkin, quoted in FRANK SCHAFFER *The New Town Story*, p. 29 (London, 1970). For a fuller description of the designation of the new towns see Chs. 2–4, and also PIERRE MERLIN *New Towns*, Ch. 1 (London, 1971).

52 HAROLD ORLANS *Stevenage*, p. 81 (London, 1952).

53 NORMAN MACKENZIE *The New Towns*, p. 1 (London, 1955).

54 See J. H. NICHOLSON *New Communities in Britain* (London, 1961).

55 For a fuller discussion, see PETER H. MANN *An Approach to Urban Sociology*, Chs. 2 and 3 (London, 1965) and R. E. PAHL

(ed.) *Readings in Urban Sociology* (London, 1968), especially papers by Gans, Durant and Pahl.

56 See RONALD FRANKENBERG *Communities in Britain* (Harmondsworth, 1965) for a comparison of the findings of a number of British surveys and for a model of 'rural' and 'urban' patterns of social organization (Ch. 11).

57 See, for example, RICHARD HOGGART *The Uses of Literacy*, especially pp. 41–52 (London, 1957; 1958 edition). See also BRIAN JACKSON *Working Class Community* (London, 1968).

58 See COLIN ROSSER and CHRISTOPHER HARRIS *The Family and Social Change*, pp. 66–72 (London, 1965), for a discussion of Swansea's 'urban villages'.

59 C. A. MOSER and WOLF SCOTT *British Towns*, Ch. VI (London, 1961).

60 JOSEPHINE KLEIN *Samples from English Cultures*, vol. I, p. 251 (London, 1965).

61 OSBORN and WHITTICK *The New Towns*, pp. 15–16.

62 J. E. D. HALL *Labour's First Year*, pp. 40–1 (Harmondsworth, 1947).

63 GLASS *Social Background of a Plan*, pp. 50–1.

64 MYRA WOOLF *The Housing Survey in England and Wales 1964* (London, 1967) and OFFICE OF POPULATION CENSUSES AND SURVEYS *The General Household Survey 1972*, p. 52 (London, 1975).

65 See, for example, TOM BRENNAN *Midland City*, pp. 158–63 (London, 1948) for a picture of youth club work in Wolverhampton.

66 J. MACALISTER BREW *Youth and Youth Groups*, p. 96 (London, 1957; 1968 edition).

67 PEARL JEPHCOTT *Some Young People*, p. 105 (London, 1945).

68 BRYAN H. REED *Eighty Thousand Adolescents: a study of young people in the city of Birmingham*, p. 28 (London, 1950). This provides detailed figures on all kinds of activities.

69 BEVERIDGE *Voluntary Action*, p. 270.

70 ELIZABETH BRUNNER *Holiday Making and the Holiday Trades*, pp. 3–5 (Oxford, 1945).

71 W. F. F. KEMSLEY and DAVID GINSBURG *Holidays and Holiday Expenditure*, p. 1 (London [1950]).

72 For a detailed discussion of leisure activities in the 1970s see MICHAEL YOUNG and PETER WILMOTT *The Symmetrical Family: a study of work and leisure in the London region*, Ch. VIII (London, 1973).

73 C. R. ATTLEE *As It Happened*, p. 166 (London, 1954); ANEURIN BEVAN *In Place of Fear*, p. 2 (London, 1952).

74 BOYD *British Politics in Transition*, p. 24.

75 HAROLD J. LASKI *The Dilemma of our Times*, p. 14 (London, 1952).

76 LIONEL CURTIS 'Political repercussions of atomic power', in M. L. OLIPHANT *et al. The Atomic Age*, p. 107 (London, 1949).

77 EDITH SITWELL *The Canticle of the Rose: selected poems 1920–1947*, p. 258 (London, 1949).

78 JEFF NUTTALL *Bomb Culture*, pp. 18–21 (London, 1968; 1971 Paladin edition).

79 BERTRAND RUSSELL 'Values in the atomic age', in OLIPHANT *The Atomic Age*, p. 83.

80 MORRIS L. ERNST and DAVID LOTH *Sexual Behaviour and the Kinsey Report*, pp. 11, 15 (London, 1949).

81 GEORGE ORWELL 'Raffles and Miss Blandish' in *Critical Essays*, pp. 146, 154 (London, 1946).

82 FILM CRITIC 'Parade of violence', in *Penguin New Writing*, No. 30, p. 126 (1947).

83 GEORGE ORWELL *The English People*, p. 17 (London, 1947).

84 HUXLEY *Science, Liberty and Peace*, p. 6.

85 Herbert Morrison, quoted in HILARY ROSE and STEVEN ROSE, *Science and Society*, p. 73 (London, 1969; 1970 Penguin edition).

86 ALMONT LINDSEY *Socialized Medicine in England and Wales*, p. 25 (Chapel Hill, North Carolina, 1962).

87 JULES HENRY *Culture against Man*, pp. 28–9 (London, 1966).

88 For a detailed discussion of work and the family see YOUNG and WILLMOTT *The Symmetrical Family*, especially Chs. IV–VI.

89 T. H. MARSHALL 'Citizenship and social class' (1949) reprinted in *Sociology at the Crossroads*, pp. 122, 127 (London, 1963).

7 Social structure, affluence and inequality

The awareness of change

'There is already a generation in existence', wrote a historian in 1964, 'for which Hitler is just as much a historical figure as Napoleon or Julius Caesar . . . between 1955 and 1960 the world moved into a new historical period, with different dimensions and problems of its own'. By 1961 American government had passed into the hands of President Kennedy and a generation which had not been involved in politics before 1939.[1] The world was aware of profound changes gaining momentum a decade after the end of the Second World War, and Kennedy's election seemed to symbolize the arrival of the new generation, the new period.

From the middle of the 1950s Britain was engaged in two major revolutions – one associated with what was described as the coming of affluence, and the other with the ending of the colonial era. Both had important consequences for the structure of social class relationships and both contributed to the 'overall euphoria of change'[2] that heralded the arrival of the 'swinging sixties'. Out of the comparative calm and restraint that marked the early post-war years, Britain at the end of 1955 suddenly entered a period of upheaval. It

*1955 —
influ of
media.*

witnessed, for example, the coming of commercial television and the spread of supermarkets and self-service; the rise of a new generation of playwrights, novelists and critics whose writing earned for them the title of the Angry Young Men; the Suez crisis; the rock and roll craze; the Campaign for Nuclear Disarmament, Aldermaston marches and rallies in Trafalgar Square; and the beginnings of much higher crime and illegitimacy rates. With the coming of the changed atmosphere to which these examples point, a mood of youthful hostility was unleashed, questioning every kind of traditional convention and authority, and preparing the ground for the more radical shifts towards a secular and permissive society. The 'bomb generation' was identifying itself.

The awareness of recent and continuing change was explicit at all levels. A Labour Party policy document in 1961, for example, began with the words: 'We live in a scientific revolution. In the sixteen years since the war ended man's knowledge and his power over nature – to create and to destroy – have grown more than in the previous century.'[3] In 1960 adult education was re-examining its role amid changes which had 'affected the home, the school, the city, the village, the factory, the world of politics and the world of leisure'. Education, like the rest of society, was aware of the kind of analysis C. P. Snow made in his famous 'Two Cultures' lectures in 1959: 'During all human history until this century, the rate of social change has been very slow . . . That is no longer so . . . There is *bound* to be more social change, affecting more people, in the next decade than in any before.'[4]

↑ in social change

It was not only at home that things were changing in 1956. Throughout colonial Africa and the Middle East nationalist movements gathered force, threatening the continued presence of British and other colonial powers. In July Egypt nationalized the Suez Canal, and in November France and Britain invaded the area, submitting after several days to international and domestic pressure and agreeing to a cease-fire. The conflict ended on 7 November, two days after Soviet tanks crushed the last resistance in Hungary, blocking any hopes of greater liberalization in the communist world. Both events strengthened the sense of alarm and political disillusionment felt by a generation already finding it difficult to visualize a world with a future.

At the same time, the association of 'The Six' was moving towards the establishment of the European Common Market in March 1957 (without British membership). Western Germany and Japan were fast recovering from wartime setbacks and establishing vigorous industry and trade. In America the civil rights movement, under its leader the Reverend Martin Luther King, was entering a new and more militant phase of protest. Throughout the world, writes Christopher Booker, 'mankind was emerging from the shadows of the forties and turning its imagination towards the future. In all parts the pattern was essentially the same – the underprivileged, the young, the colonially occupied and those who could see themselves as oppressed, were becoming fired with the same bright vision of a new world – a world of freedom and excitement, to be achieved through revolt against the established order.'[5] In Britain this new mood was reflected in countless ways – in the language and images of advertising, new styles of teenage dress and dancing, new technologies, and more militant and aggressive styles of lobbying and protest.

Perceptions of change, and of the virtues of one or another response to it, varied widely. Analyses of what was actually happening differed fundamentally. Writing about the America of the 1950s, McCarthyism and lunar probes, H-bombs and much else, one writer described the period as 'The Jittery Fifties'.[6] The description applies equally to the uncertainties and contradictions of British experience, especially from 1956. Yet there were at the same time grounds for sensing that affluence, stability, a new order were close at hand. The confrontation of opinion about social realities was sharp. The 1955 Conservative election manifesto indicated that the Party had proved, 'by re-establishing confidence in our currency, by maintaining full employment, by restoring housewives' choice and by smashing housing records, that Conservative freedom works'. It went on to aim at 'a fine and ambitious target. We believe that the British people have a real chance during the coming twenty-five years to double their standard of living. The future beckons to this generation with a golden finger.'[7] At the general election four years later the Labour Party warned that 'one of the dangers we face as a nation is the mood of complacency ... The cost of living has *not* been stabilised ... There are many millions of "have nots" in Britain'.[8]

Arguments began to take shape about the rapidly changing face of Britain itself. An old 'muddled approach to a humanist architecture' was under attack from 'The New Brutalism', a phrase current from the mid-1950s.[9] New kinds of buildings began to dominate the city sky-line. Urban and industrial sprawl and lack of detailed planning were attacked in 1955 by Ian Nairn in his challenging *Outrage*, prophesying that 'if what is called development is allowed to multiply at the present rate, then by the end of the century Great Britain will consist of isolated oases in a desert of wire, concrete roads, cosy plots and bungalows. There will be no real distinction between town and country.'[10] At all levels of discussion the confrontations focused on the confusions of people amid powerful forces of political, economic and social change.

Affluence

The industrialized West clung to the idea of affluence, expansion and stability. When the Prime Minister, Harold Macmillan, told the British people in July 1957 that they had 'never had it so good', they mostly agreed with him.

In general terms, social conditions had improved since the war. According to a survey published by the Government in 1962[11], between 1951 and 1961 the Gross National Product increased by 83 per cent. Total personal incomes almost doubled and those of teenagers quadrupled. Retail prices also rose after the war, but only by at most 50 per cent. The result was considerable improvement in living standards in some sections of the population. Those whose standards 'were previously lowest – semi-skilled and unskilled workers, the old and the sick – have benefited

most, clerical workers and salary earners least'.[12] Average
consumption per head was up by 25 per cent. By 1961
women were buying much more meat, bacon, sugar, fruit,
vegetables, beverages and manufactured food than they had
done ten years earlier, and less bread and cereals. In the
1960s, 'in nutritional terms we are better nourished than at
any previous recorded time'.[13] The pattern of food packaging and sales, and of the range of available foods, was also
changing markedly. The first supermarket opened in Britain
in 1956, and 825 opened in the next five years, as well as
several thousand self-service stores.

Much of the extra income people now earned was spent
on private housing. From 1954 to 1961 mortgage loans
doubled in volume. Between 1951 and 1961, 1,800,000 homes
were built for letting by local authorities. In addition to
their homes, families spent more on furniture and domestic
equipment. By 1961 three out of every four households had
a vacuum cleaner; two out of every five had a washing
machine and one in three had a refrigerator. Four out of five
homes by then had a television (the number of licences
issued doubling between 1955 and 1959 alone). The number
of telephones went up from some five and a half million in
1951 to eight and a half million by the end of 1962.

Nearly all of these domestic 'luxuries', as they appeared
to most families then – 'necessities' as many would term
them today, were purchased on credit. In spite of periodic
restrictions, the hire purchase debt of the country more than
doubled between the end of 1955 and the end of 1961. Cars
were a major item in this debt, for the 1950s was 'the decade
in which Britain became motorized'[14] and the first motorway developments (and parking meters) began. Between
1951 and 1961 expenditure on cars and motor cycles rose by
600 per cent. There were fewer than two and a half million
cars in 1951, but by 1961 this figure had grown to six
million.

Another index of the increasing prosperity of the late
1950s, and of the way in which it was distributed, was the
so-called 'property boom'. In 1958–9 deals in property
shares, many of them in companies controlled by the
Cotton–Clore partnership (names which became virtually

synonymous with the trend in property speculation), rose from 16,000 to 102,000. The value of ordinary shares in property companies rose in the next four years by almost eight times. Some of the new properties built during the boom were prestigious city office blocks, like the Thorn building in St Martin's Lane, and Bowater House, Knightsbridge – both in London, and the Bull Ring development in Birmingham. But these years also witnessed a vast expansion in the building of private estates, especially around the perimeter of expanding market and commuter towns, like Banbury, Swindon and Newbury.[15]

The legacy of post-war improvements in welfare, medicine and education added to people's experience of affluence at the end of the 1950s. By 1960, for example, boys and girls were, at fourteen, on average more than half an inch taller and from three to four pounds heavier than children of the same age had been in 1950. Much of the credit for this improvement lay with improved standards of housing and nutrition, as well as help and advice provided to mothers under the National Health Service before and after childbirth. Improvements in children's educational opportunities were another factor in rising standards and expectations. Between 1950 and 1960 the number of children staying on at school after fifteen nearly trebled. The number of full-time students in technical education during the decade and those on day release went up by three times. University students were still a privileged minority in 1960, mainly because of the lack of places available, not because of any lack of qualified sixth-formers.

Greater affluence and greater State benefits undoubtedly improved living conditions – especially for the families of skilled workers. Whether, by 1961, this meant that 'the dominant picture of John Bull puts him in the solid, middle class suburban range' – as the 1962 Government report claimed,[16] and sociologists like Goldthorpe and Lockwood were also beginning to suggest[17] – is more doubtful. In spite of the real gains made by some sections of the population in the post-war years, experts on social administration like Richard Titmuss and Barbara Wootton were not at all euphoric about the achievements of the welfare state. They

24 *Holidaying on the A20*

were critical of the inflexible workings of the bureaucratic machine, but were even more disappointed by the apparent failure of post-war policies to achieve a greater measure of equal opportunity and fair shares.

S/feel 'embourg v. slight

Inequalities

The accumulation of evidence on continuing inequalities led politicians and social theorists, on both sides of the Atlantic, to review their existing objectives. The reappraisal came sooner in America than it did in Britain – perhaps because there one group at least, the Negroes, was conspicuously and undeniably unequal. From 1956 this group was also increasingly articulate and militant in its campaign for equal rights. Following the big influx of West Indian immigrants to Britain through the 1950s[18] there was also racial tension. In 1958, riots between white and black youths occurred in Nottingham and in London's Notting Hill, producing fears of inevitable, prolonged conflict and demands for 'an immediate check on this unrestricted immigration'.[19] More important here, however, from the point of view of social policy, was a new perception of the nature and extent of poverty, and a continuing and characteristically British preoccupation with social justice.

By 1956 the way was clearly open for extending the kind of analysis we have seen in the last chapter, as conducted by Durbin and Burnham – the gradual erosion of social class, and the emergence of new consensus-based patterns of social organization. The outstanding post-war expression of this view, expressed in social-democratic terms, was that of Anthony Crosland. Looking at post-war developments, in social insurance and the social services, the role of the State, and the level and amount of poverty, for example, Crosland argued in *The Future of Socialism* (1956) for the abandonment of old socialist dogmas. Economic power, he suggested, was already being transferred from the business class to the State, only a small amount of residual primary poverty remained, incomes were being redistributed, and the Beveridge principles had been put into operation. Flaws in the system could be ironed out by trade union action, and

working-class living standards could be constantly improved.[20] Crosland's view was that new forms of popular
control, shaped through social-democratic policies, were
eroding privilege and inequality by peaceful means. A
future leader of the Labour Party explained to the outside
world that 'the social barriers have crumbled; the old
inequalities have greatly diminished. But this has resulted
not from the extermination of the previous dominant
classes, but through more gradual changes in the distribution of property and income, which in turn can be ascribed
partly to war and inflation, partly to the growing political
power of the masses.' [21] This kind of analysis and theory was
to come under mounting attack – Crosland's in particular
touched off a literature of controversy. From 1957 its
premises, and those of right-wing critics of the welfare state,
were to be faced with a substantial body of detailed social
investigation.

The most important focus of the movement for such
investigation was the Institute for Community Studies,
founded by Michael Young, its Director from its inception
in 1954. The best known studies associated with the
Institute began to appear in 1957, when Michael Young and
Peter Willmott published *Family and Kinship in East
London*, and Peter Townsend *The Family Life of Old People*.
Young and Willmott's *Family and Class in a London Suburb*
followed in 1960, and Brian Jackson and Dennis Marsden's
Education and the Working Class in 1962. This body of
investigation was 'in line with what has often been pointed
to as a specifically "British" tradition in sociology, with
Booth, Rowntree and the Webbs as eminent exemplars'. In
addition, the period saw a significant output of 'welfare-
centred "social studies" ',[22] the outstanding figure in this
field being Richard Titmuss.

Young and Willmott were concerned with the detailed
texture of social life, predominantly of the working class, the
poor, the old and the under-privileged. With their own kind
of methodology, they aimed – as had their distinguished
predecessors – to rediscover basic realities, and in particular
to show what continuities and discontinuities were to be
found in social institutions subject to the pressures of

230 Modern English Society

change (State intervention, population dispersal and re-organized secondary education, for example). The Titmuss style of analysis was that of the committed social administrator, close to reality, with the aim of influencing policy. In this period he published, for example, his influential *Essays on 'The Welfare State'* (1958), a pamphlet on *The Irresponsible Society* (1959) and *Income Distribution and Social Change* (1962). During the war Titmuss had already investigated the social class distribution of the incidence of infant mortality, showing how little, if anything, had been achieved in reducing class differentials since 1911.[23] From the late 1950s he sharply attacked what he called 'the myth of the "Welfare State for the Working Classes" '. The main danger in assuming that the working class was as a whole the main beneficiary of the welfare state legislation was that this had 'led to the assumption that most – if not all – of our social problems have been – or soon will be – solved. Those few that remain will, it is thought, be automatically remedied by rising incomes and minor adjustments of one kind or another.'[24] Titmuss directed attention to areas in which greater social justice had not been achieved, to the unequal distribution of benefits, to the increased tax and 'fringe' benefits of the middle class and the rich, to social changes (such as the increased number of married people and working wives, lower unemployment and higher juvenile incomes) which had concealed 'the real degree of inequality'.[25] A more detailed analysis of the distribution of social benefits and incomes meant, Titmuss concluded, that 'we should be much more hesitant in suggesting that any equalizing forces at work in Britain since 1938 can be promoted to the status of a "natural law" and projected into the future'.[26]

A great deal of related work resulted at the end of the 1950s in the 'rediscovery' of poverty. In 1962 Dorothy Wedderburn was demonstrating that although the main effect of National Assistance legislation had been 'to build in a floor in real terms at a little above the subsistence levels of the 'thirties', there were, for example, some two and a half million old people at or around the poverty line.[27] In a vivid and influential pamphlet in 1960 Audrey Harvey described increasing social divisions, defended the welfare services against 'armchair critics', pointed to the million or more pensioners living below subsistence level, described the extreme pressures of housing shortages and overcrowding on poor families, and again made the claim that the middle class had benefited most from welfare legislation. She wrote on behalf of the 'scattered and inarticulate' minority who were 'dependent upon State provision and ... those who still suffer great privation'.[28] These writers, and others like Brian Abel-Smith and Peter Townsend, forcefully supported the view that the social services should *become* a major agent in the battle against inequality.[29]

In the 1950s a similar kind of analysis and discussion began to take place with regard to education, where continuing inequalities began to be subjected to detailed investigation. An official *Early Leaving* report in 1954, for instance, showed that working-class children fared badly in competition for access to grammar schools, in school performance and in length of school life.[30] In the same year a group of sociologists based mainly on the London School of Economics began to show that working-class children were not benefiting as many people had expected from the 'secondary education for all' provided under the 1944 Act. Working-class children were under-represented in the grammar school population, and, for reasons only beginning to be explored, did less well than middle-class children in various kinds of test of intelligence and of attainment.[31] Jean Floud and her colleagues, investigating south-west Hertfordshire and Middlesbrough, reported in *Social Class and Educational Opportunity* (1956) a significant variation, according to their fathers' occupational background, in the chance of children going to grammar schools – with and without the eleven-plus examination.[32] The Crowther Report on the age group *15 to 18* confirmed that 'among the families of manual workers it is still the exception for a child to stay at school after he is legally free to do so'.[33] Optimistic forecasts of the equalizing powers of the 1944 Act were proving as disappointing as some of those relating to the welfare services. The secondary modern school was clearly identified as the school for the children who failed at eleven-plus, and failure was being increasingly shown to be closely related to aspects of family and social class background.

The London School of Economics studies also cast doubt upon the opportunity for people to move from one job level to another, in spite of theoretically open access and the myth of high levels of job mobility.[34] Certainly in the early 1950s, and for a considerable period afterwards – as other surveys have shown – the higher professional élites, such as judges, senior civil servants, company directors and bishops, were still recruited from a very narrow base.[35]

As we have seen, sociological research in the 1950s was beginning to reveal a vast reservoir of untapped potential. This was true, for example, of children who in spite of their abilities were leaving school early because their parents expected, or needed them to contribute to the family income, or as a result of other social pressures. It was true of girls who, in spite of their qualifications, were not able to go to university or to stay on in the sixth form. These high rates of wastage were discussed increasingly in terms of social justice, but also with mounting urgency in terms of economic inefficiency. This was the era of Sputnik, the armaments race, advancing technology and the consumer revolution. No nation could afford to waste its resources. To keep abreast of her neighbours Britain needed both to foster her manpower and to develop her research potential. The Labour Party printed in bold type in its 1958 election manifesto:

In this age of the Sputnik, first-rate education, open to every child, is not only desirable. It is essential to our national survival.[36]

The argument about educational equality frequently turned into an argument about manpower. The country needed to recruit talent from a much wider base, to change attitudes and expectations, as well as to remove financial and other obstacles in the path to personal and social improvement. In the late fifties and early sixties people generally experienced a sense of greater openness and opportunity, and many adjusted their expectations accordingly. Behind the consumer boom and the new ambitions of the wealthier working class, however, regional and social class differences in opportunities were still very real. One of the consequences of seeing poverty in the broader context of issues to do with inequality was to be a new concept of aid, based, as we shall see, on notions of 'positive discrimination' and 'compensatory benefits'.

Social differences in income and opportunity became an issue of major importance in the late 1950s, against the background of a widely held assumption that affluence was equalizing, that we were all becoming middle class (the theory of *embourgeoisement*). Without accepting the latter theory, Goldthorpe and Lockwood began in the early 1960s to point to ways in which a certain convergence of the middle and working class was taking place. They pointed to four main areas of change in the pattern of social stratification since the mid-nineteenth century. They suggested that: the gap separating property-owning groups and wage-earners had been reduced; the range of income differentials had narrowed; mobility had increased within and between the main social groups; and differences in consumption had become blurred.[37] Despite some narrowing of extreme differences in wealth and opportunity along the lines of their theory, the precise statistics of income and capital distribution around 1960 nevertheless revealed marked differences between the various social levels.

Inequality between occupational groups can be discussed in several different ways. Since the late 1950s, for instance, sociologists have become more interested in differences in work conditions and job prospects.[38] They have also accumulated an impressive array of statistics to prove the existence of a wide gap between the rich and the poor. John Westergaard, for instance, in a paper published in 1965, calculated that while unskilled workers received approximately 19 per cent of the average earnings of higher professional workers in 1913–14, in 1960 they still earned only 26 per cent. What is more, while they earned 31 per cent of the average income of managers in the earlier period, they earned only 29 per cent in 1960. Even these figures give only part of the story. They take no account – as Titmuss demonstrated in other connections – of such trends as the rise in the proportion of married people in the population, the growing number of mothers at work, the rise in the proportion of the elderly and retired, the move to the suburbs, the decline of unemployment in the post-war period, and the higher wages earned by teenagers. In different ways such factors had a dramatic impact in the fifties and sixties on the economy of different kinds of family, and on families at different stages in the life cycle. Among those groups which economically appeared to benefit most were middle-aged council house families where both parents were in skilled jobs and where the children had either left home or were contributing to the family economy. These same families, however, once the parents reached retirement, were no longer likely to be well off. Unprotected by a private pension scheme, still having to pay rent for their home, and not possessing any kind of capital investment, they might well find themselves living barely above the subsistence line. It is with this kind of contrast in mind that the importance of other kinds of wealth and opportunity become apparent in the discussion of social distinctions.

The statistics of capital ownership in Britain show the biggest gap between the relative economic position of different social groups – even though earnings have moved closer together for some groups. In 1960 less than 10 per cent of the population owned 83 per cent of all private wealth, the richest 1 per cent receiving over 12 per cent of the total income. At the other end of the scale, one third of all income units had no liquid assets at all.[39] The latter group was not simply under-privileged financially, it was deprived of related privileges, such as being able to buy private education and medical care, being able to choose where to live, and being able to influence one's working schedule and holiday arrangements.

The tax structure in this period, as in the present day, did little to remedy inequalities in personal wealth – and indeed in some respects reinforced them. There was, as we have seen, a net redistribution in favour of the least well-off groups. The total effect of 'perks', like a company car, telephone bills, tax avoidance and tax relief subsidies for house purchase and other expenditure, was to increase inequalities

between non-manual and manual groups.[40] In 1961 the *Stationary*
Chancellor of the Exchequer, Selwyn Lloyd, even raised the
surtax level from £2,000 to £5,000.

If the upper classes were still conspicuously better off in
all these respects, at least the proportion of the population
living in poverty had diminished since the time of Booth, as
much of the research in this period showed. By the mid-
1960s, however, the situation to which Titmuss above all
had drawn attention was clear. Using a standard of 40 per
cent above National Assistance rates as a measure of minimum subsistence, Townsend estimated that in 1964 three
million members of families whose head was in full-time
work, two and a half million persons of pensionable age,
three-quarters of a million fatherless families, three-quarters
of a million chronic sick or disabled and over half a million
families of unemployed fathers, were in poverty. This
amounted to about 14 per cent of the total population. By
basic National Assistance standards about one third of these
groups were in acute poverty. Yet many of them, for reasons
of pride or ignorance, failed to take advantage of all the
benefits to which they were entitled under the National
Assistance Act. Despite their greater objective needs these
poorer groups often failed to receive their fair share of other
kinds of allowances: only a small proportion of families
entitled to rent rebates actually obtained them, for example.
Nearly half of the children eligible for free school meals in
fact paid for them. These families also made fewer demands
on the National Health Service and derived fewer returns
from the state educational system.[41]

These statistics on income distribution and social security
payments reveal a state of affairs in which, even if most
families had 'never had it so good', by 1956 people were still
very far from being equal – whatever their politicians might
claim. John Westergaard summed up the situation in 1965
by suggesting that inequalities had only been marginally
reduced. However, he explained, since these inequalities
operated in areas of expenditure increasingly removed from
those of bare subsistence living and against a background of
generally rising levels of real income, their effect was 'less
transparent'.[42] Part of this reduced transparency was

undoubtedly due to new consumption standards. Writing in 1959, Mark Abrams, a leading market research director, described the shift in spending habits since the war:

> The proportion of families with a vacuum cleaner has doubled, ownership of refrigerators has trebled, owners of washing machines have increased tenfold; we have stocked our homes with vastly more furniture, radiograms, carpets, space heaters, water heaters, armchairs, light fittings, lawn mowers, television sets, and now tape recorders and film projectors ... all this means that for the first time in modern British history the working-class home, as well as the middle-class home, has become a place that is warm, comfortable ... in fact, pleasant to live in.[43]

The contrast with the pre-war period was remarkable; that with the middle of the nineteenth century was even more extreme. Young and Willmott comment that people who used to live in the overcrowded East End of London were 'home centred' in that they spent much of their time, at least at night, with their families: 'but people whose standards were not the lowest must have found it hard to call it a home or preserve there the old rules and sanctions of the rural communities which many of them had left. For those who emulated Queen Victoria, with her nine children but without her palaces, the room must have been something they were glad to escape from.'[44]

Whether we can infer from the trends that Mark Abrams describes that people were in any real sense more equal at the end of the 1950s is highly debatable. As Brian Jackson, in a study of northern working-class communities, points out: 'Almost everyone shops sometimes at Marks and Spencer', and 'almost everybody might have the same washing powder in their kitchen', but if the crucial element in social difference is income and working conditions, 'it is hard to see how using the same mass products as people more prosperous and powerful than yourself breaks the class barriers ... the merest glance at half-a-dozen of the major London stores – Harrods, Heals, Liberty's, Selfridges, John Lewis,

25 *Plaistow*

C & A, tells you that they reflect, serve and perhaps reinforce quite different social groups'.[45]

In the late 1950s families differed not only in terms of income level and consumption standards – their life chances also varied considerably. Differences in infant mortality, for instance, were still quite marked, although after 1960 regional differences became more significant than those based on social class alone. In 1950 the infant mortality rate was 16·9 per 1,000 in Social Class I, while in Social Classes IV and V the comparable rates were 31·7 and 36·0 respectively. By 1965 this margin had been considerably reduced. The neonatal death rate[46] was 9·2 per 1,000 for Social Classes I and II combined, compared with a rate of 13·2 for Social Classes IV and V. Only in the northern region did the traditional type of social class gradient exist, showing statistically significant differences between each of the social groups. Elsewhere in the country the effects of poverty in maintaining differences in infant mortality appeared for the first time to have been seriously weakened by the beginning of the 1960s.

Infectious diseases in childhood, and morbidity and mortality rates in general, showed parallel variations, just as they did in the 1840s or 1910s or 1930s. They also revealed changing and socially mobile fashions in treatment and diagnosis.[47] These variations hinged on the whole pattern of living of different social groups. Since these patterns were constantly changing, so did the incidence of disease. The development of preventive measures like sanitation, vaccination and immunization, improved living standards and nutrition, school and factory inspection, advances in curative medicine and surgery and more effective drugs and antibiotics, were important in reducing the overall incidence of deaths from infectious diseases and from degenerative organic conditions. But because of changing working conditions, the faster pace of life in post-war society, and changed eating, transport and leisure habits in and after the 1950s, there has been an increase in deaths from other kinds of illness. Among middle-aged, middle-class males, for example, deaths from cardio-vascular diseases and from cancer have increased considerably.

While there have been great changes in the care of the mentally ill in recent years (particularly since the Mental Health Act of 1959), significant social differences remain in this respect. The lower down the social scale one goes, the higher is the number of mental patients who are referred to hospital, and the fewer the number of 'self-selecting' patients. The kind of treatment which is available for the mentally ill is also likely to depend on social class. Middle- and upper-class patients can usually resort to private care, while working-class patients have to make do with over-crowded and often old-fashioned State-run hospitals, which may confirm illness rather than cure it.[48] Many sociologists have come to reject the medical illness analogy, and see mental illness as a form of deviance in the same way as more obvious kinds of crime and delinquency – often growing out of the same conditions. All of them show characteristic social patterns, in relation both to their incidence and to the forms of treatment (or punishment) imposed. Whereas most working-class offences are offences against property, 'white-collar crimes' include tax evasion, fraud and – most frequent of all – motoring offences.[49] While the majority of working-class 'criminals' are sent to prison or put on probation, many middle-class 'offenders' are fined or sent with a recommendation for psychiatric help. In these, as in other areas of social experience, viewpoints, definitions and categories are relative, and dependent on the perceptions of the observers. Inequalities and differences are not just a question of absolute statistics, they are relative conditions.[50]

Social class and stratification

The concept of social class, as we have seen, was a product of the large-scale social and economic changes which oc-curred at the end of the eighteenth century. Asa Briggs indicates that 'before the rise of modern industry writers on society spoke of "ranks", "orders" and "degrees", or, when they wished to direct attention to particular economic groupings, of "interests" '.[51] By the mid-nineteenth cen-tury, as the habit of classification spread from the natural to the social sciences, and as perceptions of deep and extensive social rifts sharpened, class labels had become attached to wide social groups. The labels given to the different social groups – 'upper', 'middle' and 'working' – reflected a characteristically British compromise, which attempted to avoid any implication of inferiority to those in the lowest ranks, an attempt to reconcile 'the egalitarian sentiment of democracy with the persistent fact of inequality'.[52]

What class *meant* in the nineteenth century, and what it means now, is a relationship – one which for any individual may be a constantly changing and dynamic affair, related to changes in his job situation, marital condition, the age of his children, where he lives, and what he does in his spare time. 'Class' may mean a sense of relationship, a feeling of being relatively privileged or deprived, in economic, social or political terms. It can also mean feeling some kind of solidarity with people in a similar situation and different from – and probably opposed to – other groups. In a situation of changing, and especially disappointed, expectations, people tend to identify themselves more closely with such 'reference groups'.[53]

Classically, as we have seen, the opposition between 'like' and 'unlike' social groups was expressed by Marx in terms of the confrontation between the owners of the means of production and those who were in a wage relationship under them. The realities of present-day job stratification are – and in fact always have been – a good deal more complicated than this. Since the beginning of the nineteenth century, for example, there has always been a significant group of professional workers who, while commanding little or no personal political or economic power, have always occupied an élite status in British society. If we remember that class identities are not just made up of social and economic differences, but also reflect important dimensions of choice and security (as reflected, for example, in different working conditions, promotion and retirement prospects and opportunities to determine one's life style), then the basic opposition between a minority who possess such choice and security, and the majority who are without them, still persists. Absence of such security was in the nineteenth century the mainspring from which collective trade union activities developed. In the mid-1970s it was the basis of concerted community action – for instance on behalf of welfare claimants, single-parent families and other minority groups.

Class labels tell us about one overarching aspect of people's social relationships and about one sort of interaction. In contemporary society there are a myriad status differences – to do with life style, spending habits, leisure interests, religious or voluntary group activities, manners, accent, place of residence and so on – which cut across the broad division into social class groups. These are impossible to rank in order or even to assess objectively, since they depend on subjectively perceived differences along dimensions of taste and personal preference.[54] For many families, however, they may be more important than class definitions in deciding their pattern of relationships outside the home – for example, visiting, entertaining and shared leisure pursuits.

[margin note: no longer 3 clear distinct groups.]

In order to simplify the confusion created by social class and social status labels, a number of sociologists have begun to work with new terms. Margaret Stacey, for example, who completed two major surveys in Banbury in 1948–51 and 1966–8,[55] found it useful to make a distinction between what she called the 'traditionalists' and the 'non-traditionalists'. The former were defined as those who were part of the traditional social structure (the old market town and its activities), and who lived by traditional values. They included a large proportion of families who had married locally and families with a low rate of emigration. 'Non-traditionalists', on the other hand (mainly those who had come to Banbury after 1945 to work in the new aluminium factory and at the Birds plant), had no fixed roots. They tended to be both socially and geographically mobile. With this broad categorization in the background, Mrs Stacey located two main upper-class groups in Banbury in the early 1950s – the 'county' and 'gentry'; two middle-class groups – the 'burgesses' (local tradesmen, professionals and small business owners) and the 'spiralists' (people engaged in professional and managerial work in large-scale organizations); and three working-class groups – the 'roughs', the 'ordinary' and the 'respectable'.

This kind of sub-classification within the main social levels was useful, not only for diagnostic purposes but also because of the close links it revealed between social position, aspirations, mobility and achievement. In different parts of the country, particularly in big cities, and even within the different sub-groups, other sociologists drew attention to equally important distinctions.[56] Different kinds and amounts of political and community involvement, for instance, suggest further possible sub-groupings. Take the case of two men, both working in the same place at the same job. One has no outside interests, while the other is chairman of the local branch of a national party, he is a magistrate, a school governor, a director of the football club, an elder of the church, owns his own home and has three children who have been to university. The simple class label, or even the distinction between 'ordinary' and 'respectable' is clearly inadequate in describing the social position and relationships of both of these men.

For the purpose of social planning, as well as in attempting to explore the way different groups respond, say, to educational opportunities, sociologists have continued to find it useful, nevertheless, to use some kind of objectively measurable criteria for social groups and a commonly agreed ranking order. Class description based on occupation does in a general way help in this, whatever more refined indices may coexist with it. In the presence of all the complex variables the concept of social class has continued to prove useful to sociologists because 'it captures the reality that the intricate interplay of all these variables creates different basic conditions of life at different levels of the social order'.[57]

Despite the practicality of choosing occupational criteria in this analysis, the resulting scales are not entirely satisfactory. On the fivefold occupational scale used by the Registrar General in 1961, for example, 51 per cent of the population were assigned to Social Class III.[58] Inevitably, in such a large grouping, there were considerable differences between the levels of occupation represented in this group. It was largely for this reason that a new kind of scale was introduced for the first time with the 1961 Census, distinguishing specifically between agricultural and non-agricultural, manual and non-manual, supervisory and non-supervisory jobs.[59] The table below shows how the adult male population was distributed in 1961 and 1971.

Socio-economic groups	1961 %	1971 %
1 Employers & managers (large establishments)	3·6	3·5
2 Employers & managers (small establishments)	5·9	7·9
3 Professional – self employed	0·8	0·9
4 Professional – employees	2·8	3·9
5 Intermediate non-manual	3·8	5·3
6 Junior non-manual	12·5	11·9
7 Personal service	0·9	1·0
8 Foremen & supervisors – manual	3·3	3·5
9 Skilled manual	30·4	29·1
10 Semi-skilled	14·7	12·6
11 Unskilled	8·6	7·9
12 Own account workers (not professional)	3·6	4·3
13 Farmers – employers and managers	1·0	0·9
14 Farmers – own account	1·0	0·9
15 Agricultural workers	2·3	1·6
16 Armed forces	1·9	1·4
Unclassified	2·9	3·4
	100	100

Source: Social Trends No. 6, 1975, p. 30.

Once the criteria of social grouping have been selected, as for the Registrar General's socio-economic groups, there is a second problem – that of devising an acceptable hierarchical scale. The ranking of occupations in terms of their prestige does not correspond exactly to their ranking in terms of income and education.[60] Although these three factors are normally fairly closely related, other variables (birth, for example, or inborn qualities, such as physical appearance and skin colour, or personal authority) are also important. One sociologist has noted the following assumptions which

Scale acc
to subjective
view

seem to affect status judgements: (1) white collar work is
superior to manual work; (2) self-employment is superior to
employment by others; (3) clean occupations are superior to
dirty ones; (4) the importance of business occupations
depends on the size of the business; (5) personal service is
degrading and it is better to be employed by an enterprise
than to be employed in the same work by a person.[61] But
these are middle-class assumptions, which means that most
of the scales in use today probably perpetuate a view of
society that is not necessarily consistent with the one that
would be taken by the majority of the population. Vulner-
ability to unemployment, redundancy, and ease of occupational and geographical mobility were criteria that
assumed major importance in this respect in the economic
conditions of the mid-1970s.

One of the most systematic attempts in the early post-war
years to test the acceptability of a particular ranking scale
was that carried out by Moser and Hall in preparation for
the various surveys of social mobility conducted by David
Glass and his team in the early 1950s.[62] Not surprisingly,
the researchers found that there was a wide measure of
agreement over the ranking of occupations at the extremes
of their scale. More than four-fifths of the sample agreed,
for instance, on the grades which should be allocated to the
medical officer of health, the company director, the dock
labourer and the roadsweeper. For about half of the occupations listed, at least 60 per cent of the sample were in
agreement. Occupations like fitter, coal hewer, civil servant,
minister, actor, policeman and school teacher, on the other
hand, showed a very wide spread of views. With such occupations as civil servant and actor the lack of consensus
reflects the wide range of jobs which may be included under
these titles. In other cases over which respondents
disagreed, real differences in status perceptions seem to
have been in operation.

Such differences were certainly evident in a survey which
Willmott and Young carried out among a working-class
sample in East London in 1956.[63] Their respondents fell
into two categories: the so-called 'normal' and the
'deviants'. Among the latter, who formed about a quarter of

the total, there was a marked tendency for skilled manual jobs to be elevated in status while certain marginal non-manual occupations were lowered. The reason, the authors suggested, is that in their evaluations the 'deviants' over-estimated 'social contribution', at the expense of other criteria like 'ability', 'education', 'remuneration' and 'social milieu'.

In an effort to overcome some of the difficulties involved in working with occupational scales, and because no single standard seems to fit or suit everyone, some sociologists had by 1960 already abandoned the use of objective criteria. Instead, or in addition, they asked their respondents to assess their own class position – and sometimes that of their neighbours as well. This proved particularly helpful in try-ing to distinguish between the upper-working class and the lower-middle class – groups which added up to almost half of the total population. But there were disadvantages with this method also. People's responses depend, for example, on the number and names of the alternative ranks among which they are told to locate themselves. There is a big difference between offering the choice 'upper, middle and *lower*', as against 'upper, middle and *working*' – and also between either of these scales and one comprising the more complicated 'upper-upper, lower-upper, upper-middle . . .' type of scale. A further difficulty which sociologists have become more aware of recently is that of knowing whether two people who assess themselves as belonging to a par-ticular class regard the term as meaning the same thing. A school teacher may assign herself to the middle class and think of it as consisting of educated, well-spoken, non-manual workers, while a car assembly worker does the same thing on the grounds that he considers anyone who earns, say, over £4,000 a year to be middle class. Another diffi-culty is that of bias and upgrading.

Class perspectives also vary according to the distance between the respondent and the groups of people whose position he is being asked to assess, and a very wide margin of distortion exists in judgements of marginal status – those immediately above or below an individual on the social scale. Such distortion can be explained in terms of class reference groups. Elizabeth Bott sees the individual himself as an active agent in the process of class assessment. He does not simply internalize the norms of classes that have an independent existence. He takes in the norms of certain actual groups which he encounters in his home and work life and elsewhere, evaluates them on the basis of the kinds of relationships they involve him in, and then he constructs a hierarchy of wider reference groups in the light of which he defines his own position.[64]

In the late 1950s and 1960s such discussions of class, status and stratification accompanied attempts to understand the underlying trends in affluence and patterns of inequality. Whilst poverty and inequality were being 'rediscovered', and their mechanisms analysed, there were also social theorists who pointed to the irrelevance of Marxist theories, to the 'end of ideology' and to the convergence of social groups. The theory of 'managerial revolution' continued to influence the discussion. Using the main criteria of consumer spending, home conditions and earnings, the supporters of the theory of *embourgeoisement* stressed the marked, or the gradual, acquisition of middle-class characteristics by the working class, and often denied the validity of the class concepts themselves.[65] Others continued to point to basic economic and social differences, in welfare benefits and housing, and, see table opposite, in conditions of employment.[66]

Differences were real and apparent. To John Vaizey in 1962 society was 'extremely stratified; power quite obviously lies with the possessors of vast wealth; with the hereditary and social advantages which are theirs, they rule us ... there are singularly few sources of power in this country which to any great degree are yet available to those outside the category of those born to inherited wealth or established position'.[67] To W. G. Runciman, even while pointing to important aspects of social convergence, the biggest single social difference was still 'between the so-called working class and so-called middle class ... the closer manual and non-manual workers appear to be approaching each other the more this can reinforce their difference in outlook and their disinclination to regard each other as equals'.[68] If the

Terms and conditions of employment (percentage of establishments where the condition applies)

Selected conditions of employment	Operatives	Foremen	Clerical workers	Technicians	Management Middle	Senior
Formal sick pay scheme available	46	65	63	65	63	63
Sick pay provided for more than 3 months	49	58	55	57	65	67
Coverage by formal pension scheme	67	94	90	94	96	95
Pension calculated as fixed amount per year of service	48	18	16	14	13	12
Holidays, excluding public holidays, of 15 days or more a year	38	71	74	77	84	88
Choice of time at which holidays taken	35	54	76	76	84	88
Time off with pay for domestic reasons	29	84	84	86	92	93
Period of notice of dismissal in excess of statutory requirements	13	29	26	29	53	61
Clocking on to record attendance	92	33	24	29	2	4
Pay deduction as penalty for lateness	90	20	8	11	1	—
Warning followed by dismissal for frequent absence without leave	94	86	94	92	74	67

embourgeoisement theory was wrong, it is not hard to see why it seemed so plausible in the years of affluence, and following the austerity of the early post-war years. It is similarly not hard to see why more recent studies of social class relationships have shifted from a 'convergence' back to a conflict-centred view. Instead of merely ascribing social class labels on the basis of fixed criteria like job or income, sociologists have become more concerned to take account of what people themselves feel about their social position. This has resulted in a more complex, less idealized, picture of social relationships, based both on social class and on different patterns of status, style of life and social activities and opportunities.

What this analysis reveals is not just a conflict of data, but one of attitude and ideology. Uncertainties within the social sciences reflected wider political and social uncertainties. The period of upheaval, as we described the late 1950s earlier in this chapter, was one in which social and political ideologies came into direct confrontation. The late 1950s and early 1960s was a period in which protest took on a new dimension, and in which the bomb generation became identified with a new culture to match its new politics. Everything discussed in this chapter was paralleled by and enmeshed with this range of political and cultural phenomena. Although in the late 1960s and 1970s different emphases were to emerge, the cultural and political legacies of the earlier period were to be strong. It is to these features of the 1950s and 1960s that we turn in the next chapter.

Notes

1 GEOFFREY BARRACLOUGH *An Introduction to Contemporary History*, pp. 13, 35–7 (London, 1964; 1967 Penguin edition).

2 CHRISTOPHER BOOKER *The Neophiliacs: a study of the revolution in English life in the fifties and sixties*, p. 79 (London, 1969).

3 LABOUR PARTY *Signposts for the Sixties*, p. 7 (London, 1961).

4 WORKERS' EDUCATIONAL ASSOCIATION *Aspects of Adult Education*, p. 3 (London, 1960). See also C. P. SNOW, *The Two Cultures and the Scientific Revolution* (Cambridge, 1959), especially section 4, 'The rich and the poor'.

5 BOOKER *The Neophiliacs*, p. 108.

6 ROBERT BENDINER 'The jittery Fifties', *New Statesman*, 2 January 1960, p. 7.

7 CONSERVATIVE PARTY *United for Peace and Progress*, p. 7 (London, 1955).

8 LABOUR PARTY *Britain Belongs to You*, p. 1 (London, 1959).

9 REYNER BANHAM 'The world of the Brutalists: opinion and intention in British architecture, 1951–60', *The Texas Quarterly*, Special Issue, 2 (*Image of Britain*), 1967, p. 2.

10 IAN NAIRN *Outrage*, p. 1 (reprint of June 1955 special number of the *Architectural Review*). See also the companion volume, *Counter-Attack against Subtopia*.

11 *Social Changes in Britain: the full survey*, in *New Society*, 27 December 1962, pp. 26–8.

12 BURNETT *Plenty and Want*, p. 267.

13 Ibid., p. 280.

14 *Social Changes in Britain*, p. 27.

15 See, for example, MARGARET STACEY *Tradition and Change*, Ch. 1 (London, 1960).

16 *Social Changes in Britain*, p. 27.

17 JOHN H. GOLDTHORPE and DAVID LOCKWOOD 'Affluence and the British class structure', *The Sociological Review*, Vol. 11, 1963. See also their 'Not so bourgeois after all', *New Society*, 18 October 1962, pp. 18–19, and JOHN H. GOLDTHORPE *et al. The Affluent Worker in the Class Structure* (Cambridge, 1969).

18 See RUTH GLASS *Newcomers* (London, 1961).

19 PHILIP GIBBS *How Now, England?*, p. 46 (London, 1958). (Ch. III is entitled 'The invaded island'.

20 C. A. R. CROSLAND *The Future of Socialism*, especially Chs. I–III, VI (London, 1956).

21 HUGH GAITSKELL *Recent Developments in British Socialist Thinking*, pp. 1–2 (London [1956]).

22 CHARLES MADGE 'From small beginnings', *Times Literary Supplement*, 4 April 1968, pp. 338–9.

23 See RICHARD M. TITMUSS *Birth, Poverty and Wealth* (London, 1943).

24 RICHARD M. TITMUSS *The Irresponsible Society*, p. 3 (London, 1960).

25 RICHARD M. TITMUSS 'The incomes of the rich', *New Statesman*, 31 August 1962, pp. 249–50. See also *Irresponsible Society*, p. 11, and *Income Distribution and Social Change*, *passim* (London, 1962).

26 *Income Distribution and Social Change*, p. 198.

27 DOROTHY COLE WEDDERBURN 'Poverty in Britain today – the evidence', *Sociological Review*, Vol. 10, 1962, pp. 265–79. See also, for discussion of attempts to define the 'poverty line', pp. 257–8, 276–9.

28 AUDREY HARVEY *Casualties of the Welfare State*, pp. 3–4, 7, 11 (London, 1960).

29 BRIAN ABEL-SMITH *Freedom in the Welfare State*, p. 9 (London, 1964).

30 CENTRAL ADVISORY COUNCIL FOR EDUCATION *Early Leaving* (1954), extract in HAROLD SILVER (ed.) *Equal Opportunity in Education*, pp. 129–35 (London, 1973).

31 See contributions by H. T. HIMMELWEIT and others to D. V. GLASS (ed.) *Social Mobility in Britain* (London, 1954). Extracts from this and some of the following are contained in SILVER *Equal Opportunity in Education*.

32 J. E. FLOUD (ed.), A. H. HALSEY and F. M. MARTIN *Social Class and Educational Opportunity* (London, 1956).

33 MINISTRY OF EDUCATION *15 to 18*, p. 9 (London, 1959).

34 See GLASS *Social Mobility in Britain*, Chs. VIII–XII.

35 See T. J. H. BISHOP with RUPERT WILKINSON *Winchester and the Public School Elite*, Ch. 2 (London, 1967) and ANTHONY SAMPSON *The New Anatomy of Britain* (London, 1971).

36 LABOUR PARTY *The Future Labour Offers You* (London, 1958).

37 GOLDTHORPE and LOCKWOOD 'Affluence and the British class structure', pp. 133–5.

38 See, for example, DOROTHY WEDDERBURN and CHRISTINE CRAIG 'Relative deprivation in work', in DOROTHY WEDDERBURN (ed.) *Poverty, Inequality and Class Structure*, pp. 141–64 (Cambridge, 1974).

39 See A. B. ATKINSON *Unequal Shares, Wealth in Britain* (London, 1972), p. 24, and for a general account of more recent trends BARBARA WOOTTON *Contemporary Britain*, pp. 11–26 (London, 1970).

40 See TITMUSS *Income Distribution and Social Change*.

41 See RICHARD M. TITMUSS *Essays on 'The Welfare State'*, Ch. 2 (London, 1958).

42 JOHN WESTERGAARD 'The withering away of class: a contemporary myth', in PERRY ANDERSON and ROBIN BLACKBURN (eds.) *Towards Socialism*, p. 84 (London, 1965).

43 MARK ABRAMS 'The home-centred society', *The Listener*, 26 November 1959, p. 914.

44 YOUNG and WILLMOTT *The Symmetrical Family*, pp. 37–8.

45 BRIAN JACKSON *Working Class Community*, p. 164 (London, 1968).

46 That is, deaths at birth and during the first week of life. Post-neonatal deaths are those occurring for the remainder of the first year of life. The infant mortality rate is equal to neonatal plus post-neonatal deaths.

47 See MICHAEL SUSSER 'Social medicine in Britain: studies of social class', in A. T. WELFORD et al. (eds.) *Society: Problems and Methods of Study* (London, 1962).

48 See THOMAS SCHEFF *Being Mentally Ill* (London, 1966).

49 See EDWIN H. SUTHERLAND 'White collar crime', in ALEX INKELES (ed.) *Readings on Modern Sociology* (New Jersey, 1966); and DAVID M. DOWNES *The Delinquent Solution* (London, 1966).

50 See LAURIE TAYLOR *Deviance and Society*, Chs. 2–4 (London, 1973).

51 ASA BRIGGS 'The language of "class" in early nineteenth-century England', in ASA BRIGGS and JOHN SAVILLE (eds.) *Essays in Labour History*, p. 43 (London, 1967).

52 YOUNG and WILLMOTT *The Symmetrical Family*, p. 11.

53 W. G. RUNCIMAN *Relative Deprivation and Social Justice*, pp. 25–6 (London, 1966; 1972 Penguin edition).

54 See J. A. JACKSON (ed.) *Social Stratification* (London, 1968), especially papers by EDWARD SHILS, MARK ABRAMS and T. H. MARSHALL.

55 STACEY *Tradition and Change*; MARGARET STACEY et al. *Power, Persistence and Change* (London, 1975).

56 See ELIZABETH BOTT *Family and Social Network* (London, 1957) and R. E. PAHL 'The two class village', *New Society*, 27 Feb. 1964, quoted in ERIC BUTTERWORTH and DAVID WEIR (eds.) *The Sociology of Modern Britain*, pp. 234–8 (London, 1970).

57 M. L. KOHN, 'Social class and parent–child relationships', quoted in D. F. SWIFT 'Social class and educational adaptation', in H. J. BUTCHER (ed.) *Educational Research in Britain*, p. 290 (London, 1968).

58 See CENTRAL STATISTICAL OFFICE 'Social commentary: social class', pp. 10–32 in *Social Trends*, No. 6, 1975.

59 See OFFICE OF POPULATION CENSUSES AND SURVEYS *Classification of Occupations 1970* for an explanation of the way occupations are classified in detail.

60 See J. H. GOLDTHORPE and K. HOPE *The Social Grading of Occupations: a new approach and scale* (London, 1974).

61 THEODORE CAPLOW *The Sociology of Work*, pp. 42–9 (New York, 1964 edition).

62 See C. A. MOSER and J. R. HALL 'The social grading of occupations', in GLASS *Social Mobility in Britain*, Ch. 2.

63 PETER WILLMOTT and MICHAEL YOUNG 'Social grading by manual workers', *British Journal of Sociology*, December 1956, p. 337.

64 ELIZABETH BOTT *Family and Social Network*, p. 167 (London, 1957). See also W. M. WILLIAMS *The Sociology of an English Village*, pp. 107–9 (London, 1956) for distorted judgements of class position in the north-country village of Gosforth.

65 For the theme of *embourgeoisement* see F. ZWEIG *The Worker in an Affluent Society*, London, 1961. For a discussion of some parallel American themes, see the widely discussed DANIEL BELL *The End of Ideology* (New York, 1960). The most detailed analysis of British experience is in the various books and articles by Goldthorpe and Lockwood.

66 From CHRISTINE CRAIG *Men in Manufacturing Industry*, quoted in WEDDERBURN and CRAIG 'Relative deprivation in work', p. 144.

67 JOHN VAIZEY *Education in a Class Society: the Queen and her horses reign*, p. 1 (London, 1962).

68 W. G. RUNCIMAN 'Towards a classless society?', *The Listener*, 15 July 1965, p. 77. Runciman advised anyone who thought that 'we're all middle-class now' to go canvassing in a working-class district, drink in some public bars, spend a day in an engineering works or walk down to the dockside.

8 Authority and opposition

Cultural change

Two fundamental features of the late 1950s and early 1960s
– cultural and political change – merit separate discussion.
We have sketched in the background to these changes, but it
is important to emphasize how deeply they in turn
influenced the context of social opinion, action and structure
in the period after 1956. Many seemingly settled elements in
post-war society were being called into question at levels,
and in ways, which were profoundly disturbing to some of
those who had become adult in the years before the atomic
bomb and the cold war 'balance of terror'.

In the late 1950s and early 1960s cultural and political
changes were closely related, and at the heart of both was a
protest, articulated more or less explicitly, against dominant
cultural and political values. Both were associated with the
inter-generational differences revealed and sharpened after
1945, but which became most clearly expressed in terms of
conflict from 1956. In cultural terms the importance of the
year 1956 is measured by the arrival of skiffle and rock-and-
roll, by Elvis Presley's *Heartbreak Hotel* and the launching
of Tommy Steele. Concepts such as 'teenage culture', 'pop

music' and 'youth' suddenly acquired new meanings. A new awareness rapidly developed of an autonomous world of cultural activity peopled by the younger generation and their idols, engaged in new kinds of ritual and rhythm, seeking different standards for their activities, dress and behaviour. That it did so was an indication of the disjunction between the forms of mass culture available in the early 1950s and the needs of a generation coming to maturity in a different world, and with a different economic basis from that of their parents.

One of the important aspects of the mid-1950s was a growing sense of duality, of a coexistence and confrontation between old and new. Richard Hoggart, publishing his *The Uses of Literacy* in 1957, offered the time what it recognized as a picture of some of its basic social features. Hoggart divided his book, in fact, into two parts – 'An "Older" Order' and 'Yielding Place to New', contrasting the warm cultural world of traditional working-class life with that of 'The Newer Mass Art', the 'Candy-Floss World', the 'Juke-Box Boys'. Hoggart and others went on to explore in detail the world of mass culture, and the difficulties of relating it to the accepted standards of 'high culture'.[1] The New Left, a movement of socialists discontented with the rigidities of communism or with the half-heartedness of the Labour Party on major issues like nuclear disarmament, was sharply aware of the pains of a society caught between conflicting international and internal forces. Stuart Hall, describing the marked visual contrasts in old and new architecture, captured the sense of astonishment at the way 'old and new physical environments coexist within a single borough. Here are the old two-storey brick dwellings of a working-class suburb . . . there are the new eight-storey flats of an L.C.C. housing estate, enclosed in a grass-and-concrete jig-saw', the 1880s-built school, and the glass-and-steel comprehensive school under construction.[2]

Social and ethical questions relating to the right use of leisure were coming under increasing scrutiny. 'Instead of worrying about other people's living conditions,' said Sir John Wolfenden, 'those with a "social conscience" now worried about other people's leisure, about films, about whether it was right to spend money on football pools, about the increase in juvenile crime and so on.'[3] In the late 1940s and early 1950s, however, questions of mass culture were relatively ignored and not areas of important public controversy. 'Trends' and 'fashions' were noticed, but a sense of major change did not develop until the middle of the 1950s. The spread of television was now paralleled by a serious decline in cinema attendance. Whereas in 1950 4·3 per cent of homes had television sets, the figure was 49·4 per cent in 1956 (and was to be over 90 per cent by 1964).[4] Cinema attendance declined accordingly, from 1,635 million admissions in 1946 to 1,396 million in 1950 (and then down to 515 million in 1960). In 1950 77 per cent of cinemas were still changing their programmes two or three times a week.[5] Behind this struggle for allegiance, however, lay a firmly established overall pattern of mass communications and culture, in which a shift was taking place from the verbal to the visual, and from the public place of entertainment to the home. The radio and the cinema, while eclipsed, maintained strong positions and, as one commentator put it in 1962, with 10 million visits a week the cinema remained 'a social and cultural force'.[6] What the cinema and the television and other forms of popular entertainment had to offer, however, had not kept pace with the appetites of a younger generation inheriting a new sort of world. Much of the popular culture was still either post-war escapism or already nostalgia about the war itself. A list of the best British films of 1954–5, for example, included *The Dam Busters*, *The Deep Blue Sea*, *Summer Madness*, *Doctor at Sea*, *Escapade*, *Footsteps in the Fog*, *Carrington V.C.* and *Out of the Clouds*, and the best of American films included *The Barefoot Contessa*, *The Rear Window*, *Dragnet* and *The Kentuckian*.[7]

We shall return in a later chapter to developments in mass communications. For the moment the point is the failure of the younger generation to adjust to a widely disseminated visual and oral popular culture, in which they found too few points with which to identify. Nowhere was this more true than in popular music, in an era still dominated by American and British crooners, and an output of radio programmes and gramophone records geared to a

predominantly courting and young-married audience. The
big band, dance music and the Palais were central to the
popular musical life of the late 1940s and early 1950s.
Nothing announced the inter-generational break more emphatically than skiffle and rock-'n'-roll. Ray Gosling experienced the shock waves in Northampton: 'when Bill Haley's
Rock Around the Clock got shown, and the first Elvis . . . It
was the start of something. Everyone felt this – with the
James Dean pictures, and the start of the teenage thing. It
was like the start of a revolution; coming with the big noise
right at the beginning of the whole thing.' In the sixth form
at school he was conscious of 'the whole new thing that was
coming through James Dean and money and Elvis and
Steele and how the world of the back streets was breaking
up and this new was coming through, superimposed on top
of the old. To me the new was something so great, so
wonderful, something that one just had to be part of. For
many of the others it was an attack on both the old they
knew as kids, and the learning and higher things they were
only just beginning to acquire.'[8]

By the end of the 1950s everyone was aware that a cultural transformation had taken place – though not everyone
was as enthusiastic as Ray Gosling about it! The impact he
describes was a lasting one, self-sustaining and continually
challenging. If in the mid-1950s there was a sense of 'the
new', by the end of the decade there was a sense of the
irretrievable passing of at least part of the old. Interpreting
the new age, Royston Ellis wrote in 1961:

The early nineteen-fifties were grim, dull years. There
were no coffee bars, no commercial television stations, no
juke boxes, and no teenage singing stars. The young
people of those years were the same as they had been for
generations previous. They were quiet, ordinary embryo-
adults . . . Their spare time was spent on sport, ballroom
dancing, or on visits to the cinema . . . face to face with
celluloid glamour . . . Their idols were film, not record,
stars. And one of the young film actors the teenage public had started to follow was a boy called . . . James
Dean.[9]

The new generation turned to Dean and Elvis, records and fashions and attitudes which were 'ribald and contemptuous of this modern age into which they have regrettably been born'.[10] A whole new vocabulary became necessary to describe and discuss the youth 'counter-culture' of the fifties and sixties. George Melly called it *Revolt into Style*, Kenneth Leech (borrowing a word from Richard Neville) called it *Youthquake*, and Nik Cohn titled it *Awopbopaloobop Alopbamboom*.[11] From the 1950s the route of teenage self-assertion, a thoroughly international phenomenon, twisted and turned, to be called 'Youth Revolution, Drug Revolution, Sexual Revolution, Political Revolution, Jesus Revolution'.[12] Without profoundly shared class, wartime, post-war and other solidarities and identities, the generation who became 'teenagers' or 'adolescents' in the mid-1950s created their own.[13] Commercialized though the new culture was, it vibrated to the needs of the teenage customer.

Authority under attack

The very existence of a self-reliant youth culture was seen as a threat by many members of older generations. Not until the early 1960s, to some extent with Bob Dylan and then with the Beatles and other teenage heroes, was the pop phenomenon assimilated by a significant proportion of the older generation. In the meantime teenage culture was becoming securely established, on the basis of full employment and teenage affluence. Defining teenagers as young people 'who have reached the age of fifteen but are not yet twenty-five years of age and are unmarried', Mark Abrams analysed the substantial income of Britain's five million teenagers, which in 1959 was 'spent mainly on dress and on goods which form the nexus of teenage gregariousness outside the home. In other words, this is distinctive teenage spending for distinctive teenage ends in a distinctive teenage world.' Nearly 20 per cent of teenage incomes went on clothing and footwear, over 10 per cent on cigarettes and tobacco, 6 per cent on alcohol and 2 per cent on records and gramophone equipment (the last figure being enough to account for 42·5 per cent of all consumer spending under this heading).[14] The adult generation of the early 1950s had seen 'youth' or 'young people' as objects of a cultural and moral responsibility on the part of their elders.[15] The latter were disconcerted to find a new phenomenon, the teenager, not only inhabiting a strange new cultural world, but also exercising influence over major areas of cultural and social changes. When G. M. Carstairs gave the B.B.C.'s Reith lectures in 1962 he described the world of adolescents and their relationships with their parents as having undergone dramatic changes: 'I believe this adolescent world deserves attention not only as a source of trouble, of public concern; but also because adolescents are themselves among the most active, as they are the most vociferous, agents of social change.'[16]

The general consensus about the exercise of authority, and about legitimate ways of challenging it, appeared to be undermined. Writers began to analyse 'the widespread rejection of "established" authority in most developed countries'[17] – even in the Soviet Union. The feature of the teenage phenomenon which aroused anxiety was the wide range of activities associated with it that threatened established values. The rock heroes and music were more explicitly and aggressively sexual than the more home-spun and escapist varieties that had appealed to those reaching adulthood between and during the wars. Violence and delinquency were associated with the teenage revolt – which went on in the early 1960s to produce 'inexplicable' gang warfare between mods and rockers, 'senseless' invasions of seaside towns, vandalism and increasing delinquency of various kinds. The teenage consumption spree included the high-speed motor-cycle and the Italian-style scooter. T. R. Fyvel, writing about *The Insecure Offenders* in 1961, saw the whole phenomenon as related to the break-up of the established bourgeois order, a revolution against the values associated with 'the age of bourgeois exclusiveness which launched what we know as Western industrial civilization'. At the beginning of the sixties 'one had to recognize that not only the privileges of yesterday are being swept away. The whole structure of authority of the bourgeois order has

26 *Teenage 'caff'*

today become suddenly tenuous and is crumbling.' Not all
teenagers participated with the same degree of economic
freedom. Whilst some were impelled towards Presley and
the coffee bars, others were driven to delinquent behaviour.
Teenage culture was part of a range of changes brought
about by the welfare state, affluence and related shifts of
balance in the social structure.[18]

Since the new teenage culture implied or expressed a
rejection of established values, the extent and seriousness of
its anti-parent, anti-Christian, anti-tradition ethic were
received with exaggerated alarm. Its amoral and delinquent
overtones were overstated, and other causes of social disturbance were overlooked. 'The current adult image of youth,'
wrote J. B. Mays in his study of youth culture in 1965, 'if
we may judge by newspaper reports, is one of comparative
irresponsibility, hooliganism and disrespect for established

authority. It is a picture which can only be described as a caricature and one which most young people, naturally enough, resent very strongly. Probably at no other time in the nation's history has there been so much adverse criticism of youth as there is today, and so little understanding, also, of what really is its role and function in society.' There was a real danger of 'inter-generational alienation', with serious social consequences.[19] The over-response to these developments, and the dangers forecast, proved to have been over-simplifications, though the youth phenomenon itself was real enough. If authority was under attack, it was not, however, only from 'youth culture' and what it implied.

The consensus situation was being challenged from other quarters and for other reasons. Different battles were being waged against 'the Establishment', against accepted moral and political values. An intellectual and literary disenchantment had already in the early 1950s produced an explicit attack on the 'normality' of the way things were. In the United States, the Beat Generation of Jack Kerouac and John Clellon Holmes had from the early fifties extolled an underground society which sought experience of all kinds and refused to take part in the power and control structures of American life. Beat literature had a following in Britain, but between 1953 and 1956 a British literary movement labelled the Angry Young Men more explicitly rejected conventional social standards and conventional 'middle-class' behaviour. In John Wain's *Hurry On Down*, in 1953, for example, the hero established a pattern for the movement by accepting and acting on his own sense of disorientation in modern society. He is a graduate rejecting all that his university education implies. He acts impulsively (towards his landlady, his family, the people in the pub) when he cannot tolerate the conventional and meaningless rituals of people with whom he cannot communicate. He is insulting. He refuses to 'wallow, at every crisis, in the emotional midden that his parents had spent twenty-two years in digging'. Wain has no difficulty in explaining his anti-hero: 'He had been equipped with an upbringing devised to meet the needs of a more fortunate age, and then thrust into the jungle of the nineteen-fifties.' He thinks about how to use the first twenty-two years of his life 'as a foundation for the next fifty; and the mushroom-shaped cloud that lived perpetually in a cave at the back of his mind moved forward for a moment to blot out everything else'.[20]

Disorientation, bitterness, refusal to accept old 'normalities' – these were the marks of the Angries. Kingsley Amis offered another version of the theme in *Lucky Jim* in 1954, and in May 1956 the Royal Court Theatre staged the most famous and symbolic product of the movement, John Osborne's *Look Back in Anger*. The hero, Jimmy Porter, incoherently – and to large numbers of people incomprehensibly – violating all the standards of the bourgeois world in which he felt imprisoned, became the standard-bearer of the Angry generation. Others established signposts in ways equally threatening to the established order. A new literature and cinema of working-class life, for example, was heralded by Alan Sillitoe in *Saturday Night and Sunday Morning* in 1958, and a disarming extolment of the virtues of the rebel followed the next year in his *Loneliness of the Long-Distance Runner*. *Roots*, staged and published in 1959, was Arnold Wesker's outstanding picture of the suppressed potential of working-class life. The rebel, the outcast, the outsider (popularized in Colin Wilson's book of that name in 1956), had become central themes of the arts. *Look Back in Anger* coincided with rock-'n'-roll, Suez and Hungary. It typified another reaction against and weakening of traditional forms of authority.

Wain and Osborne spoke for people already uneasy about dominant social and political attitudes, and ready to respond to this kind of protest. That traditional values were under threat was recognized far more widely when, in October 1960, Penguin Books went on trial for its decision to publish D. H. Lawrence's novel, *Lady Chatterley's Lover*, banned in Britain since its first appearance on the continent thirty-two years earlier. The trial was a test of the Obscene Publications Act of the previous year, designed to suppress pornography, but enabling works of artistic merit to go beyond previously permitted publication frontiers. The acquittal of Penguin Books, the sale of the novel, the public

discussion of the 'four-letter words' and descriptions of the
sex act it contained, were a step to further legislation and
relaxation of the concept of 'obscenity' as applied to printed
literature, the cinema and the theatre.[21] There were other
signals of a reinterpretation of sexual and moral values –
notably the Wolfenden Report of 1957 on homosexual
offences and prostitution. By the mid-1950s Brigitte Bardot
was the internationally recognized symbol of eroticism in
the cinema.[22] The 1960s were to see a considerable widening
of the frontiers of sexual and fantasy literature, and an
acceleration of what came to be called the 'permissive
society'.[23] Between 1956 and 1963 pressures for a more liberal approach to sex in the arts, in mass culture and in
society, were increasing, but until the mid-1960s the 'sexual
revolution' was associated predominantly with teenage culture and with the liberal literary intelligentsia (including, for
example, Richard Hoggart and the Bishop of Woolwich,
who appeared for the defence in the *Lady Chatterley* trial).
By the mid-sixties attitudes were polarizing around issues
relating to sexual freedom, and around other aspects of controversial social behaviour – notably smoking marijuana. In
the late 1950s, it is true, tough attitudes were being expressed (for example, on the importation and effects of
American horror comics).[24] But in general the established
criteria for judging works of the printed and visual imagination, and for judging public behaviour, were a subject of
confused and uncertain discussion. Things were 'associated'
with adolescents or with adults, but since no-one was certain about the permanence (or even the extent) of new forms
of expression and behaviour, firm judgements were not
easily made. G. M. Carstairs expressed the situation clearly
in 1962:

> I am going to talk about teenagers and that means, almost
> inevitably, that I am going to talk about violence and sex;
> but . . . I regard the present increase of crimes of violence
> and the present state of confusion in the rules governing
> sexual behaviour as problems not only of adolescence
> but of our society as a whole. I believe that juvenile
> delinquency and sexual promiscuity can be regarded as

27 Brigitte Bardot, 1958

pointers to areas of uncertainty, of confused values, in contemporary adult life.[25]

To established values, however, even uncertainty is a threat. To a post-war middle-aged generation seeking security, the confusion of values represented by teenage and other phenomena, was indeed a threat. In important areas of social and cultural life, authority had come seriously under attack.

Politics and protest

At no time since the seventeenth century (except in the heyday of radical politics in the period 1830–50) has Britain experienced a closer and more obvious association between social, cultural and political change than it did in the late 1950s. The changes we have discussed in this chapter were accompanied by and related to changes in the political climate. Political values were as open to challenge as others. Continuous Conservative government from 1951 to 1964, identified with the 'you've never had it so good', 'I'm alright Jack' philosophy, provoked increasing hostility to aspects of the very affluence it vaunted. Hostility was directed likewise against the complacency and apathy associated with confidence in, and reliance on, economic expansion. It was directed against related 'established' values in international policy, against 'bomb politics', against the testing of atomic (and from 1954 hydrogen) bombs, against complacency about radioactive fallout, and against the dangers of cold war 'brinkmanship'. The political responses of the 1950s and 1960s therefore included strong, and increasingly public, opposition to all forms of established political and economic power. To the new radicalism the traditional organizations of the left were no longer adequate – the Labour Party was too identified with Establishment political manoeuvring, and the Communist Party too discredited by its long identification with Soviet policy – now under sharp attack from the post-Hungary generation of radicals. The political symbol for the new radicalism was the Campaign for Nuclear Disarmament, which, from 1958, expressed a new dimension in extra-parliamentary opposition and protest.

Focused on a single issue, C.N.D. achieved enormous publicity for its fervent rejection of the moral and political implications of atomic warfare. The movement expressed, and won wide support for, a philosophy of positive neutrality, a refusal to take sides in big-power politics, an attempt to identify Britain with the as yet weak association of emergent and uncommitted nations. Bertrand Russell, one of the key figures in the movement, explained that since the late 1940s 'hate was considered synonymous with patriotism, and preparations for war were thought to be the only safeguard of peace. The world was set upon the wrong course, and, in coming years, it travelled further and further along the road towards disaster.'[26] Policies of disaster required emergency and even unconstitutional measures. Russell and others created the Committee of 100, which went beyond C.N.D. in courting prosecution, making direct action and passive resistance significant and lasting features of British political protest movements. Demonstrations and Aldermaston marches were now accompanied by sit-downs in Whitehall and elsewhere. The world moved to the brink of nuclear holocaust when, over Cuba, American and Soviet nuclear missiles confronted each other in October 1962. 28 October of that year was probably the moment in history. when humanity came closest to extinction.

Although nuclear disarmament was the symbol and focus of the new style of political agitation, it also meshed in with another kind of protest. The teenager, the Angry Young Man, the C.N.D. protest marcher, were part of a movement directed against the Establishment. Nothing, in the sustained attacks of a decade or so from 1956, was sacred. Traditional values came to be identified with the Establishment, a more comprehensive concept than the élite or the ruling class. In a symposium he edited on the subject in 1959, Hugh Thomas wrote that 'to those who desire to see the resources and talents of Britain fully developed and extended, there is no doubt that the fusty Establishment, with its Victorian views and standards of judgement, must be destroyed'.[27] Kingsley Martin, in 1963, wrote about *The Crown and the Establishment*, and concluded that the monarchy was 'still the head of the Establishment rather than

28 CND March, 1958

the nation; it still represents a social class and apparently still takes for granted, as Lord Esher had carelessly remarked, that it is "naturally bound to the Tory Party" '.[28] In the same year, with enormous impact, Dr John Robinson, Bishop of Woolwich, published *Honest to God*. In it he strongly questioned the gamut of Church doctrine and opinion on ethical issues, suggesting that Christians were now in conflict with 'the guardians of the established morality, whether ecclesiastical or secular'. The Christian 'may often find himself more in sympathy with those whose standards are different from his own and yet whose rebellion deep down is motivated by the same protest on behalf of the priority of persons and personal relationships'.[29] The mood of challenge was producing a spectrum of attacks on the credentials, ethics and policies of established authority. *Private Eye* magazine and television satire like *That Was the Week that Was*, as well as the creation of life peers (from 1958), were other aspects of the erosion of such authority in the 1960s.

Uncertainty and insecurity coexisted in the late fifties and early sixties with obvious new economic and social potential. On the one hand were Sputnik, launched in 1957, and Gagarin in space in 1960, advances in computer and communications technology, the cracking of the D.N.A. code, and dramatic improvements in medicine and surgery. On the other were H-bomb tests, missile confrontation and the twists and turns of big-power politics. In America and Europe the mood of suspicion and insecurity was heightened by the paranoia of the McCarthy anti-Communist hysteria in the United States, and by the increasing bureaucracy of everyday life. This mood was reflected in the number of influential studies published (especially in the U.S.A., but popular in Britain) on the twin themes of alienation and mass society – in some respects the academic counterparts to *Look Back in Anger*.[30] Existing signposts were untrustworthy. 'They' had made a mess of everything. The counterculture and the protest movement merged (nowhere more than in such songs as Bob Dylan's *Blowing in the Wind* and *The Times they are a-changin'*). In Britain one of the results was a more sustained awareness and analysis of the nature of power and privilege.

Economic and political power

Richard Titmuss pointed out in 1959 that the subject of power had not been fashionable in recent years. He bitterly attacked the reversal of social values that had taken place:

> The iniquities of public bureaucrats have been repeatedly exposed to the greater glory of private bureaucrats. The makers of public policies have been decried to the advantage of the makers of private fortunes. A national press which, as a whole, has steadily taught the public for fifteen years to sneer at public order and public service and to admire cupidity and acquisitiveness has no doubt had some effect . . . Values matter less; what does matter is the kind of show that people put on.

If there had been a shift in the exercise of power in our society, concluded Titmuss, it had not been towards a more accountable use of it: it was now 'concentrated in relatively few hands, working at the apex of a handful of giant bureaucracies, technically supported by a group of professional experts, and accountable, in practice, to virtually no-one'.[31] Titmuss was in this case not so much inaugurating as reflecting a growing unease about political and economic power.

'Affluence', insisted the New Left in particular, but also the Labour Party in opposition, had affected very little. The managerial revolution was a myth. Power remained where it had always been in capitalist society – in the same place as the bulk of industrial and financial ownership. *Universities and Left Review*, one of the founder journals of the New Left in 1957,[32] had produced two analyses of the realities of economic power a year before Titmuss referred to the 'unfashionable' nature of the subject. The first, a pamphlet entitled *The Insiders*, attacked the myth of 'the firm nobody owns', and underlined the dominant shareholding and directorship structures of such firms as I.C.I. and the Metal Box Co. The second, an article on 'The Controllers' by Michael Barratt-Brown, looked at the inter-connections amongst commercial and merchant bankers and industrial directors, and suggested 'a close connection between private

and commercial bankers and the largest insurance and industrial concerns with a quasi-monopoly of the market, both
at home and overseas'.[33] The 'power élite' revealed in these
analyses indicated that the trend towards a more classless
society suggested by Burnham, Durbin and Crosland was
illusory, and that the centres of economic and financial
power were in fact being strengthened. Even new economic
and business moralities were being sanctioned, as Ralph
Samuel underlined:

> Prestige has followed power. Business has been carried to
> the Top, enjoying, today, greater esteem than at any
> other time in English history. In the nineteenth century
> new branches of industry were often suspect and had to
> wait two or three generations before they acquired
> respectability and upper-class acceptance . . . Today, how-
> ever, new branches of business win immediate Establish-
> ment recognition. The take-over bid, the most revolutionary
> development in company finance since the war, has been
> accepted by even the most conservative City houses . . .[34]

The Labour Party itself was led, in 1961, officially to attack
'the growth of new forms of privilege and the rapid concentration of economic power' since it had left office in 1951.
The economy, it pointed out, was still 'dominated by a
small ruling caste . . . The top one per cent of the population own nearly half the nation's private wealth and
property'. The result was a powerful 'compact oligarchy':
roughly a third of the directors of the Bank of England,
Ministers, directors of the 'Big Five' banks, of large City
firms and of large insurance companies had been educated
at one school – Eton.[35] A study of the 'descent from 1945'
by Clive Jenkins showed that the control of nationalized
industries displayed similar characteristics: by 1951 it had
become clear that 'while the owners of certain industries
had been displaced from the direct exercise of their power
the balance of social forces had remained unchanged in the
nationalized sector and the same class relationships existed
there as in the private-enterprise firms'.[36] Public ownership,
to the New Left, did not therefore in itself go far enough in
attacking the roots of privilege.

The discussion of economic realities and Establishment power was also one of politics and democracy. C.N.D. and the New Left made explicit, and intensified, the younger generation's rejection of party politics and formal confrontations at various levels. Raymond Williams, whose *The Long Revolution* in 1961 was a peak in the new cultural–political analysis, pointed to the loss of meaning of 'socialism' in modern society. It was 'not surprising that many people now see the Labour Party merely as an alternative power-group, and in the trade union movement merely a set of men playing the market in very much the terms of the employers they oppose'.[37] One of the features of the trade union movement from the late fifties was to be, in fact, the displacement of key right-wing trade union officials by more radical and militant leaders, some of whom had participated in C.N.D. and allied movements.

In relation to questions of democracy the certainties strengthened by the Second World War and by victory had also been weakened. The war had been one to protect democracy, and post-war nationalization and welfare improvements had been in the name of democracy, but visible polarities of wealth and privilege were now seen as undermining that very concept. 'The strength of the democracies is the existence of civil and political liberties as organic parts of the State structure', wrote former Labour minister Richard Crossman in 1959. 'Their weakness is the complete failure to subject irresponsible economic power to public control.'[38] The cross-currents in this discussion were complicated, partly because the majority of Conservatives continued to accept the increased role of the State as a necessary part of the new democracy, though without much conviction, choosing 'from one school of thought or another, without much consistency and mainly in response to changes of fashion in public opinion'.[39] Only Enoch Powell among leading Conservatives was consistently opposed to State participation in and aid to industry, urging vigilance in a situation 'where it is the Government that takes the vital decisions on development and in investment, thereby lifting these decisions out of the plane of a free economy'.[40] There were few Conservatives in this period willing to be unfashionable enough to portray the aggrandized State role (not just nationalization) as hostile to democracy. One, Lord Percy of Newcastle, did launch a major attack on the extension of the concept of democracy from political to social levels of discussion, attacking the subordination of morality to Physical Welfare, and protesting that 'the individual has been incited to sink his conscience and his will in a monster of State sovereignty where he may forget his identity in the intoxication of corporate power'.[41]

The new radicalism, on the other hand, did wish to take the concept of democracy out of politics in the narrowest sense, and infuse it with a sense of social purpose, to bring democracy into everyday life, not just to reinvigorate the ballot box. The literature of the New Left, for example, was concerned prominently not only with nuclear weapons and power élites, but also with the popular arts and people in urban environments, social relationships in new towns and youth clubs, the trade union branch and the high street shops. Raymond Williams in particular underlined the failure of democracy to permeate the crucial area of work: 'it is difficult to feel that we are really governing ourselves if in so central a part of our living as our work most of us have no share in decisions that immediately affect us ... It is clear, on balance, that we do not get enough practice in the working of democracy, even where its forms exist.'[42]

In the late sixties and the seventies the discussion of democracy was to become less sharp, and to alter its focus. Some of the main social and political tensions receded, others were settled or absorbed into the workings of society. Some international agreements (on nuclear tests, for example) were reached, and the cold war subsided. Public ownership became less of a major political issue. Forms of protest (such as the sit-in and squatting) became either institutionalized or simply familiar. Questions of economic and industrial efficiency for the most part overwhelmed that of worker participation, as salient industrial issues began to be approached through State-sponsored bodies, and as questions of trade union power became more central to public consciousness. Interests in the nature of citizenship and democratic living went in new directions in the 1970s especially, in connection with community and neighbour-hood movements, and with problems of the poor, the Black, the young, women and other sections of the community. It was in the melting pot of the late 1950s and early 1960s that the ability to focus on community problems, and to devise new ways of establishing democratic commitments towards them, had developed significantly in British society.

Political institutions

While pointing to the challenges of the 1950s and after, it is important also to stress that patterns of political activity have for most people remained relatively stable since the Second World War. Over a longer time-scale, however, we can now recognize important changes. Until the end of the eighteenth century the landed aristocracy exercised virtually complete control over English society: they were the State. Their authority was shared between three agencies – those of government, the army and the Church. With the expansion of industry and commerce in the early nineteenth century the class of wealthy businessmen and independent property owners grew and challenged the supremacy of the established élite. In England, unlike France, no revolution was necessary for this new class to gain a share of power in the existing political hierarchy. The more successful were absorbed into the dominant class, while the remainder were appeased by an extension of the franchise. As they moved up, the successful burghers took with them the capitalist ideals of self-help and *laissez-faire* which had already, in large part, secured them their economic strength. These ideals, too, were absorbed by the ruling élite, until, as we have previously seen, they became the cornerstone not only of social policy generally but also of the continued stability and political effectiveness of the upper class itself.[43]

The established aristocracy maintained its former positions of authority even into the twentieth century. But new power groups emerged – those of the large corporation, of organized labour and of mass communications for example. The influence of the army and of the established Church was considerably eroded. Unlike some societies, the legitimacy of political institutions has not had to be secured in Britain by direct force. The survival of some political groups and the attrition of others is part of a continuous process of revaluation by members of the society of different modes of authority and submission. Survival also depends on the relative financial strengths of the groups contending for power. Membership of the élite in the government, as in the army and in the established Church, is still, as we have seen, largely based on the possession of private wealth and a private education. This was the historical and contemporary pattern being called in question in the events of the late 1950s and 1960s.

In the nineteenth century, as we have also seen, a number of popular demands for reform were acceded to in one form or another – in education, in public health, and in working conditions and labour relations (thereby containing the potential revolutionary challenge of the urban working class and, in the process, securing valuable electoral support). Most members of the working class, while continuing to agitate for further extensions to their democratic rights, nevertheless held to traditional patterns of deference and submission. This is an illustration of the British amalgam of conflict and consensus politics, which has also been illustrated by the discussion of changes in the late 1950s. Conflict means 'a struggle over ruling positions, challenges to parties in power, and shifts of parties in office'. Consensus, on the other hand, allows the peaceful 'play' of power, the adherence of the 'outs' to the decisions of the 'ins' and the recognition by the 'ins' of the rights of the 'outs'. Without it 'there can be no democracy'.[44] The discussion of conflict and consensus provides a framework in which to view, for example, the changing focus of the debate about equality since the war, and the discussion of democracy in the 1960s and 1970s. It raises sharp questions. How much 'real' freedom of action do different individuals and groups possess in contemporary society? How far are the institutions of government 'really' democratic? What degrees of freedom of choice exist within modern bureaucratic organizations? What rights do minority groups possess? How effective is public opinion in influencing major political decisions? How far are people 'manipulated' by the mass media? To what extent do consensus politics imply 'managed' politics, the 'institutionalization of opposition' and the coercion of the majority?

All of these questions were brought into particularly sharp focus in the late fifties, demonstrating yet again how wide a range of meanings 'democracy' can carry. For Burke, the conservative political theorist, and for Ostrogorski, one of the earliest writers to attempt a study of party organizations, it was a sufficient condition for democracy that:

> a group of citizens first organize themselves into a political party on the basis of some principle or set of principles; they then deduce a political programme from these principles and their candidates proceed to lay this programme before the electorate; if the party secures a majority in Parliament, it then implements the 'mandate' given it by the electors. If issues arise not covered by the 'mandate', then it is for the M.P.s to use their own judgement in deciding what to do.[45]

To more radically minded political thinkers this model lacks the element of continuous accountability and participation. Robert McKenzie insists that any explanation of the democratic process which ignores the role of organized interest groups 'is hopelessly inadequate and sterile in that it leaves out of account the principal channels through which the mass of the citizenry bring influence to bear on the decision makers whom they have elected'.[46] This difference is crucial, for according to the second model voters undertake to do far more than simply choose their elected representatives; they exercise their right, through the enormous range of pressure groups in our society, to advise, cajole and argue with government about the policies that it seeks to adopt. What the nuclear disarmament movement, for example, raised as a central issue was that of how far pressure groups can go in their extra-parliamentary opposition to policies they may consider wrong or even leading towards international disaster – how far conflict can go in attempting to produce a new consensus.

In various ways and fields governments have tried to

respond to such questions, and to the radical pressures we
have outlined, for example by attempting greater 'consultation', through agencies for consumer protection, in joint
economic and planning bodies, issuing consultative
documents, and even – for the first time in Britain –
through a referendum in the case of the Common Market.

With the vote for all over eighteen the electoral pattern
has itself come under attack in the 1970s only in two connections. First, the Liberal Party has consistently sought to
change election procedure to a form of proportional
representation, and with the ailing fortunes of the
Conservative Party in the early 1970s won some support for
the principle on the right. Second, the improved fortunes of
nationalist parties in Wales and Scotland in the early 1970s
thrust regionalism into new prominence, and the Labour
Party into a commitment to devolution. Despite both of
these, and the confirmation of membership to the European
Economic Community in 1975, the majority of the British
people experienced politics primarily, as previous generations had done, in terms of the polling booth.

Most people continued, at the same time, to experience
some form of interest group activity, however limited or
remote from the centres of influence it might appear. Interest groups, of course, pre-date the democratic franchise.
Some of them, such as the Anti-Corn-Law League, expired
once their purposes were achieved, leaving behind, however,
important traditions of popular organization. Others, such
as the T.U.C., which was founded in 1868, have gained in
importance over the years. New groups come into existence
almost daily so that scarcely an interest or cause does not
now have its body of organized defenders (or opponents) –
and very often they have several such bodies to represent
them. Approximately half of the electorate belong to one or
more interest groups, varying in size and influence, and in
the proportion of their membership playing an active part in
their affairs.[47]

The strongest interest groups today are those of sectional organizations. In the mid-1970s, for example, the
Confederation of British Industries represented the interests
of some 12,000 companies and over 200 trade associations

and employers' organizations – as well as most of the nationalized industries. The labour lobby was in 1971 made up of 469 unions of employees and had a total membership of 10·9 million. On matters of common concern to all the unions negotiations are conducted by the T.U.C., which in 1975 had an affiliated membership of 10,363,724. An increasingly important role of the T.U.C. in the 1970s has been the co-ordination of trade union responses to government initiatives, especially with regard to incomes policy, budgetary policy and related economic and social affairs.

In addition to the major sectional groups (including also, for example, the British Medical Association) there are large numbers of important promotional groups, like the Howard League for Penal Reform, the National Council for Civil Liberties and the Consumers' Association. There are groups representing special sections of the population, such as the British Legion and the motoring organizations. There are religious and evangelical groups, and a multitude of educational, cultural and recreational groups, including organizations like the National Trust. One of the most successful interest groups created in the 1970s was the Campaign for Real Ale, which succeeded in reversing a basic commercial trend away from traditional brewing and dispensing methods. The day-to-day activities of many of these groups relate to government domestic and foreign policies, as in the case of the Anti-Apartheid Movement, and organizations which, since the Second World War, have sought to recruit public support against, for example, German rearmament, the Common Market, and the wars in Korea and Vietnam. C.N.D. was, as we have seen, the outstanding example.[48]

Pressure groups permit the establishment of intermediate links between government and electorate. They help to check and balance the power of the ruling élite, and they supply M.P.s and civil servants with specialized advice and information. In several respects, however, the system is imperfect. Groups do not have equal influence – and some sections of the population are simply not represented in this way. The general public – and even the membership of these organizations – are cut off from the decision-making machinery. Even more important, the operation of pressure groups may in itself conceal some fundamental issues. Even if the problems of power and privilege, political and social democracy, which were central to the new movements of the 1950s, have altered in many ways, in fundamental respects they remain intact and impervious to public pressure.

The discussion of politics and culture involves a concern both with change and with permanence, with institutions and with ideas. It is important, looking at the period after 1956 and at the issues which it raises, to detect the survival value of institutions, alongside profound changes in attitudes and policies, and in the institutions themselves.

Notes

1 See RICHARD HOGGART 'Mass communications in Britain', in BORIS FORD (ed.) *The Pelican Guide to English Literature*, Vol. 7: *The Modern Age* (Harmondsworth, 1961).

2 STUART HALL 'A sense of classlessness', *Universities and Left Review*, No. 5, 1958, p. 26.

3 Quoted in ASA BRIGGS *Adult Education and Mass Culture*, p. 9 (Nottingham, 1958).

4 W. A. BELSON *The Impact of Television*, p. 213 (London, 1967; 1968 edition).

5 JOHN SPRAOS *The Decline of the Cinema*, p. 14 (London, 1962): H. E. BROWNING and A. A. SORRELL 'Cinemas and cinema-going in Great Britain', *Journal of the Royal Statistical Society*, Series A (General), Pt II, 1954, p. 143.

6 SPRAOS *The Decline of the Cinema*, p. 165.

7 WHITAKER'S *Almanack 1956*, p. 1008 (London, 1956).

8 RAY GOSLING *Sum Total*, pp. 71, 75 (London, 1962).

9 ROYSTON ELLIS *The Big Beat Scene*, p. 15 (London, 1961). See also ROYSTON ELLIS *Rebel* (London, 1962) for a study of James Dean.

10 GIBBS *How Now, England?*, p. 127.

11 GEORGE MELLY *Revolt into Style: the pop arts in Britain* (London, 1970); KENNETH LEECH *Youthquake: the growth of a counter-culture through two decades* (London, 1973); NIK COHN *Awopbopaloobop Alopbamboom* (London, 1969). For the folk element in the new music and some of the background see DAVE LAING et al. *The Electric Muse: the story of folk into rock* (London, 1975). There is a useful chapter on Britain in

278 Modern English Society

CHARLIE GILLETT *The Sound of the City: the rise of rock and roll* (New York, 1970).

12 LEECH *Youthquake*, p. 1.

13 For the way the politicians 'discovered' the adolescent generation of the late 1950s see STUART HALL 'Politics of adolescence?', *Universities and Left Review*, No. 6, 1959.

14 MARK ABRAMS 'Teenage consumer spending in 1959 (Pt II): middle class and working class boys and girls', pp. 3–5 (London, 1961).

15 KING GEORGE'S JUBILEE TRUST *Citizens of Tomorrow*, especially Pt IV (London, 1955).

16 CARSTAIRS *This Island Now*, pp. 39–40.

17 LEECH *Youthquake*, p. 1.

18 T. R. FYVEL *The Insecure Offenders: rebellious youth in the welfare state*, pp. 111–23 (London, 1961; 1963 Penguin edition).

19 JOHN BARRON MAYS *The Young Pretenders: a study of teenage culture in contemporary society*, p. 15 (London, 1965).

20 JOHN WAIN *Hurry On Down*, pp. 17–29 (London, 1953; 1960 Penguin edition).

21 See C. H. ROLPH (ed.) *The Trial of Lady Chatterley* (Harmondsworth, 1961). For the legislation details see H. STREET *Freedom, the Individual and the Law*, pp. 129–40 (London, 1963), and H. MONTGOMERY HYDE *A History of Pornography*, pp. 195–233 (London, 1964), including an appendix on the *Fanny Hill* case.

22 See SIMONE DE BEAUVOIR *Brigitte Bardot and the Lolita Syndrome* (English edition, London, 1960).

23 GILLIAN FREEMAN *The Undergrowth of Literature* (London, 1967). For the later 1960s developments see the GUARDIAN *The Permissive Society* (London, 1969).

24 See FREDRIC WERTHAM *Seduction of the Innocent* (London, 1955), an American book published in London with an introduction by Randolph Churchill.

25 CARSTAIRS *This Island Now*, p. 45.

26 BERTRAND RUSSELL *Has Man a Future?*, p. 26 (Harmondsworth, 1961).

27 HUGH THOMAS (ed.) *The Establishment*, p. 18 (London, 1959).

28 KINGSLEY MARTIN *The Crown and the Establishment*, p. 179 (London, 1962; 1963 Penguin edition).

29 JOHN A. T. ROBINSON *Honest to God*, p. 120 (London, 1963).

30 See, for example, C. WRIGHT MILLS *The Power Elite* (New York, 1956); WILLIAM H. WHYTE *The Organization Man* (New York, 1956); HANNAH ARENDT *The Human Condition*

(Chicago, 1958); DAVID RIESMAN *The Lonely Crowd* (New York, 1950).

31 TITMUSS *The Irresponsible Society*, pp. 3, 17.

32 The other was *The New Reasoner* (also founded in 1957). The two merged to become the *New Left Review* in 1960.

33 *The Insiders* was reproduced as an insert to *Universities and Left Review*, No. 3, 1958; MICHAEL BARRATT-BROWN, *Universities and Left Review*, No. 5, 1958, pp. 53–61.

34 RALPH SAMUEL ' "Bastard" capitalism', in E. P. THOMPSON (ed.) *Out of Apathy*, pp. 31–2 (London, 1960).

35 LABOUR PARTY *Signposts for the Sixties*, pp. 9–10.

36 CLIVE JENKINS *Power at the Top*, p. 19 (London, 1959).

37 RAYMOND WILLIAMS *The Long Revolution*, pp. 301–2 (London, 1961).

38 RICHARD CROSSMAN *Labour in the Affluent Society*, p. 17 (London, 1960), a 1959 Fabian lecture.

39 HARRIS *Competition and the Corporate State*, p. 268.

40 Quoted in ibid., p. 245.

41 LORD PERCY OF NEWCASTLE *The Heresy of Democracy*, pp. 232–3, 238 (London, 1954).

42 WILLIAMS *The Long Revolution*, pp. 306, 309.

43 See PETER WORSLEY 'The distribution of power in industrial society', *Sociological Review Monograph* No. 8, 1964.

44 S. M. LIPSET *Political Man*, p. 21 (London, 1959).

45 R. T. MCKENZIE 'Parties, pressure groups and the British political process', in RICHARD ROSE (ed.) *Studies in British Politics*, p. 257 (London, 1966).

46 In ibid., pp. 258–9.

47 For an account of the history and tactics of various kinds of pressure groups, see S. E. FINER *Anonymous Empire* (London, 1958) and J. D. STEWART *British Pressure Groups* (London, 1958).

48 For an account of pressure group politics see H. ECKSTEIN *Pressure Group Politics* (London, 1960).

9 New critiques: the social system and the family

Options of the 1960s

If 1956 announced a new world, 1963 marked a decisive turning point. It saw the end of the Macmillan era, the death of Hugh Gaitskell, and the brief period of Tory leadership under Lord Home. Abroad, old alliances and relationships were under strain. Like other Western nations Britain was still recovering from the shock of the Cuban missile crisis, as well as facing the rapid loss of former African colonies, and suffering the humiliation of being refused membership of the European Common Market by General de Gaulle. The assassination of President Kennedy in Dallas, Texas, a world-wide wave of *coups d'état*, and natural disasters, added to the feeling of fatalism and uncertainty in foreign affairs. Britain's former status as a major power was now clearly eclipsed. The consolidation of post-Stalinist Russia and the wind of colonial change had wrought profound and irreversible shifts in the world balance of power, including a self-conscious alignment among the so-called 'Third World' nations of Africa, South America and the Middle East. Communist China was playing a more active international role, and new revolutionary

29 *Biba*

theorists, from Guinea to Cuba, from Vietnam to Paris, were influencing a generation of young radicals and revolutionaries across the world.

In Britain, consumption continued to expand from 1963–8, bringing a rising rate of inflation, a Prices and Incomes Board and a worsening financial crisis. But until the bubble burst life for large sections of the population, especially for the young, was full of new experiences and a common feeling of optimism and opportunity. The demand for goods was insatiable. All over the country dull high streets were transformed into brash, noisy, bustling worlds where supermarkets replaced family drapers and grocers, and old-style corner shops vied desperately with their competitors to offer more attractive prices, trading stamps, piped music, customer carry-out services or free parking. New boutiques and clubs (the Playboy Club in London's Park Lane opened in 1966) and new kinds of eating places also appeared (including Wimpy Bars, Golden Eggs and Steak Houses), appealing to the young, affluent and uncommitted. King's Road, Chelsea and Carnaby Street epitomized this trend and won

30 *Mary Quant*

for themselves the status of places of pilgrimage for an increasing number of visitors to 'swinging London'.[1] Well-established firms like Boots, W. H. Smith and Woolworth's learned to adapt to new styles of packaging and marketing, adopting more ruthless standards of profitability, often at the expense of personal service and choice.

Skilled market judgements were the basis of commercial success. They relied on two ingredients – flair, of the kind that successful pop groups like the Beatles and the Rolling Stones, and that designers like Mary Quant, displayed (and which could in turn be 'managed' and made highly marketable), and accurate information about potential customers. The early 1960s saw the arrival in Britain of large-scale market research, a branch of applied social science with ethical standards that did not go unquestioned, which permitted firms to research the acceptability of new products, to identify trend setters, and to check on the effectiveness of advertising campaigns.[2]

In the 1960s technology continued to transform people's lives, and at a faster pace than ever before. It affected health prospects and made possible an improvement in the length and quality of life. The pharmaceutical industry was particularly successful, marketing new drugs that helped to control heart disease, psychotropic drugs that helped patients suffering from depression, and, perhaps most important, the contraceptive pill. The 1960s also saw the arrival of better and cheaper television sets. The standard of cinema production improved, with bigger screens, better colour and more powerful amplification systems. While fewer people went to the cinema, what they saw (for example the James Bond films) was more spectacular. People relaxed with the all-pervasive portable transistor radio or greatly refined hi-fi equipment. This new world of consumer opportunities and hitherto unfelt needs was confirmed and extended in the media. In 1962 the *Sunday Times* brought out its first colour supplement, to be followed by the *Observer* and *Telegraph* supplements. Trend-setting articles were unobtrusively interwoven with lavishly designed advertisements (and it was sometimes hard to tell which was which). The myth of affluence was sustained – at least for a few more years.

With a continued improvement in living standards for many families, more and more followed the example of the Sunday supplement trend-setters by taking holidays abroad. More people bought cars and improved their homes, more ate out, went to concerts, galleries and museums, and more bought paperback books and glossy magazines. The magazines were often important because of the overt hints (for example on entertaining and home decoration) they provided to insecure lower-middle-class groups aspiring to be like their more established neighbours. For younger groups, the magazines offered guidance in a world where sexual and moral standards were no longer clearly defined.

Progress in the commercial and industrial fields was not evenly distributed. Thus, while the chemical, pharmaceutical and electronics industries prospered in the mid-1960s, older industries were in decline. In the State-run industries especially there were large-scale redundancies. On the railways, following Beeching's rationalization plans, whole depots were closed down, so that jobs were lost in the workshops as well as among drivers and station staff. The mines went through a similar process of contraction. There was a growing suspicion of State control and bureaucracy – including within the trade union movement.[3] The number of official and unofficial strikes dramatically increased. Relations between workers and managers were extremely delicate, and so, after 1964, were those between the Labour government and the trade unions. The level of exports, the balance of payments, the value of the pound, were increasingly recurring themes, reflecting an underlying economic malaise.[4]

The resignation of Harold Macmillan, coming after the unedifying drama of the long-drawn-out Profumo affair in 1963 (in which a British cabinet minister was implicated, with other members of the Establishment, in a call-girl scandal linked to a possible espionage network) meant that old-style political authority in Britain was now decisively on the wane. The deference due to the traditional ruling classes because of their inherited 'fitness' to govern, already weakened by their enforced withdrawal from the colonies and by the processes discussed in the last chapter, was seriously called in question by this affair. In a brief interregnum the Fourteenth Earl of Home was tempted back from the House of Lords to create a new image of stability and calm, but his failure, and the relentless satirical outpourings, for example, on the popular weekly television series, *That Was the Week That Was*, that it led to, further weakened aristocratic and Establishment authority. Standards of political morality and the exercise of political authority were being challenged at the same time as the Bishop of Woolwich was challenging the notion of absolute moral standards, and the Beatles and the Rolling Stones were confirming that the youth challenge was not evaporating – and was in fact still gathering momentum.

Harold Wilson, who had been elected to the leadership of the Labour Party after Hugh Gaitskell's death early in 1963, was a generation younger than the Tory leaders and came from a very different background – born in Huddersfield and educated at a grammar school. With the reputation of the Home administration in tatters and the rumblings of financial and industrial unrest close at hand, he launched an unambiguous appeal in his pre-election speeches for 'a chance for change . . . a time for resurgence. A chance to sweep away the grouse-moor conception of Tory leadership and refit Britain with a new image, a new confidence.' He appealed for help in creating a Britain that 'believes in its power to make a distinctive and decisive contribution to the world, a Britain that breaks down the barriers of colour and class – of occupation, skill and age'. For Wilson socialism meant 'applying a sense of purpose to our national life: economic purpose, social purpose and moral purpose. Purpose means technical skill – be it the skill of a manager, a designer, a craftsman, an engineer, a transport worker, a miner, an architect, a nuclear physicist, a doctor, a nurse or a social worker.'[5] The slogans which helped to make Wilson Prime Minister in 1964 were unmistakable – change, technology, automation and the scientific revolution.

The mid-sixties were indeed years of change, but they were marked as much by disappointment as by optimism or revolution. There were better training opportunities, especially for scientists and technologists. Plans for a

31 *Harold Wilson's Labour victory, 1964*

comprehensive system of secondary schooling were also hurried along, although their full impact was delayed until late into the 1970s because of the continued existence in many parts of the country of old-style tripartite arrangements. However, given the high birth-rate of the immediate post-war years, much of the expansion that occurred in the 1960s only served to maintain the existing rate of recruitment to higher education. Following the Robbins Report on *Higher Education* in 1963 university intakes more than doubled (to about a quarter of a million) in the next ten years, but this did not improve the relative chances of children in different social groups.[6] Nor did it increase the proportion of the age group attending college or university, or satisfy the demands of industry for more highly trained manpower and better managers.

The hoped-for transformation in social conditions and the creation of greater equality between different social groups were slow to appear. The Labour Party, in office

after a long period in opposition, found itself confronted
with as many difficulties as its Conservative predecessors. It
met, for example, a deep conflict over the need to balance
the principles of social democracy with those of intervention
and control – especially in the monetary sphere. It had to
decide between the priorities of high public spending (and
therefore high rates of taxation) and the need to redistribute
wealth fairly. It found itself, above all, having to govern by
consensus – to work with the Bank of England and the
major industrial corporations, and to reckon with world
trading patterns and priorities – and hence having to persuade the unions to abandon some of their ideals or accepted procedures in the interests of the nation 'as a whole'.
In fact, during the sixties, while grappling with financial
crises by short-term financial policies, on the social front
politicians concentrated on long overdue, politically non-
controversial reforms – for example, the Homosexual Law
Reform and the Abortion Act.

The mood of optimism which had greeted the arrival of
the new Labour government in 1964 was over by 1967. The
Party suffered a series of by-election defeats and its leader's
rating dropped heavily in the polls – those instant guides to
the nation's political temperature which had themselves
only begun to be a regular part of the news media since 1961
– when the *Daily Telegraph* took over regular publication of
Gallup Polls and the *Daily Mail* regularly published
National Opinion Polls. Using techniques similar to market
research, and, like it, taking advantage of the speed and
complexity of analysis permitted by computers, the public
opinion polls were the inheritors of the long empirical tradition of survey research in the British social sciences. Now,
however, the humane and carefully trained skill and sen-
sitivities of early survey workers were overtaken by the skills
of computer programmers and data analysts.

Discontent with consensus government was at its most
bitter among young people – and university students in
particular. Unlike the protests of the Angry Young Men in
the 1950s, which had class privilege and conventions as their
main target, and in complete contrast to the increasingly
anarchic, psychedelic fantasies of the pop era, the students'

movement of the late 1960s had sharply focused political concerns. They joined arms internationally against oppression and exploitation – in government, industry and education for example, and in support of the continuing wars of colonial liberation in Africa, South America and the Far East.

In the later sixties the pop music boom collapsed, boutiques closed, and among the more affluent and better educated adolescents there followed a succession of escapist crazes based on yoga, zen, transcendental meditation, flower power and drug-taking – each generating its own esoteric world of jargon, music and dress, and each representing a deliberate decision to opt out of existing society and its norms. Among less privileged groups, the skinheads, bovver boys, greasers and rockers, organized, fought, disbanded and regrouped, acting out their aggressive fantasies in overt acts of violence. As they did so, they fulfilled middle-class and middle-aged fantasies about teenage violence, irresponsibility and unreason.[7]

The hollow vision

That young people erupted into hostility to existing forms of government in 1968 was no accident. The years from 1963 had been, above all, years when new styles, new trends and new faces occupied the public consciousness. English society had shrugged off the domination of the old-style aristocracy, and seen the wavering security of old-style religious and social certainties dealt damaging blows. In the shape of its new generation of politicians and television pundits, it fostered for a few years a deliberate climate of youthful iconoclasm. There was a decisive shift to a more secular, permissive, plural society. Its values had at first been adopted only among sections of the younger generation, but during the 1960s spread more widely through the population. By 1969 Christopher Booker was reminiscing about the almost Victorian feel of the early 1950s – especially its dominant belief in social progress through technological advance – a vision which had

underlain the advance of twentieth-century civilisation. In the first fifty years of the century it transformed the world, with advances in science, with the disintegration of traditional ways of life and social structures, with the rise of mass-communications as a major factor in the social and psychic life of the age. And yet today ... even that world of 1950 seems curiously old-fashioned, almost safe and cosy. With its Victorian city centres, its New Look clothes, its steam trains, its map of Africa still painted red, its almost Victorian standards of decorum in public entertainments and the orthodox arts, it seems in some ways more closely linked with the nineteenth century than with our own time.

Modern technology, from the space probe to the television set, had accelerated the pace of development towards the vision of progress. The vision was coming closer, but 'the real fruit of the Fifties and Sixties lies in the fact that, as never before, its hollowness has been exposed'.[8]

The new cultural and intellectual movements, and the groups which espoused them, had a hard, cutting, critical edge. The Beatles were demonstrating that reality mattered (for example, with their powerful evocation of loneliness and futility in *Eleanor Rigby*, in 1965), and some popular and folk music in the United States and Britain increasingly echoed political opposition to America's involvement in the Vietnam war, which began in 1964. 'Progressive' pop music, whatever its content, carried an incisively critical and even cynical appeal – looking for new ways of announcing more fully a rejection of accepted society, and establishing new international cults – including Led Zeppelin, Frank Zappa and Leonard Cohen – with an important British dimension. New social theorists, whose influence was felt particularly through the political protest movements of 1968 and after, joined issue with the whole apparatus of industrial (and not only capitalist) society. Herbert Marcuse, writing in the United States, was listened to throughout Europe. His *One-Dimensional Man*, for example, published in 1964, became a focal point in the protest movements of the United States and Europe, offering an alternative radical buttress to that of orthodox Marxism. Its basic message was that people in advanced industrial societies had no control over politics,

290 Modern English Society

intellectual and cultural life, indeed any major part of their lives. In the name of technical and economic progress they had forfeited freedom. Industry, the mass media, economic and political machineries had 'absorbed' all aspects of the individual: 'a comfortable, smooth, reasonable, democratic unfreedom prevails in advanced industrial civilization, a token of technical progress'. Industrial societies had become 'totalitarian' – which was 'not only a terroristic political coordination of society, but also a non-terroristic economic – technical coordination which operates through the manipulation of needs by vested interests'. A 'pluralistic' society, with its multiple parties, newspapers and 'counter-vailing powers', could still be deprived of basic choices and freedoms. Advanced industrial society suffocated all 'needs which demand liberation' and liberty was transformed into an instrument of domination.[9] Unlike earlier condemnations of State encroachments, Marcuse's critique was a basically revolutionary message, arguing for the establishment of a society of Reason. On the basis of a 'critical theory of society' he threw open to scrutiny and new challenges the totality of modern society, and provoked new conceptions of its repressive techniques and realities. The new radical anarchist, Black Power and left-wing movements and groupings of the late 1960s and 1970s, as well as the student movements of the U.S.A. and Europe, directed their anger against targets different from those of earlier movements – the police, university authorities, liberals, the repressive machineries of schools and social security services, as well as political parties and governments.

A vital feature of the 'critical' approaches to society adopted in the 1960s was the new emphasis on existing social organization as a network of subtle-forms of repres-sion. 'Society' was being interpreted on the left, not in relation to forms of 'solidarity' or cohesion, consensus or conflict as formerly understood, but as oppression and war-fare, unfreedom and unreason. When the police became 'pigs' and the State was seen as an instrument of violence even more sharply than in older Marxist analysis, the nature of 'society' was being called into question perhaps more basically than at any time we have discussed. The fact that

the political groups formally involved were (especially after
the peak of student unrest in the late 1960s) extremely small
minority organizations is less important to us here than the
fact that they formed part of a spectrum of critical commen-
taries on society and on aspects of society. 'Society', to
Marcuse and the student left, abounded in dangers and
threats. 'Society', to the 1960s pop culture, was inadequate,
unsuccessful, hopeless. 'Society', to many folk singers, was
what its leading 'democratic' exponent, the United States,
was doing to its black population and to Vietnam. The
confusions, protests, innovations of the 1950s led to the
scepticism of the 1960s about the functioning of society
itself.

Other processes reflected this development. In the world
of learning, for example, the younger and more socially
'relevant' social sciences moved ahead in popularity against
the natural sciences and more traditional economics. The
new universities (especially Essex and Sussex) and polytechnics played a part. A new and rapidly mounting concern
with environmental issues was another part. 'Conservation'
and 'pollution' were becoming topics of daily discourse. The
deep feeling of disillusionment with science and technology
and its products, resulting in a 'swing' away from science
among university entrants, was perceptively analysed in the
1968 report of the Dainton Committee on *The Flow of
Candidates in Science and Technology into Higher Education*,
acknowledging that

> For many young people science, engineering and tech-
> nology seem out of touch with human and social affairs.
> It is significant that biological and medical studies have
> not suffered the decline of the physical sciences: and part
> of the attraction of the social sciences is that they deal
> with people and with society. The objectivity of science
> and the purposefulness of technology have become iden-
> tified, for some, with insensitivity and indifference.[10]

One of the apparent advantages (and hidden dangers) of
the newer, or newly popular, social sciences – including
sociology, social anthropology and social psychology – was
their accessibility. Unlike the pure sciences, they appeared

to use ordinary language in ordinary ways and to argue on the basis of commonsense knowledge. At the same time, however, a reaction against this and earlier traditions gave rise to a new interest in theoretical orientations in the social sciences. This was based precisely on the questioning of commonsense views of the world, of opening up apparent truths for deeper inspection. Revolutionary, Marxist, existentialist and other critical theoretical positions (such as phenomenology) attracted increasing attention. Rather than being seen simply as the objects of particular external events or effects, the 'subjects' of social research were now acknowledged to have 'intentions' and perspectives of their own. Theory was no longer being seen as geared to action in an unambiguous way. New perceptions were being sought in the social sciences in ways which paralleled the fundamental reorientations of Marcuse, and built on the humane and radical traditions of earlier books like C. Wright Mills's *The Sociological Imagination* (1959). Peter Bergher's *Invitation to Sociology* in 1963 emphasized the subject's basically 'debunking motiff', an effort to see behind apparently permanent facades.[11] David Cooper and R. D. Laing were in the late sixties also bringing psychiatry into the arena of critical debate occupied by Marcuse, Black Power and radical sociology. In 1967 Laing, for example, introduced his *The Politics of Experience*:

> There is little conjunction of truth and social 'reality'. Around us are pseudo-events, to which we adjust with a false consciousness adapted to see these events as true and real, and even as beautiful. We who are still half alive, living in the often fibrillating heartland of a senescent capitalism – can we do more than reflect the decay around and within us? . . . The requirement of the present, the failure of the past, is the same: to provide a thoroughly self-conscious and self-critical human account of man.[12]

Not all theory, of course, was 'critical' in this sense. In all fields of social inquiry, however, more empirical traditions were being joined by a sharper interest in theoretical perspectives.

The family

One example of this trend can be found in studies of the family, which, with its ramifications, offer a case study of changing social perspectives in the 1960s and 1970s. From the early 1960s research on the family became increasingly sophisticated, shifting from a concern with the effects of community and social class on different kinds of family life to more anthropologically based studies that often centred on aspects of socialization or on family roles. This related also to the studies of the 'youth phenomenon' we have discussed, and, in the light of the new independence of teenage groups, and the comparative freedom of women resulting – most directly – from the contraceptive pill, studies focused on the likely future of the family. Underlying the changing trends in youth protest and women's work and family roles were important demographic changes. The immediate post-war years had witnessed a dramatic rise in the birth-rate (from 15·8 per 1,000 in 1931, to a peak of 20·5 per 1,000 in 1947, falling in the 1950s, and climbing to 17·7 per 1,000 in 1966). For related reasons there had been a similar increase in divorce. More families were planned and more women found, as a consequence, that having married in their early twenties, by thirty-five or forty they were free of child-minding responsibilities. Thus, at a time when their children were ready to embark on independent careers and begin adult relationships, they were themselves also looking for jobs and perhaps envying the freedom and opportunities available to their children.

Since late Victorian England, and especially during the two world wars and in the 1960s, a series of profound changes has altered the shape of family life for all classes and all age groups. There is no human society in which some form of the family is not found, given its role for its own members and for the continuance of society at large. The family ideally values all its members equally, and creates for the individual 'the sort of order in which he can experience his life as making sense'.[13] Families are automatically involved in equipping new generations for survival, as well as with particular, and interlocking, kinds of status (son, Welsh, black, aristocrat, worker and so on).

Families perform these jobs on behalf of the wider society, and are themselves influenced by other institutions and groups. At different times, particular cultural traditions define the form of relationships between husbands and wives and between parents and children. They also prescribe what come to be regarded as acceptable norms of behaviour within the family, the wide range of which can be seen in different groups which have at some time immigrated to England – for example, Pakistani, West Indian, Irish and Jewish. Such variations are reinforced by legal and religious sanctions and by informal pressures within the different groups, although there may be a time-lag during which 'official' norms are out of step with actual standards of behaviour. During the 1960s, for instance, pre-marital sex was increasingly common but the official response to a girl having and keeping a baby was unhelpful, not to say punitive. In the 1970s the time-lag in standards was felt particularly acutely by the teenage offspring of immigrant families.

Perhaps the most decisive way in which society has influenced the form and functions of the family has been in taking over areas of responsibility for matters that were formerly its exclusive or primary concern – health, infant welfare, education, the care of the elderly. It appears, however, that differences in size and structure between the family in industrial and in pre-industrial society have been exaggerated. Until new research findings in historical demography appeared in the late 1960s and 1970s it had been assumed that the growth of public involvement in functions formerly associated with the family had coincided, in industrial society, with a contraction in the size of the family household. What the new research showed, in Peter Laslett's words, was that this had been a mythical belief in 'the rise of individualism as the universal explainer of familial change'. The pre-industrial household had been assumed to be large and complex, precisely in order to contrast it with the more 'progressive' modern family, with the 'triumph of individualism' in the modern world: 'the wish to believe in the large extended household as the ordinary institution of an earlier England and an earlier Europe, or as a standard feature of an earlier non-industrial world, is indeed a matter of ideology'.[14] The presence of servants in pre-industrial households had been real but exaggerated. Too great a uniformity between regions and nations had been assumed. Changes in family size and structure had been over-simplified. Conclusions from research up to 1972 into the pre-industrial family, particularly in Europe, pointed to the basic feature being 'the nuclear family, the simple family household'. At the same time, 'surprisingly high proportions of persons appearing in a list of inhabitants can have had some experience of the extended or even of the multiple household, even though the nuclear family is in a commanding position numerically'.[15] While many serious studies of political parties, trade unions and religious bodies have existed for decades, by the mid-1970s there had as yet been no history of the family. Historical research of this kind was still in its infancy.

Of the more recent changes the most important has been the emergence of 'childhood', 'adolescence' and 'old age' as distinct stages and statuses. The status of women too has been transformed, to a large extent as a result of the improved expectation of life and the greater degree of control over births. While few would deny the enormous impact of changes in the family over the past thirty years, sociologists are far from agreed on what the consequences are – or on what the implications for the future may be.

One characteristic change since the coming of industrialization has been the transformation of the family from being a unit of production to a unit of consumption – noticeably from the late 1950s. One functionalist view of this change is that the separation of work and home, the extension of State education and the existence of the national health and welfare services, mean that the family is left with no really useful jobs to do, and is therefore bound to collapse. Families, runs this argument, are no longer responsible for assigning individuals to particular statuses in social and occupational hierarchies because, thanks to the 1944

Education Act and greater job mobility, these are now distributed on the basis of personal achievement. Families no longer help individuals in the process of 'role bargaining' either (that is, using their influence to secure jobs or privileged contacts).[16] Finally, the family's 'values are collectivist while those of society are competitive and individualistic', and it is 'diffuse in its functions when the functions of the institutions of society are specific'. It is, in short, 'a thoroughly bad preparation for life'.[17]

Against this view, which rests on some questionable assumptions, a number of alternative arguments can be put. Raymond Williams, for example, has suggested that the present structure of family and community relations is only a temporary phenomenon, and that as it adapts itself to the consumer revolution, to better educational opportunities, greater rates of mobility and the longer life span, the family can be expected to reconstruct itself.[18] Rosser and Harris, in their study of the family and social change in Swansea in the early 1960s, offer another view:

> The facts seem to point to the emergence of a modified form of extended family, more widely dispersed, more loosely knit in contact, with the women involved less sharply segregated in role and less compulsively 'domesticated', and with much lower levels of familial solidarity and a greater internal heterogeneity than was formerly the case in the traditional 'Bethnal Green' pattern. It is a form of family structure in which expectations about roles and attitudes are radically altered – and in particular, in which physical and social mobility are accepted. It is the form of extended family which is adjusted to the needs of the mobile society.[19]

Since this study was completed there is evidence that the family has continued its process of adaptation and reconstruction. Indeed, Young and Willmott in the mid-seventies confidently announced the arrival of a new family type based on symmetrical relationships between the spouses which, they claimed – according to the principle of 'stratified diffusion' – would soon spread from the middle to the lower social groups.

What is perhaps most salient in all of this is, despite the changes, the durability of traditional kinship and residential patterns. 'Visiting is still the most common social activity, even though the kin may live further from each other than they would have during the preindustrial era. And kin are still the first people turned to for help, financial or otherwise.'[20] Clearly there is not just one family type in existence in Britain today. There are still important social class and ethnic variations. Some families are paternalistic in the Victorian mould, whilst others are egalitarian and based on communal living. And while the ideal suggests greater companionship and sharing of roles, the reality is often very different. Over 6 per cent of the children surveyed by the National Children's Bureau were from families that had only one parent present, while 14 per cent were living in conditions of serious poverty.[21] Much that is said about the family is still, indeed, ideology.

Marriage and family size

A feature of the period from 1945 to the mid-1960s in Britain was high marriage rates and early ages at marriage. Whereas 552 of every 1,000 women in the age group 20 to 39 were married in 1911, in 1951 the figure was 731 and in 1961 it had reached 808 – which was as high as demographers expected it to go.[22] Taking a slightly longer age span, we find that while in 1921 88 per cent of men and 83 per cent of women were or had been married by the age of 45, by the mid-1960s these percentages were 95 and 96 respectively. A number of factors influenced this change, one of the most important being the equalization of the number of spinsters and bachelors at the relevant combination of ages. After the First World War there were some three million 'surplus' women. The Second World War caused many fewer casualties, so that in contrast to the earlier period the sexes were more nearly balanced. Indeed, by 1961 there were 976 females for every 1,000 males aged 20 to 39, and in 1974 the ratio of males to females was 1,041 : 1,000 for the under 45s, and 811 : 1,000 for the over 45s.

This fact helps to explain the earlier age at marriage. In

1921 the proportion of husbands who had married before they were 21 was less than 5 per cent: it was 15 per cent for wives. By 1973, however, the mean age at marriage for men was 24·8 and for women 22·7. 15 per cent of husbands and 45 per cent of wives were married before they were 21. While similar proportions of men and women marry from all social classes, age at marriage varies considerably according to educational and social background. It is comparatively low in Social Class V and comparatively high in Social Class I where, especially for young men, the period of training for professional and other specialist occupations, and the subsequent period of establishing a secure economic position in the profession, tend to result in the postponement of marriage.

One of the reasons for the younger age of working-class marriages is the improved standard of living which teenagers have enjoyed since 1945. With incomes higher than ever before,[23] with the extension of hire purchase facilities, and with more jobs for married women, many of the former economic barriers to early marriage were removed. The earlier onset of puberty[24] and the large number of pre-nuptial conceptions were perhaps an even more significant encouragement to early marriage. In 1964 approximately one-third of brides under 21 were already pregnant when they married. While only 5 per cent of the children born in 1955 were illegitimate, by 1967 the proportion had risen to 8 per cent (and remained at roughly that figure – it was 8·6 per cent in 1973).

The marked rise in the birth-rate immediately after the Second World War was not sustained during the 1950s, though there was an upward movement in the mid-1960s, followed by another decline. It seems likely that average family size is now stabilizing at just over two children. This figure is much smaller than for the typical Victorian family (over half of married women had five or more live children, and nearly one fifth bore ten or more), but it represents an increase over the families characteristic of the 1920s and 1930s. What is more, these changes in family size conceal quite significant social class variations. According to Glass and Grebenik,[25] throughout the period 1900 to 1924 the wives of manual workers had consistently higher fertility than wives of white-collar workers (although the absolute differences in family size fell considerably). Since 1945 a new trend has appeared, and it is among the professional classes that increases in family size are most noticeable, although fertility is still highest in Social Class V. Kelsall,[26] for example, demonstrates that whereas the average number of children born to marriages which had only lasted five years at the time of the 1961 Census was 1·74 for parents in Social Class V, the comparable figure for wives of self-employed professional men was 1·69. The lowest average figure was for the families of routine grades of non-manual workers, clerks and shop assistants who, in 1961, had had only just over 1·2 children. When marriages have lasted longer the class (and opportunity) differential is more clear. The National Children's Bureau, for instance, in 1973 estimated that at the age of seven or eleven more than one in every six children (18 per cent) lived in a family where there were five or more children. Overall, the proportion of eleven-year-old children who came from a large family or who had only one parent-figure was one in four (23 per cent).[27]

The reasons for the recovery in fertility after 1945 are, in many cases, the same as those for higher marriage rates – improved real wages, the extension of the social welfare services and of health, housing, educational and recreation facilities, as well as the availability of easy credit and hire purchase. Changing, less superstitious and less sentimental, attitudes towards pregnancy and childbirth, improved hospital facilities for confinement and the alleviation of some of the drudgery associated with the care of infants and small children (with – for those who could afford them – ready-prepared baby foods, disposable nappies, washing machines and launderettes) have also helped to create a more favourable climate for young parents.

By the late 1960s, in spite of these gains, attitudes to family-building again began to change – especially among women. For the first time female contraceptive techniques were readily available and widely publicized. No shame was attached to seeking professional advice about their use –

either from the family doctor or from a family planning clinic. In the mid-1970s such advice was made available free of charge. The availability of legal abortion (after April 1968) was for some women a further defence against unwanted pregnancies. Legal abortions soon accounted for about 150,000 terminations of pregnancy a year. By the mid-1970s the climate of opinion towards conception and child birth had changed so dramatically that a number of women's groups were even demanding 'Do it yourself abortion kits'. By 1975 the birth-rate had dropped to 12·2 per 1,000, below the level of the slump in 1933. Inflation, high mortgages, fewer council houses being built and related difficulties of family budgeting, clearly contributed to this depression of the birth-rate – how permanently cannot be predicted. Nor is it clear how much the decline represents a 'retreat from motherhood'. It is perhaps significant that the women's movement, with its demand for instant abortion and women's right to control over their lives, should have become prominent in the United States and Britain at a time when world-wide over-population and a scarcity of food supplies, conservation of the environment and of energy resources were tangible problems and important subjects of international debate.

Divorce

Many of the social changes which led in the 1950s and 1960s to earlier marriages contributed also to a higher incidence of divorce. In 1969 petitions for the dissolution of marriage reached a record number of 61·2 thousand (and the number almost doubled, to 115·5 thousand, by 1973). The 1969 figure was an increase of 140 per cent on the post-war low point of 1958, marking an annual average rate of increase of 9 per cent in the 1960s. While divorce has been explained historically by reference to legal and administrative reforms, demographic changes and factors such as war, 'it is hard to see ... how the recent rapid rise can be explained in such terms. Explanation must now probably look to changes in marital values and behaviour.'[28] This change of values, which is reflected in the press and on television, and is buttressed by psychological theories deriving from Freud and his successors (now widely popularized in weekly magazines and paperbacks), has resulted not only in big increases in petitions for divorce, but also in high rates of remarriage.

Another index of changing attitudes to marriage is the high incidence of separation in today's marriages, often occurring long before divorce.[29] Before the Second World War, legal separation was the only possible escape from an unhappy marriage – except for those fortunate enough to be able to afford the legal costs involved in proving a matrimonial offence. Thus, in 1937 the proportion of marriages terminated by divorce was less than 2 per cent. Immediately after the war, thanks to free legal aid and advice for those in lower income groups (as well as to the strains of war), the divorce rate shot up to over 7 per cent. It dropped slightly in the mid-fifties, but since then has been increasing again, both as a consequence of a relaxation in the rules governing divorce and the changing attitude among married couples about what marriage ought to be like.

O. R. McGregor and Ronald Fletcher, the authors of two widely influential studies of the family and divorce written in the 1950s,[30] have argued that the increasing rate of divorce (and remarriage) in the post-war period was an indication that far from being on the verge of collapse, the family was more popular than ever. Others believe that a high divorce rate, together with a growing illegitimacy rate, the increasing proportion of pre-nuptial pregnancies and high levels of venereal disease, are evidence of irresponsible attitudes which undermine marriage and the family.

It is difficult to generalize. Divorce figures on their own do not tell us anything about the quality or stability of family life. We need to know how long marriages last before breaking up – at what point separation occurs, and how long this occurs before divorce. We need to know how many children are involved, their age, and what arrangements are made for them after a separation or divorce. Given, today, the possibility of divorce by consent (after two years' separation or without consent after five years apart), it has been calculated that something over one and a quarter million adults will have been involved in divorce proceedings in the 1970s, affecting more than half a million children under school age.[31]

From the few small-scale studies of divorce undertaken since the Divorce Reform Act of 1969 (implemented from January 1971), we know something about the kinds of marriage most at risk. The rate of divorce is affected by age, length of marriage, social class and pre-marital pregnancy. The two social groups most prone to divorce are white-collar workers and those in unskilled jobs. Early marriage is another strong indicator of divorce, especially if the bride was pregnant at the time of her marriage. One researcher has estimated that 30 per cent of women who marry before the age of 20 will be divorced within seven years.[32] These data do not necessarily imply that a past family security and stability has been lost. We know that Victorian middle-class families were often far from happy and united. Prostitution was at its height in the mid-nineteenth century, and a double standard of morality denied women the right to express their sexual feelings. In working-class homes, for much of the last century, poverty, overcrowding, promiscuity and undernourishment made a mockery of what today are considered family values. Before industrialism conditions for the family were also harsh and unstable. Peter Laslett, analysing family life in the seventeenth century in the village of Clayworth, for example, estimated that in 1688 no fewer than 28 per cent of the children came from homes broken by death. Twenty-six of the sixty-five married couples in the village had been married before: there were three third marriages, four fourth marriages and one fifth – all in a village of about 400 people.[33]

Women and work

In the prevailing conditions of urban, industrial and commercial life, and given the monotony of many people's jobs, it is commonly felt that the family's main task should be to provide secure emotional support. Whereas in the nineteenth century it was exclusively women who were expected to fill the supportive roles (the men being more distant, authority figures), husbands also are now beginning to share the more nurturant and expressive roles. At the same time, as we have seen, family life has for most groups become more home-centred and 'privatized'. Rehousing and new community developments, which have meant that most families are separated geographically from their wider kin, have been one important reason for changed marital roles, as was shown by various studies in the 1960s and 1970s.[34] The longer span of most marriages and the growing tendency for married women to work are further reasons for changing attitudes – giving them more independent lives, more to share and a greater expectation of help from the husband in the home.

In the past, discussion about working wives tended to centre on the conflict between women's two roles – as housewives and mothers, and as workers outside the home.[35] The scope of this discussion is now being enlarged to encompass the two roles of men, and the conflict between the demands of the 'instrumental' order of the world of work and the more 'expressive' demands of family life. Prejudice and confusion remain, however, in judgements of married women's status. The expectation that women will be primarily responsible for the therapeutic and caring roles in the family creates considerable difficulties for married women wanting to return to work.[36] While many of the legal and political barriers to equal status between men and women have been removed and, since 1945, many of the restrictions on the employment of married women have similarly disappeared, other barriers remain. These involve deep-rooted attitudes, ideals and expectations held not only among husbands and wives but also among employers and co-workers. A survey of management attitudes in 1975, for example, found that the vast majority of those responsible for personnel in British industry thought that women were inferior to men in all the qualities considered important when making a job appointment.[37] Such prejudices are continually reinforced by the mass media.

The origin of this ambiguity and confusion of views lies partly in the existence of two distinct ideals of womanhood – both of which date from the nineteenth century. The first

32 *Women's demonstration*

of these is the idealization of the middle-class lady of leisure, still sanctified in some middle-class families. The second is based on the ideal of the hard-working wife. In post-war Britain women have been expected to combine both roles. Another frustrating legacy from the nineteenth century is the idea that it is basically wrong to be a career woman, since this threatens the sanctity of the home and denies the ideal of the child-centred family.[38]

None of this has prevented an increasing proportion of women from going out to work. (In the 1930s only 10 per cent of married women were employed; in 1951 the proportion was 26 per cent, and in 1971 41 per cent.) One obvious explanation is that because of a higher marriage rate and the earlier age at marriage, the number of single women available for recruitment is much lower than before. The growth of family planning, smaller average family sizes and the concentration of child-bearing during the early years of marriage also mean that, whereas at the end of the nineteenth century a mother spent twelve to fifteen years of her life in pregnancy and lactation, today this period is over after only four or five years on average.[39] Compulsory schooling after the age of five (and for some, the existence of nursery schools and play groups before this age) has also helped to reduce the mother's responsibilities. Given these changes, as well as the increased longevity of women, most mothers can look forward to at least thirty years of active working life after the completion of their families.

Economic changes have also helped to alter the pattern of women's work. In the early 1960s, in some sectors of the economy, developments in productivity depended entirely on there being an adequate supply of women workers, though this is less so in the harsher economic climate of the 1970s. The growth of retail trading and light manufacturing industries engaged in the production of consumer goods, and of clerical and office jobs, was important in providing opportunities for women to work. There was also an increase in the number of women, particularly married women, employed as social workers and medical and teaching auxiliaries. Although nearly half of all women workers in the 1960s were in non-manual jobs, their representation among the higher ranks of professional and administrative occupations was disproportionately small. Less than five in 1,000 women were in the higher professions and, while women accounted for one-third of those employed in the manufacturing industries, not more than one in a hundred was in a supervisory post. Women in most occupations received lower pay than men (in offices, for example, two-thirds of the men's rate, even on equivalent work).[40]

In the early 1970s conditions improved in principle. An Equal Pay Act was passed in 1970. In October 1973, however, it was calculated that in mechanical engineering the hourly rate for women workers was 61·73p, while for men it was 89·3p. In food, drink and tobacco manufacturing, women earned a rate of 58·76p an hour, while men earned 85·44p. In some trades women were more fortunate – in the retail meat trade and groceries, and in the Ford Motor Co., they had been given equal rates of pay. Even in these trades, however, women did not have equal opportunities for training and promotion, and often they were equal only to the lowest-paid male workers.[41]

If women are still unfairly treated at work, jobs are none the less apparently what they want – for reasons which include finance, escape from housework, and companionship. Concern was being expressed in the post-war decades that the growing proportion of mothers at work was contributing to lower standards of child care. The spectre of thousands of 'latch-key kids' was presented, with children left to hang around until late at night, fed only on crisps, bubble gum and chips bought from local shops, and liable to get involved in all kinds of delinquency. Evidence from a number of surveys of married women at work suggested that this was a serious exaggeration. Most mothers who go out to work make careful arrangements to see that someone looks after their small children during the holidays and when older members of the family are not at home. Many women deliberately choose shift work so as to be at home when their children are there – although this can create other family and marital problems.[42] In returning to paid employment women have in fact regained a status that had been theirs until the end of the eighteenth century.

The young and the old

The changes we have discussed have had advantages and disadvantages for the various family members. Small families, for instance, offer a less diverse range of emotional experiences, although relationships may be deeper and more fully integrated than are possible in larger families. Another consequence of small families is the wider gulf between the generations which, in the 1960s, became the focus of attempts to explain the 'youth phenomenon'.[43]

Adolescence has, in fact, been central to discussions of the family since 1945, one important reason being the expansion of the adolescent population following the high birth-rate at the end of the war. On Mark Abrams's definition of adolescents as 'anyone between fifteen and twenty-four who is unmarried',[44] this group amounted in the early 1960s to about one tenth of the population. Adolescents have also had more leisure and income than in the past: Abrams calculated that while the average real wages of adults increased by 25 per cent between 1938 and 1958, those of adolescents went up by twice that amount. Since the early 1960s the range of choice – in goods, entertainment, clothes and life styles – has become unprecedentedly wide, as sociologist Frank Musgrove testifies:

> The biggest single difference from my parents' youth is one of choice: there are far more alternatives open to me than there were to my father. Hence I tend to be less decided and single-minded, but at the same time less prepared to take a specialist attitude to anything. The rate of change in my parents' life-time has been staggering . . . One effect has been to give me a great sense of separateness from my parents through history.[45]

For such reasons, parents, like teachers and others of the older generation, are often seen to be ineffective and out of date.[46] In the absence of very meaningful contacts with their wider relatives, and lacking older brothers and sisters, adolescents have no alternative to the society of their peers – with the inevitable conflicts involved. Teenagers, suggested Peter Laurie, 'stand in the same relationship with adults as explorers do to settlers – the one has to travel light, acquire information, react flexibly to any chance; the other has to stay put, narrow his gaze, concentrate his energies, and hoe his furrow'.[47] The early age of puberty, longer formal schooling and uncertainty about jobs in a world of rapid occupational shifts, have added to the strains of adolescence. It is not surprising that some young people who failed (as well as some who were successful) in the competitive educational and occupational system, discovered how to drop out or rebel.

The variety of distinct adolescent groups in the 1960s included not only the mod and the student militant, the addict and soccer hooligan, but also the sixth formers still at school and the newly-weds. Whatever the bizarre behaviour of some adolescent groups in the 1960s – for instance in the so-called seaside riots or at pop festivals – according to a Gallup Poll survey published in 1966 only one in 500 teenagers was actually delinquent; one in three went to church regularly; one in three attended evening classes, and not more than one in twelve was continually changing jobs.[48] Indeed, as the authors of the Latey Report on *The Age of Majority* observed in 1967, when recommending the reduction of the voting age from 21 to 18 (effected in the Law Reform Act of 1969), what was most surprising about the younger generation as a whole was its conformity. In the 1960s, in spite of the impression that may have been created by the media, the majority of adolescents probably differed little or not at all from their elders in any important political or ideological sense.[49] The rebelliousness of the minority, however, was due to more than youthful high spirits. For many of them, as we have seen, it represented a serious and committed opposition to forms of social life and institutions which they felt they could no longer respect. Many of the younger generation participated in the youth culture without adopting some of its implications of social militancy.

Since the early 1960s the proportion of young people opposed to existing laws and conventions has undoubtedly grown, although there have been few dramatic confrontations to match the student revolts at Hornsey College of Art, Essex University and the London School of Economics in 1968. Indeed, as we saw earlier, the seventies have seen a more fundamental process of erosion of the authority of institutions like the school, work, the police and established government.

In the 1960s old people were the subject of far less sociological analysis and public concern than were adolescents. Their problems were still receiving scant political attention, and the Labour government's pension policies between 1964 and 1970 were inadequate to meet the needs of the growing number of retired people, especially in periods of economic difficulty. From the beginning of the 1970s the old moved to the centre of the stage. The over-65s now accounted for one in seven of the population and, as a group, were becoming progressively older. Like adolescents, pensioners are not a uniform group – but are separated by differences based on social class, age and health. So far, the

33 *Student demonstration, 1974*

majority of the elderly have been in the 65 to 74 age group and have therefore been comparatively mobile and healthy. For them social policies have centred on opportunities for part-time work, modified pension and earnings rules, retraining and preparation for increased leisure. In the future the balance of concern is likely to shift to the growing proportion over 75. Their needs mainly relate to hospitals, doctors, nursing homes, day-centres and community care agencies, like Task Force and Meals on Wheels. They raise delicate questions of social budgeting and priorities, questions to which organizations not traditionally involved in this area of policy – the trade unions, for example – have turned their attention in the 1970s.

Within the family, for those who retain their health, the role of grandparents is still often an important one – involving visiting and help, financial or practical. Demographic changes have meant that most grandmothers are not only younger, but different in other ways. As Young and Willmott point out, today's grandmothers have not practised their craft continuously. They may be at work, and their role reduced for other reasons too. They are less likely to advise daughters on health and child care, or to find rented accommodation for their married offspring – matters now taken care of by local authorities or other agencies. In working-class families particularly, the result has been to turn 'the trio of mother–daughter–husband into a duet'.[50]

Although more old people are able to enjoy a fully creative life, the strains imposed by enforced retirement (when many are still capable of work) and by housing and financial difficulties cannot be overlooked. Poverty among old people is an ever-present problem, especially in periods of high inflation. To these and related practical issues, as well as to the hardship of loneliness, considerably more attention has been directed in the 1970s both by the public authorities and by agencies like Age Concern.

Socialization

Social investigation and analysis has attempted to understand these and other complex changes in the family, its

relationships, its narrower and wider generational structures, its functions, needs and inadequacies – and to consider the implications for social policy. In the field of family
policy there can be no uniform solutions for there is increasingly no 'compact majority', only a steady profusion of
divergent minorities.[51] Social policy, whose role in the past
has been primarily egalitarian, may increasingly have to
accept diversity and to accept it as a social value, constantly
to re-evaluate its assumptions.

Most of the family research we have discussed so far has
been based on a descriptive model. Researchers have attempted to show how family relationships and expectations
have altered as a result of new social conditions – for
example, the move to the suburban estate, the increase in
married women at work, and the growing number of old
people.[52] In all of these studies the method employed has
been empirical and based on questionnaires. In most cases,
as in the early social surveys, there have been underlying
policy issues that the research aimed to clarify or expose.
There is, however, another area of research centred on the
family which has used different and more narrowly focused
and more radical methods – that is, research in the area of
socialization. Some of the most influential work in this field
has been based on the empirical tradition, for example
that of John and Elizabeth Newson, with a sample of
Nottingham children.[53] There have, however, been widely
different approaches to the understanding of how children
are socialized. Some of these, like Jean Piaget's studies of
language and concepts in children, derive from observations
of normal children and concentrate on the development of
cognitive skills. Others use case studies, such as Bruno
Bettelheim developed in his work with autistic children, and
described in *Love is not Enough* (1950), and have roots in
psychoanalytic explorations of the emotionally disturbed.
Still other theories, notably the influential ideas of Ruth
Benedict and Margaret Mead, have focused on investigations of child-rearing practices in more primitive societies.[54]

Among sociologists there are two main theories of
socialization. One of these (represented, for instance, in the
theories of the American sociologists Gerth and Mills) relies

on the concept of social roles. Action, on this view, is ultimately reducible to patterned institutional expectations (roles) to which the child is ascribed or which he learns as he grows up in the family. These determine the permissible range of social behaviour for given individuals in particular situations. Although roles can vary widely between different cultural (including social class) groups, accepted norms of behaviour have fairly narrow limits within a particular setting.[55] From such a starting point wider descriptions are possible. Although the family is the primary agency in socialization, other groups can be seen to play a considerable part in this process. The school, the peer group, and institutions such as the church have functions with regard to allocation to adult occupational status, egalitarian relationships or other aspects of the child's growing vocabulary of social conduct.

Since the 1960s social role theory has been amplified by what is known as the transactional view.[56] According to writers like Erving Goffman, character is not straightforwardly determined by external role demands. The individual himself can choose how to act – whether to conform to expectations, to rebel or to create new roles.[57] The family was also an institution which came inside the range of interests of radical critical theory. Since Marcuse and the radical psychiatrists in particular were arguing for liberation from repressive capitalist affluence, it was natural for them to look critically at such a powerful institution for mediating the values of existing society. In 1971 David Cooper argued that the family 'reinforces the effective power of the ruling class in any exploitative society'. It strengthens conformity: 'the family, since it cannot bear doubt about itself and its capacity to engender "mental health" and "correct attitudes", destroys doubt as a possibility in each of its members'. The family's role was to induce 'the base of conformism – normality through the primary socialization of the child'. The family prevents creative individuality, 'specializes in the formation of roles for its members rather than laying down the conditions for the free assumption of identity'.[58] Cooper's argument illustrates how far theoretical critiques of social institutions went in the 1960s and 1970s, focusing on the family as well as political protest, the nature of knowledge[59] and the functions of technology.

Like other institutions, the family has also remained an area over which conflicting theories and methodologies do battle. If the family has a mediating function, how, to what end and with what penalties, does it perform that function? Is it, as Barrington Moore and Edmund Leach suggest, a 'true relic of barbarism'?[60] Is it a necessary *rite de passage*, a socially and morally binding force in society? The profusion of studies since the early 1960s by sociologists, demographers, psychiatrists and others[61] indicates that the family is in one sense a thriving social institution. It is also controversial, open to plural interpretations, and presents an increasing variety of types, functions and influences. It has raised, as have other social institutions, sharp questions about methods and purposes of inquiry. It has been a major participant in processes of social change in the 1960s and 1970s, and has been, like politics and protest, technology and the environment, moral values and economic power, an invitation to re-examine our perceptions and ideologies.

Notes

1 See JOHN CROSBY 'London – the most exciting city', *Daily Telegraph*, Supplement, 30 April 1965.

2 See DANIEL J. BOORSTIN *The Image* (New York, 1962); JEREMY TUNSTALL *Advertising Man* (London, 1964).

3 See GRAHAM WOOTTON *Workers, Unions and the State* (London, 1966).

4 See MICHAEL SHANKS *The Stagnant Society* (Harmondsworth, 1961); REX MALIK *What's Wrong with British Industry?* (Harmondsworth, 1964); ERIC WIGHAM *What's Wrong with the Unions?* (Harmondsworth, 1961).

5 Speech at Birmingham Town Hall, 19 January 1964, reprinted in *The New Britain: Labour's Plan outlined by Harold Wilson* (Harmondsworth, 1964).

6 See GUY R. NEAVE *How They Fared: The impact of the comprehensive school upon the university.* (London, 1975).

7 See STANLEY COHEN *Folk Devils and Moral Panics* (London, 1972).

314 Modern English Society

8 BOOKER *The Neophiliacs*, p. 299.

9 HERBERT MARCUSE *One-Dimensional Man: studies in the ideology of advanced industrial society*, pp. 1–7 (London, 1964).

10 COUNCIL FOR SCIENTIFIC POLICY *Enquiry into the Flow of Candidates in Science and Technology into Higher Education*, p. 79 (London, 1968).

11 PETER L. BERGER *Invitation to Sociology*, pp. 44, 51 (New York, 1963; Penguin 1966 edition).

12 R. D. LAING *The Politics of Experience* and *The Bird of Paradise*, p. 11 (Harmondsworth, 1967). For radical psychiatric and political critiques see DAVID COOPER (ed.) *The Dialectics of Liberation* (Harmondsworth, 1968), containing contributions by Laing and Cooper, Black Power leader Stokely Carmichael, Marcuse and others. For the radical sociology of the 1960s and early 1970s, see MARTIN SHAW 'The coming crisis of radical sociology' in ROBIN BLACKBURN (ed.) *Ideology in Social Science: readings in critical social theory* (London, 1972), discussing ALVIN GOULDNER *The Coming Crisis of Western Sociology*.

13 PETER BERGER and HANSFRIED KELLER 'Marriage and the construction of reality', *Diogenes*, 46, 1964.

14 PETER LASLETT 'Introduction: the history of the family', in PETER LASLETT (ed.) *Household and Family in Past Time*, pp. 5, 7, 73 (Cambridge, 1972).

15 Ibid., p. 67. See ANDERSON *Family Structure in Nineteenth-Century Lancashire* for an example of family analysis in a nineteenth-century industrial area.

16 See WILLIAM GOODE 'The process of role bargaining in the impact of urbanisation and industrialisation on family systems', *Current Sociology*, Vol. XII (1), 1963–4.

17 FRANK MUSGROVE *Ecstasy and Holiness*, p. 154 (London, 1974), summarizing the views of the American sociologists Eisenstadt and Parsons.

18 WILLIAMS *The Long Revolution*, pp. 331–2.

19 ROSSER and HARRIS *The Family and Social Change*, p. 301.

20 MICHAEL GORDON (ed.) *The Nuclear Family in Crisis: the search for an alternative*, p. 6 (New York, 1972).

21 PETER WEDGE and HILARY PROSSER *Born to Fail?*, pp. 11–13 (London, 1973).

22 See R. K. KELSALL *Population*, p. 21 (London, 1967).

23 ABRAMS 'Teenage consumer spending in 1959'.

24 Estimates for the average age of the onset of puberty are notoriously difficult to arrive at. However, whereas the present age is around thirteen for girls and fifteen for boys, in 1854 puberty

for girls seems generally to have occurred between fourteen and sixteen years of age. (See GEORGE R. DRYSDALE *The Elements of Social Science*, p. 65 (London, 1854; 1881 edition).

25 D. V. GLASS and E. GREBENIK 'The trend and pattern of fertility in Great Britain', *Papers of the Royal Commission on Population* (London, 1954).

26 KELSALL *Population*, pp. 56–7.

27 WEDGE and PROSSER *Born to Fail?*, p. 11.

28 ROBERT CHESTER and JANE STREATHER 'Taking stock of divorce', *New Society*, 22 July 1971, p. 153.

29 Ibid.

30 O. R. MCGREGOR *Divorce in England* (London, 1957); RONALD FLETCHER *The Family and Marriage* (Harmondsworth, 1962).

31 CHESTER and STREATHER 'Taking stock of divorce', p. 153.

32 COLIN GIBSON 'The association between divorce and social class in England and Wales', *British Journal of Sociology*, Vol. XXV (1), 1974, p. 79.

33 PETER LASLETT 'What is so special about us now?', *The Listener*, 7 February 1963, p. 236.

34 See YOUNG and WILLMOTT *The Symmetrical Family*; ROSSER and HARRIS *The Family and Social Change*; ELIZABETH BOTT *Family and Social Network*.

35 See ALVA MYRDAL and VIOLA KLEIN *Women's Two Roles* (London, 1956).

36 EDMUND DAHLSTRÖM and ROTA LILJESTRÖM *The Changing Roles of Men and Women*, Ch. 5 (London, 1967).

37 AUDREY HUNT *Management Attitudes and Practices towards Women at Work* (London, 1975).

38 For detailed case studies of the frustrations (and advantages) felt by professional career wives see RHONA and ROBERT RAPAPORT *Dual-Career Families* (London, 1971). For the views of working-class wives see Hannah Gavron *The Captive Wife* (London, 1966).

39 See TITMUSS 'The position of women', in *Essays on 'The Welfare State'*.

40 See NAN BERGER and JOAN MAIZELS *Woman – Fancy or Free?*, Ch. VI (London, 1962).

41 ANNA COOTE and TESS GILL *Women's Rights: a practical guide*, pp. 21–49 (Harmondsworth, 1974).

42 See S. YUDKIN and A. HOLME *Working Mothers and their Children* (London, 1965).

43 See MARGARET MEAD *Culture and Commitment: a study of the generation gap* (London, 1970).

44 ABRAMS 'Teenage consumer spending in 1959'.

45 MUSGROVE *Ecstasy and Holiness*, p. 109.

46 See BARRY SUGARMAN 'Youth culture, academic achievement and conformity', *British Journal of Sociology*, Vol. 18,
1967.

47 PETER LAURIE *Teenage Revolution*, p. 11 (London, 1965).

48 See MICHAEL SCHOFIELD *The Sexual Behaviour of Young
People* (London, 1965).

49 See also EDGAR FRIEDENBERG *The Vanishing Adolescent*
(Boston, 1959).

50 YOUNG and WILLMOTT *The Symmetrical Family*, p. 93.

51 See RICHARD MILLS *Young Outsiders*, pp. 189–90 (London,
1973).

52 For suburban estates see, for example, WILLMOTT and
YOUNG *Family and Kinship in East London* and *Family and
Class in a London Suburb* (London, 1960). For women at work
see PEARL JEPHCOTT *et al. Married Women Working*
(London, 1962) and VIOLA KLEIN *Britain's Married Women
Workers* (London, 1965). For old people see TOWNSEND *The
Family Life of Old People*.

53 JOHN and ELIZABETH NEWSON *Patterns of Infant Care in an
Urban Community* (London, 1963); *Four Years Old in an Urban
Community* (London, 1968); *Seven Years Old in the Home
Environment* (London, 1976).

54 JEAN PIAGET's seminal study was *Language and Thought of the
Child* (first published in English, London, 1926). See RUTH
BENEDICT *Patterns of Culture* (London, 1935); MARGARET
MEAD *Coming of Age in Samoa* (New York, 1928), and *Growing
up in New Guinea* (New York, 1930).

55 HANS GERTH and C. WRIGHT MILLS *Character and Social
Structure* (London, 1954).

56 See DICK ATKINSON *Orthodox Consensus and Radical
Alternatives* (London, 1971). Chapter 5 contains a full
statement of this development in sociological theory.

57 See ERVING GOFFMAN *The Presentation of Self in Everyday
Life* (New Jersey, 1956), and *Interaction Ritual* (New York,
1967).

58 DAVID COOPER *The Death of the Family*, p. 6, 9, 12–13, 25
(London, 1971; 1972 Penguin edition). See also R. D. LAING
The Divided Self (London, 1960); R. D. LAING and A. ESTER-
SON *Sanity, Madness and the Family* (London, 1964).

59 Underlying much of this discussion is an increased interest in
the sociology of knowledge. See PETER L. BERGER and
THOMAS LUCKMAN *The Social Construction of Reality* (New

York, 1966). See also BERGER and KELLER 'Marriage and the construction of reality'.

60 J. BARRINGTON MOORE, jr., 'Thoughts on the future of the family', in STEIN et al. (eds.) *Identity and Anxiety*, p. 393; EDMUND LEACH *A Runaway World?* (London, 1968).

61 See, for example, MICHAEL GORDON *The Nuclear Family in Crisis*; KATHERINE ELLIOTT (ed.) *The Family and the Future* (London, 1970); SUZANNE KELLER 'Does the family have a future?', *Journal of Comparative Family Studies*, Spring 1971.

10 Citizenship and education

Civil, political and social rights

Writing in the late 1940s, T. H. Marshall described 'the modern drive towards social equality' as merely 'the latest phase of an evolution of citizenship which has been in continuous progress for some 250 years'. In Marshall's view, this improved 'citizenship' could be divided into three elements: civil, political and social. He saw the following pattern in their development:

> Civil rights came first, and were established in something like their modern form before the first Reform Act was passed in 1832. Political rights came next, and their extension was one of the main features of the nineteenth century, although the principle of universal political citizenship was not recognised until 1918. Social rights, on the other hand, sank to vanishing point in the eighteenth and early nineteenth centuries. Their revival began with the development of public elementary education, but it was not until the twentieth century that they attained to equal partnership with the other two elements in citizenship.[1]

Marshall's judgements broadly summarize the changes we have traced in earlier chapters, and they offer a useful basis on which to examine the shape of society, community and 'citizenship' in Britain today. They lead us also into a discussion of the role of education in modern English society. This will be the subject of our last case study.

The three phases in the acquisition of rights, identified by Marshall, mark the transition to formal democracy in England. The right to protection against the arbitrary use of personal and public power, and the right to participation in the processes of government, were features of social and political debate from Magna Carta to the twentieth century. At different times, to different extents, and for different groups in society, they became realities. Political and social democracy, legal and civil rights have, however, become more than formalities only in the twentieth century. In such fields as divorce, women's suffrage and legal rights, consumer protection, and popular access to secondary and higher education, the formal structures of democratic life have been filled out only comparatively recently – and many of them still only partially. Indeed, by the mid-twentieth century, as we shall see, the notion that political rights were unrelated to 'social' rights was being increasingly challenged.

Central to developments in Britain during the 1970s was the question: who governs? The discussion of political democracy increasingly involved reference to the trade unions and big business, as well as to international influences on the British economy and way of life.

The question 'who governs?' involved an appraisal of the nature of power and of the role of government and the State in exercising it. 'Power in Britain today', wrote Anthony Sampson in 1971, 'depends on a confederation of interests, which rarely work together ... contemporary political scientists are inclined to see parliament's essential role not so much as a legislature, but as a means of mobilizing consent or a communications centre'.[2] The structural changes we have discussed in the period since 1945 did not weaken non-parliamentary sources of power. On the contrary. In the late 1960s and 1970s successive governments tried to 'mobilize' (or neutralize) the power both of big business and of the trade union movement. In doing so, they found themselves in dramatic confrontations.

In the 1960s and 1970s, industrial, commercial, insurance and banking interests continued to consolidate their power. This happened for three reasons. First, individual large units continued to grow larger, as a consequence of mergers and take-overs. In 1967, for instance, the 300 largest companies held 87 per cent of all assets.[3] The men involved in this close network of inter-locking directorships acquired enhanced roles in the processes of economic consultation and bargaining. Second, the role of multi-national companies gained in importance as economic difficulties mounted and jobs and foreign investments required protection. In key manufacturing sectors, including the motor, shipbuilding and aircraft industries, multi-national companies were increasingly able to wield power and dictate terms for their survival – as in the case of the Chrysler UK rescue operation in 1976. Third, as the British economy became even more threatened, those in charge of major manufacturing and exporting firms seemed crucial to a solution – indeed, to the survival of the nation as a whole.

Politics in the 1970s, therefore, involved a large area of direct bargaining between government and leaders of the Confederation of British Industries, of individual industries, commercial interests and firms. Consultation and co-operation over budgetary and financial measures, tax relief or changes in Value Added Tax, for example, were highly publicized. The ability of governments to 'handle' or collaborate with the leaders of finance and industry became an important parliamentary and electioneering bargaining counter – as, of course, was the government's ability to obtain trade union backing for its financial and related policies.

The question of trade union power achieved new prominence in January 1974. Attempts by the Wilson government in the late 1960s to introduce legislation on industrial relations had undermined the traditional basis of trust between the trade union leadership and a Labour government. Now, in 1974, in a situation of strict wage controls, a miners' wage

34 *Miners' strike, 1974*

claim brought them into a direct clash with the
Conservative government of Edward Heath. Rather than
yield to the miners' strike, the government put the country
on a three-day working week. Heath called a general election and lost. The Wilson government, back in office,
conceded the miners' demand as a 'special case'. The miners
had won. A Labour government had shown itself better able
to 'deal with' (or as many felt, to surrender to) the miners –
but at what cost, and with what implications for the question 'who governs?'. The question was debated frequently as
new situations arose to indicate the strength – or at least the
importance – of the trade union movement and its leaders.
Government and opposition trod cautiously – both wishing
to show their ability to 'talk to the unions', and both aware
of the crucial role of the T.U.C. and the unions in

producing a workable solution to the problems of economic setback, high inflation and unemployment – especially in the middle of the decade. By negotiating an agreement on an incomes policy with the unions, the Labour government was acknowledging the paramount need to mobilize the 'consent' of the unions. At a particularly critical point in 1975, with inflation at its height, the old questions were again asked:

> Until a few months ago there was little doubt that our true masters were a handful of trade union leaders. Now it appears that the more reasonable of these masters have allied themselves with the Government in a programme, supported by the Opposition and the majority of the public . . . Who will our masters be next spring? Will the trade union leaders be more firmly in the saddle, with the Government once again out in the cold? . . . The Government has brought to an end the era of thirty and forty per cent wage demands. Its methods have very little to do with democracy as it would have been understood in Britain only ten years ago.[4]

The T.U.C., now relating to government in new ways, found itself, as a result of national economic difficulties, in a central position. Although the processes of decision-making had not changed decisively or permanently in the early 1970s, there had been visible shifts in the roles of the leaders of the trade union movement and of industry. Government had in the 1970s become even more of what Anthony Sampson called a 'communications centre'. The political aspects of citizenship in the 1970s have to be seen in this markedly changed economic and political context.

Three other aspects of the changed political context of the 1970s – the European Common Market, regionalism and Northern Ireland – require mention in the discussion about the nature and functioning of democracy in Britain.

From the early British attempts to enter the Common Market, after application for membership was initially made in 1961, opinion in Britain had been divided about the economic merits of entry, about the terms and about the political implications. The majority of Conservative and Liberal opinion favoured entry and it was a Conservative

Prime Minister, Edward Heath, who successfully completed negotiation for entry on 1 January 1973. Labour opinion was more divided. As early as 1962, for example, the Party's leader, Hugh Gaitskell, offered the annual conference a typically hesitant Labour view. The economic arguments, as he presented them, were unclear, and the terms so far negotiated seemed inadequate. Britain, already a member of the European Free Trade Area, was torn between Europe and the Commonwealth. Politically, federation with Europe could mean the end of Britain as an independent European state, and the end of the Commonwealth. On the other hand, association with Europe might mean greater international influence and the possibility of building a bridge between Europe and the Commonwealth.[5] It was such hesitations about the terms of entry, trading agreements, and the loss of sovereignty to the institutions of the E.E.C. that underlay the Labour Government's submission of the question of continued membership to a referendum – the first in British history – in June 1975. Strong opposition to British membership was expressed within the Labour Party (and Cabinet) and on the political Right (outstandingly by Enoch Powell).[6] Support for continued membership among the majority of political leaders and the electorate, however, indicated acceptance of the new terms negotiated. It was clear that arguments about the threat to traditional institutions commanded less interest than the possible trading advantages of membership. In this field too, therefore, economic worries were shaping political responses and structures.

A second area in which serious inroads into old conceptions were made in the 1970s was that of regionalism. We have concentrated in this book explicitly on English society, while recognizing that much of the description and discussion applied throughout the United Kingdom. The growth of nationalism in Scotland and Wales cannot, however, be excluded from a discussion of political rights and processes, especially in the 1970s.

Before the Second World War, both the Scottish and Welsh nationalist parties had pursued policies of independence in one form or another. The Welsh Nationalist Party,

for example, declared its policy in the 1930s as being 'to
secure Dominion Status for Wales, to protect and to foster
the economic and cultural life of the nation, and to secure
for Wales the right to become a member of the League of
Nations'.[7] Nationalism in Wales was a tiny force but during
and after the war parallel pressures for a measure of autonomy were exerted, including pressure by the Liberals, calling for a Welsh Parliament with powers over home affairs.[8]
A spate of pamphleteering offered rival schemes for Welsh
progress. Support for Welsh nationalism or indeed any form
of Welsh regional autonomy continued to be weak, however,
until the 1960s. The activities of the Welsh Language
Society, using direct action in its campaign for Welsh language culture, achieved similar publicity to that of other
direct action groups over other issues. In the early 1970s,
with increased support and representation in Parliament,
the Welsh Nationalist Plaid Cymru was in a position to
influence events more directly. Its success was one factor in
the plans for devolution which the Labour Party first outlined in its manifesto of 1974.

Scottish nationalism before the war was a more important
force, though still weak. It suffered from splits and expul-
sions in the 1930s and again in 1942, but during the wartime
political truce between the Labour and Conservative parties
it received a substantial protest vote. From 1942, however,
it was organizationally of little significance: 'the great
achievement of the S.N.P. from 1942 to 1964 was simply to
have survived'.[9] But by the 1970s Scottish nationalism was
rivalling, and defeating, other parties, and gaining substantial representation at Westminster. The Labour government
responded with a devolutionary policy which the S.N.P.
(and Plaid Cymru) rejected as insufficient.

While sharing the same central aim, there were important
differences between the Welsh and Scottish movements.
Wales, as an official report put it in 1944, was conscious that
after the First World War 'victory in the field ... was
followed by virtual defeat at home'.[10] Even in the 1970s it
was difficult to argue that Wales could look forward to
greater prosperity as an independent economic unit. Arguing from a claim to North Sea oil, however, Scottish nation-

alists could present an economic case. Both the Welsh and the Scots could continue to point to their own strong political and cultural traditions.

The 1970s, especially over the devolution issue, saw the emergence of widespread concern not only about rights and the quality of citizenship, but about primary allegiances. Were we now citizens of Europe, and if so in what real sense? Would independence for Scotland and Wales, or the establishment of regional governments of some kind, lead to a total revision of the concepts of 'English' and 'British'? Economics, national and international politics, along with ancient regional traditions, all coincided in raising major questions about the nature and limits of citizenship.

Similar questions were built into the dramatic developments in Northern Ireland at the end of the 1960s and in the 1970s. The political, religious and economic issues involved in the re-emergence of Irish Republican Army militancy, and the Protestant political and para-military response, lie outside our terms of reference. It is important to note, however, that in the British consciousness the community rivalries and violence in Northern Ireland, and the involvement of British troops, produced further conflicting notions about the nature of the total British or United Kingdom society. Could Northern Ireland cut itself adrift, or be cut adrift, to fight its own battles? How indefinite was a British responsibility and commitment to police such bloody conflict, given the Irish sectarian dimension and hostility by both major political groups to basic aspects of British policy? When I.R.A. atrocities spread to Britain, the dilemma became acute. What was involved was not just a search for political solutions, or attitudes towards military involvement, but the very concept of citizenship within a larger community, responsibilities within a set of economic and social structures, and the special and difficult questions not only of Ulster, but also of regionalism or nationalism in Wales and Scotland. Being a citizen in the 1970s involved all of these considerations that had not been envisaged by T. H. Marshall in the 1940s, and were not prominent even in the 1950s and early 1960s.

The seventies and social change

An increasingly familiar feature of Britain in the 1970s was a sense of crisis – both on the grand scale, involving the national economy and the very survival of basic aspects of British society, and in personal terms, concerning, for example, purchasing power, job security, the quality of secondary schools and the declining value of savings. When international oil prices quadrupled in 1973, when international demand and shortages in raw materials drove up the price of coffee, or paper, or sugar or beef to unprecedented extents, the impact on the domestic consumer in Britain was direct – and often dramatic. Slowly and grudgingly, in the course of the seventies, the nation accustomed itself to constant economic uncertainties and to cuts in public spending which affected such things as the quality of local library services, public transport, nursery school places and roadworks. The euphoric mania of the 1960s for spending, building, planning and improving had disappeared.

When the Prime Minister resigned in March 1976, Peter Hall outlined some of the changes that had taken place since Wilson first entered office in 1964. The rate of population growth had dramatically declined. What is more, by the mid-1970s there were signs of an even sharper fall in the birth-rate. Some big cities, outstandingly London, were losing jobs and population at a rapid rate. Meanwhile, smaller towns (like Reading and Taunton) were growing. Private car ownership was still increasing and at the same time public transport had declined (from carrying a third of total passenger miles in the mid-1960s to a fifth in the mid-1970s). Manufacturing industry had declined along with opportunities for semi-skilled work. White collar jobs and the service industries, on the other hand, had expanded. Great physical changes had taken place:

> The housing managers, restrained from building outwards by green belt policies, built upwards – until the rising pressure of public and professional opinion brought the end of the high rise era. The city fathers willingly entered into partnership with the property developers to

bulldoze and comprehensively redevelop their cores – until growing conservationist protest and economic stagnation brought at least a partial change. The result has been the greatest physical transformation that British cities have ever known since the industrial revolution.

The Wilson era might, in retrospect, suggested Hall, 'come to seem a kind of golden age of material affluence, of economic growth . . . and of physical metamorphosis. We may never see its like again in Britain.'[11]

This analysis, even if it over-states the changes of the 1960s, does not exaggerate the sense of the end of an era that pervaded the mid-1970s. In other ways too the sense of crisis was pervasive. Crime began to assume dimensions associated previously only with the biggest American cities. In the two years from 1973 to 1975 the number of burglaries reported in London increased by 35 per cent. Violent theft increased by 87 per cent and increases were recorded in all forms of crimes of violence, in shoplifting, fraud and auto-crime. Even more worrying was the finding that of all the police arrests made, over half involved people under twenty-one, and 29 per cent involved youths between ten and sixteen.[12]

How far these massive increases in crime reflect a real increase in criminal activity and how far they are a reflection of greater police vigilance and readiness to make arrests is impossible to tell. To some extent the increase may be an artefact of new labelling devices. 'Mugging', for instance, was an offence unknown in Britain until the name was imported from the United States in the early 1970s. At this point it was enthusiastically taken up by both the police and the mass media and used to cover a wide range of offences of varying degrees of violence against the person. Not surprisingly, the public reacted with great concern to the new phenomenon.[13]

For these and other reasons, change was frequently seen as crisis: even as breakdown. Widespread publicity attended occurrences of violence in school playgrounds, picket demonstrations, vandalism, football hooliganism, racial fights and incidents typifying the alleged decline in moral standards. The growth of more permissive approaches to sex and pornography which we discussed earlier were, in particular, producing a concerted defence of traditional standards. The campaign begun by Mary Whitehouse in the late 1960s against permissive trends in the media, for instance, grew into a gathering of 35,000 in Trafalgar Square for the first meeting of the Festival of Light in September 1971. In 1974 Sir Keith Joseph took up Mary Whitehouse's theme and related it to the post-war growth of collectivism. Although his attack was on socialist policies, it also represented a return to the classic Tory doctrine of free competition. (This was a trend that undoubtedly contributed to Edward Heath's defeat by Mrs Thatcher in the Conservative leadership election of 1975.) The new Tory message was unequivocal: the 'new establishment' of post-war Britain had 'preferred the permissive society, and, at the same time, the collectivized society'. There was nothing unusual in this combination, Sir Keith explained, since socialism took away from the family 'the responsibilities which give it cohesion', including responsibility for 'education, health, upbringing, morality, advice and guidance, of saving for old age, for housing'.[14] The family was the foundation of civilization, and was being undermined.

The mass media

A powerful force in shaping people's perceptions of the way they live and how they relate to the wider processes of government has been the mass media. At different times, either press, television or radio have been influential both in building a sense of shared national identity and common interests and in reinforcing divisions between different social groups. In particular, in the recent past, because of their virtual monopoly on 'news' and their generally conservative political standpoint, they have been held responsible for manipulation of a quite overt political nature. A brief examination of the history of the media in the country may help to clarify and extend our discussion of citizenship.

The press began life and developed for the transmission of messages 'along other than official lines. Early news-

papers were a combination of that kind of message –
political and social information – and the specific messages –
classified advertising and general commercial news – of an
expanding system of trade.' As the nineteenth century progressed, the press gained in influence: 'as the struggle for a
share in decision and control became sharper, in campaigns
for the vote and then in competition for the vote, the press
became not only a new communications system but, centrally, a new social institution'.[15]

Before the mid-nineteenth century newspapers were
mostly local or dependent for their national circulation on
slow and expensive postal services. By the 1880s, however,
greater efficiency in news-gathering, the new tradition of
snippet presentation, the greater scale and monopolization
of industry and commerce, and the possibility of exploiting
the advertising side of newspaper production, all contributed to the development of the mass circulation newspaper as we know it. Northcliffe's halfpenny *Daily Mail*
rolled off the press at the rate of 200,000 copies an hour in
1896. At the beginning of the twentieth century the *News of
the World* reached a Sunday circulation of three million. In
1938 national daily newspaper sales totalled 11·5 million.

The fact that the sales of national dailies fell by 8 per cent
in the decade from the mid-1960s (from approaching 15·7
million to under 14·4 million) did not seriously diminish the
place and functions of the newspaper. Nevertheless, when
this decline is taken along with a 12 per cent drop in Sunday
newspaper sales over the same period (from 23·7 to 20·8
million), a drop of about 42 per cent in the sales of the two
London evening papers, the disappearance of the *Daily
Sketch*, and the difficulties of the *Daily Express*, *Daily
Mirror*, *Daily Mail* and other papers in the 1970s, the
changing balance of popularity between press, radio and
television can be judged more clearly.[16] It is important not
to overlook, however, the increasing sales of local newspapers, carrying a massive volume of commercial advertising, and also the flourishing weekly periodicals, including
many which appeared for the first time in the 1960s or 1970s
(for example, those concerning home improvement, leisure,
mothercraft, car maintenance and the occult).

A discussion of the media in the 1970s inevitably focuses on television, which Brian Groombridge described in 1972 as 'a major educational force in society, perhaps the chief one', and as 'the chief means of communication in a society desperate for effective communication'.[17] But the story is not simply one of television versus the newspaper. It involves other factors we have already discussed, including the technological changes which produced the long-playing gramophone record and which influenced the pop era. The story is also one of the fortunes of the cinema and theatre, of the paperback book and the public library, new styles of teenage publications, and family magazines and the balance of programmes in the reconstruction of B.B.C. sound broadcasting. The story extends from the end of 1973, to local commercial radio and beyond. We cannot consider all this range of phenomena, or the implications of trends such as portable and colour television, increasing concentration of ownership in the commercial media, and the effects on them of

35 *Power of TV*

sales pressures and advertising needs. Here we are more concerned with questions of citizenship in relation to the media.

In the complex and changing circumstances of modern
society, the media – perhaps uniquely – are capable of per-
forming an important mediating function. A socially mobile
person, or a newcomer to this country, has no ready source
of knowledge about how to assume a new style of life.
His guides therefore become popular magazines, advertisements, radio and television. The media do not simply
enable people to adjust more readily to their changing social
environment, gradually they begin to alter their perceptions
and demands. They have a particularly strong influence on
children and adolescents – now the focus of a highly
specialized market in goods as well as entertainment – and
are increasingly inducing changes in school curricula and
teaching methods, for example, putting pressure on teachers
to make what they teach more relevant and responsive to the
changing impact of television in particular.

The media make another kind of contribution to life in modern society through the enormous fund of shared experiences which they provide. They 'establish contact among people even if they stay put. They bring about some uniformity of attitude and a blending of customs and beliefs.'[18] To some extent this process represents a measure of consensus (based on shared perceptions and shared experiences) which is necessary for the survival of any society. On the other hand, there is a danger that the massive weight of editorial selection which the media necessarily impose results in serious distortion. Evidence submitted to the Annan Committee on the Future of Broadcasting, for example, expressed concern at the way television coverage of the Glasgow dustmen's strike early in 1975 had been highly partial. It had focused on 'where the action was', filming dramatic incidents like soldiers chasing and killing rats among the accumulated heaps of garbage, rather than workers and corporation officials talking round the negotiating table. By setting up the terms of the discussion in its own particular way, therefore, television presented a biased version of what was happening in the city. This style of editing matters less in newspaper reporting, since most people are aware of the bias in the paper which they read (and which they probably choose for that reason). Television, however, in monopolizing the main channels of public discussion, has considerable power to make its images stick, often preventing people from making informed judgements. Experiments with cable television in places like Swindon and Greenwich in the early 1970s, offering opportunities for local participation in the making of community television, and the B.B.C.'s *Open Door* programmes, offering minority groups a chance to advertise their work or interests, have not affected the overriding pattern and power of the established media.

From the point of view of concepts like citizenship, there is a need to see the relationships between individuals and the media in terms of the total political and social context. The communicators are not necessarily manipulators, and the viewers or readers are not necessarily manipulated. Communication is not between automata. It is between real people who belong to real families and groups and who have real likes and dislikes. The picture of an undifferentiated audience is misleading because it 'ignores the fact that individuals *use* the media to realize their own varying purposes and *choose* to some extent among the media between various possible ways of satisfying their needs'.[19] The response to such choices, and the use made of them, are part of a pattern in the individual's social experience.

Social rights and community

Citizenship, like poverty, is rarely absolute. People feel more or less able to exercise their rights and to function as members of a community. There are, of course, social situations in which participation and democratic action appear, if not impossible, at least valueless, but both conditions are relatively diminished in our society by comparison with the past. People in poverty or without a sense of citizenship are not concerned with the past, however, they are relatively deprived in the present.

Throughout this book we have been tracing implicitly changes in the concept of community, from the 'mechanical solidarity' of pre-industrial communities to relationships established in industrial towns and cities. In its modern sense the term 'community' has two main meanings, as Raymond Williams explains: 'Community can be the warmly persuasive word used to describe an existing set of relationships, or the warmly persuasive word to describe an alternative set of relationships.' The ambiguity is made clearer in his discussion of 'community politics' which, Williams says, is separate 'not only from *national politics* but from formal *local politics* and normally involves various kinds of direct action and direct local organization "working directly with people", and which is distinct from "service to the *community*", which has an older sense of voluntary work supplementary to official provision or paid service'.[20]

For most of the nineteenth and twentieth centuries 'community' as a concept was most relevant to descriptions of working-class life.[21] Since the 1960s in particular, however, this sense of community has been eroded in many parts of the country so that people now have a different sense of 'belonging'. Having been rehoused away from the dense inner urban areas where they grew up, people are 'on the move' not just physically but, as Stuart Hall points out, from one kind of class 'ideal' to another: from 'solidarity, neighbourliness, collectivity' to a world of 'individualism', of 'competition' in the social struggle to 'get on', of 'privatization'.[22] The consequences for their feeling of citizenship are considerable – as for their feelings about class.

As we have seen in previous chapters, awareness of class, and the value of the concept in social analysis, have remained intact in spite of profound social and political changes. The reality of class differences remains too. In 1969, for example, the existence of extremes of wealth and status was reflected in the fact that 1 per cent of the population owned 20 per cent of the personal wealth, and that 'whatever criteria are used it is probable that between 5 and 15 per cent of the British population may be said to be living in poverty'.[23] The *General Household Survey* published in 1974 by the Office of Population Census and Surveys revealed that unskilled workers' families were ten times more likely to suffer over-crowding in their home than professional families, and were five times more likely to lack sole use of both bath and lavatory. They were only half as likely to be covered by occupational sick-pay schemes when ill, though three times more likely to be absent from work due to illness or injury. Even more damaging was the revelation, confirming what Richard Titmuss had pointed out as early as the 1950s, that public expenditure and public services are often geared not to the reversal of these inequalities, but to their extension.[24]

In the 1970s perceptions of social class differences were sharpened by, among other things, the impact of inflation and unemployment, the wages freeze, the reduction of food subsidies and cuts in the welfare and education services. These, along with the move to a new town or housing estate, focused people's response to social differences not so much on their *shared* deprivation (their solidarity with others in similar circumstances), but on their *relative* economic and social status compared to other families.

The discussion of relative deprivation, represented most clearly in the 1960s by W. G. Runciman's *Relative Deprivation and Social Justice* (subtitled 'A study of attitudes to social inequality in twentieth century England'), became a significant element in the examination of class experiences in the 1970s.

A key to this approach can be found in a passage in *Poverty*, published by Coates and Silburn in 1970.

> ... once abandon a stringently calculated subsistence level as the yardstick for adequate wages, and substitute the appropriate scales of public relief which will take direct account of individual and household circumstances, and once we have some limited awareness of the minimum standard of life that social convention (rather than physical survival) demands, then we must expect low wages and/or large families to become a much more significant factor.[25]

Two points are important. For a 'scientifically' calculated subsistence yardstick the authors substitute something less stringent, but which can take account of the complex variables of 'household circumstances'. In addition, the notion of 'social convention' as the guide to minimum standards is introduced. This, by definition, is a 'relative' and changing standard.

In the 1970s the sense of inequality and relative deprivation, rather than absolute poverty, pervaded discussions of social policy. A major example of the approach is *Poverty, Inequality and Class Structure*, edited by Dorothy Wedderburn in 1974. In it, to take one example, Peter Townsend analysed the difficulties of using 'absolute' definitions of poverty, and argued the case for criteria which acknowledged subtly changing social standards and culturally defined needs:

> Tea is nutritionally worthless but in some countries is generally accepted, even by economists, as a 'necessity of life'. For many people in these countries drinking tea has been a life-long custom and is psychologically essential. And the fact that friends and neighbours expect to be

offered a cup of tea (or the equivalent) when they visit helps to make it socially necessary as well.

Other items in diet, clothing and social activity could illustrate the use of accepted convention as a yardstick rather than basic survival.[26]

People's perceptions of their status on varying scales of social measurement clearly affect their view of 'community' and its interlocking institutions. They affect how they see the operation of the church and the welfare services, the schools and local political parties. They affect their willingness to take part in organizations and activities designed for or by particular social groups – pensioners, mothers, sportsmen, trade unionists or film makers. From the late 1960s attempts were made to recruit wider participation in such groups – especially those whose purposes included community self-help and a share in local planning.[27]

These attempts must be seen in relation to two salient factors – the continuing decline in agencies which had been traditionally concerned in certain kinds of community activity – notably the churches – and the increasing scale of public institutions, including local government.

Reviewing the evidence on church membership, Barbara Wootton concluded in 1971 that the 'secularization of the community' was continuing with great speed, and that the 'decline in the influence of religion undoubtedly represents one of the most significant social changes between this century and its immediate predecessor'. Baptisms, confirmations, ordinations, church and Sunday school attendance, were declining rapidly in all the main denominations – except for the Roman Catholics.[28] However, among the multitude of small voluntary agencies that grew up in the seventies to supplement the provision made by statutory bodies, groups run by the clergy and church volunteers were prominent – especially, for instance, in the field of homelessness, the care of old people and the prevention of suicides.

The scale of local government had been growing in Britain ever since its creation at the end of the nineteenth century. The number of elected councillors had risen to

43,000 and paid local government officers to almost one million. At the same time local authority expenditure had risen from 5 per cent of the Gross National Product to more than 15 per cent. If, however, from the point of view of the ordinary citizen, local government operations often appeared too remote and bureaucratic, the Government's view was different. Introducing a white paper on local government reorganization and boundary changes in 1970, the then Environment Secretary, Anthony Crosland, presented the Government case as follows:

> Firstly, the areas of the new authorities must be large enough for planning. Secondly, to be able to afford the skilled manpower and other resources, needed to provide services of the highest standard, an authority should have a population, in our view, of no fewer than about 250,000. Thirdly, wherever possible, each authority should be responsible for all the services in its area.[29]

This view can be seen as a necessary development in the equalization and efficiency of local services and a further instance of the intrusion of economic considerations into questions of citizenship and political rights. It can also be seen as further distancing public authorities from their local population, weakening even more any sense of community based on representative local government.

Like many other policy-makers, Crosland linked his local government proposals with a call for more 'local participation'. The Seebohm committee on local authority and allied personal services also argued strongly in 1968 for greater attention to the needs of communities, and to 'the feeling of identity which membership of a community bestows', deriving from 'the common values, attitudes and ways of behaving which the members share and which form the rules which guide social behaviour within it'. Community development work formed part of its recommendations.[30] The Skeffington Report on *People and Planning* went further. Following the Act of 1971, it established that local residents must be informed by the council of any planning developments likely to encroach on their homes. They must also be given a chance to air their views about the proposals.

In some parts of the country, often in connection with motorway development proposals, local groups mobilized themselves most effectively to this end.[31]

In the 1970s many local authorities sought ways of encouraging local participation, including through neighbourhood councils and community health councils. After the first two years of their operation, however, only fifty neighbourhood councils had been created, mostly in Liverpool, Stockport and Lambeth. Their work was uneven. According to one observer they might be 'anything from a talk shop for the middle classes, a public relations job for the local council, an effective pressure group for local interests, or a powerful movement mobilizing people to do things for themselves.[32] Occasionally their achievements were unintentional. In one part of Liverpool, for instance, where the neighbourhood council worked particularly well and was responsible for a big tree-planting scheme, residents later complained of birdsong waking them up.

Most community action developments in the mid- and late-1970s were based on informal, non-official and often anti-official networks. Many tenants organizations, community newspapers, environmental groups, advisory services, women's and other community action and amenity groups were formed precisely to act as pressure groups *against* local government and public agencies. From time to time, as in Liverpool and Newcastle in 1975, national organizations, such as Shelter and Save the Children Fund, as well as community development projects explicitly set up by the government, found themselves joining sides with residents against their local authorities.

To establish a comprehensive picture of attitudes towards the local and wider community, it would be necessary to follow many earlier threads into this discussion – including housing and the social services, work and the family. One indicator of the sense of belonging to a community which we can consider briefly, however, is participation in leisure pursuits.

A summary of recreation demands in 1970 underlined five main trends in the period since 1950: a greater interest in cultural pursuits; a growth of social recreation (dining

36 *Fathers at play*

out, drinking together, parties); increased participation in sports and physical recreation (together with a drop in attendance at many spectator sports); increased use of the countryside for leisure; and an increase in the proportion of the population taking holidays away from home.[33] The fall in attendance at spectator sports coincided with the fading interest in pop festivals in the early 1970s, and with the continued fall in cinema audiences (from 395 million in 1962 to 157 million in 1972).[34] All five trends coincided with a massive increase in the ownership of record players, tape equipment and gramophone records. By the mid-1970s some three-quarters of homes possessed some form of recording equipment, and over half had tape equipment.[35] Gardening, seaside visits, games of skill at home, going into the country, and gambling were the most popular leisure activities, in that order.[36] The general trend is clear: most leisure in the 1970s was private, shared only with the family or close friends. Community involvement was the preserve of a highly committed (mainly professional) minority.

An essential ingredient in this pattern of leisure interests was the desire to work overtime rather than take increased time off. At the end of the sixties two studies showed that 'as "official" working weeks have shortened (to 41 hours for the men in the sample) people have become more prepared to barter leisure for income: one in ten of all men have second jobs, about one in three factory workers do regular overtime. In spite of his 41-hour week the average man commits at least 50 hours to economic ends.'[37]

None of these data explains the nature of people's perceptions of themselves in, or alienated from, communities. They indicate levels at which people establish their priorities and make their judgements. Citizenship, social rights and community are concepts which operate at these various levels and bring together many of the strands in our earlier discussion.

Minorities

Discussion of broad concepts of the kind we have introduced in this chapter are complicated by particular problems relating to minority groups, and much of the discussion is indeed explicitly generated by them. The existence of minorities, such as students, single parent families, battered wives, homosexuals and different ethnic groups, with objectives or codes of behaviour which set them apart from the rest of the community, is the point at which the very concepts raised in this discussion are presented most sharply. In this context words like community, democracy, tolerance and rights, come most closely under scrutiny.

In the 1960s and 1970s a wider pattern of minority 'spokesman' groups became established, and an 'alternative' cultural and information network emerged to foster their interests. Radical and alternative publications, for example, became strongly enough established to enable individuals and groups to communicate and to extend their influence. Thus, in the 1970s regular journals were appearing, offering radical alternatives in the fields of education, social work, environmental protection, women's and gay liberation and race relations. Alternative bookshops and distribution machineries were set up, providing outlets for these publications, as well as for the pamphlets and books of other small political and philosophical groups. Other groups offered advice and help, for example, to the consumer, the social benefits claimant, the wives of prisoners.

For minority groups and isolated individuals, the concept of community involves the possibility of identifying with similar people outside their immediate environment, and of organizing and communicating with them. It also means resistance and hostility to such movements and minorities. One feature of the 1970s was, indeed, the growth of attempts to halt what were considered to be inroads into 'established' or 'traditional' or 'Christian' or 'British' ways. The movement associated with Mary Whitehouse, Lord Longford and the Festival of Light, as we have seen, sought to counter the work of the 'permissive lobby'. Tory M.P. Rhodes Boyson and the *Black Papers* sought to combat 'progressive' methods in education. The fascist National Front sought to defeat liberal attitudes towards immigration and race. For the majority of the population all such clashes of opinion remained marginal to their experience of society, but in the centres of cities with immigrant populations, among radical groups of teachers and social workers, and among the minority groups themselves, the subject of minority rights was a matter of serious debate.

This is particularly true of questions relating to race, ethnic minorities and immigration. This is not the place to discuss even the general pattern of immigration from the West Indies, East Africa, India and Pakistan, and the differences between the reception given to these groups and to Irish, Jewish, Cypriot, Chinese and other earlier immigrants. Nor can we discuss the specific problems of housing, employment and education and the national distribution of the immigrant population in the second half of the twentieth century. We are concerned here with questions of citizenship and community, and the arrival of new ethnic groups in the 1960s and 1970s made a sharp impact on the discussion of these issues. 'All studies of minorities', points out an Institute of Race Relations report, 'must logically imply a concern with the majority. No analysis which takes as its starting point the notion of "immigrant problem" can be complete: for what is at stake is essentially the outcome not of a unique encounter but of another in a long series of disputes about who belongs within our society.'[38]

Whereas earlier groups of immigrants had been more or less completely 'assimilated' to British cultural and social traditions, the black immigrants, some people argued, could not be absorbed in this way.

Two crucial points about immigrant and ethnic minorities need to be made. First, in the 1960s and 1970s the problems they presented were primarily those of urban society itself: specifically, they were those of the inner city, already undergoing upheaval, disintegration and decline.[39] The second point is that questions of absorption or alienation, acceptance or prejudice, involve questions of class and status as well as those of colour. As Sheila Patterson found in Brixton and elsewhere in the early 1960s,

problems of adaptation and acceptance have been increased by the fact that the 'dark strangers' moving into this area are predominantly a lower-class group moving into a highly status-conscious lower-middle-class or upper-working-class area. Preconceptions linking colour with low social status, as well as with an alien, primitive, and uncultured way of life, have received considerable support from first hand, though often superficial, observation of the newcomers' behaviour.

Her report on Brixton at that point suggested that coloured people had 'become an accepted part of the British urban landscape, if not yet of the community'.[40]

The late 1960s intensified the distinction between landscape and community. A crisis in 1967 involved large-scale immigration of Kenya Asians with British passports. The Labour government responded the following year with legislation to restrict the right of entry. At the same time it introduced a Race Relations Act to increase protection for minorities against various forms of discrimination.

The chief spokesman against immigration, and the focus of British anti-immigrant fears, was Enoch Powell. He warned, for example, in a speech in April 1968, of white Britons becoming a minority. 'As I look ahead,' he confided, 'I am filled with foreboding. Like the Romans, I seem to see "the river Tiber foaming with much blood".' Powell received a flood of support, including token strikes and demonstrations by some dockers and other workers, while attempts to rally anti-Powell feeling won little public trade union support.[41] The National Front welcomed this exposure of the immigrant 'menace' and the 'treason' involved in permitting it. Powell's apocalyptic approach, condemned by leading politicans as provocative and racialist, lost him his position in the Shadow Cabinet, and ultimately separated him from the Conservative Party. He did not, however, stop campaigning against immigration or warning of racial disasters ahead.

It has been extremely difficult to establish reliable figures about the exact size of the various immigrant populations in Britain. It has also been hard to analyse attitudes by and towards black and coloured minorities, though detailed studies have been made across a range of situations – for example, immigrants and churches, children's racial attitudes and experience and the extent of prejudice.[42] These are not, as we have suggested, so much problems of the minority as those of the majority – of the history, shape and adaptability of the community in which established or new minorities exist: 'ultimately, the determining element in deciding the future of race relations in Britain is the character of British society and the manner in which it responds to the stresses set up during the process of adaptation and change'.[43]

Immigration, like Chartism, industrialization, the women's suffrage movement, or other social movements or changes we have discussed, underlines basic questions about the prevailing definitions of society and community. Questions of the conditions and rights of minorities, and of attitudes towards them, are basically familiar questions about the nature of the whole society and of the interlocking relationships of its component parts.

Education

Nowhere have questions of rights, society and community been more extensively debated than in relation to education. No institution in the nineteenth and twentieth centuries has been more confidently – and perhaps more mistakenly – viewed as a means of promoting a greater sense of community. Education is our final case study of modern English society because, after the mid-1950s, it was the focus of discussion of social inequalities and disharmonies. The late 1960s and early 1970s produced sustained attempts to analyse and use education to remedy economic and social disadvantage. It is important to outline the processes by which education had in the twentieth century assumed so central a position in social analysis and planning.

The principle of universal elementary education had been established in 1870, although it was not until 1880 that the School Boards were obliged to make attendance compulsory and not until 1891 that elementary education became virtually free. In 1902 the State and local authorities became involved in the provision of secondary education. There continued, however, to be little formal connection between these parts of the educational structure. The newly created local education authorities were obliged to provide facilities for elementary education as a result of the 1902 Act, but their powers to provide facilities or grant aid for education 'other than elementary' were at first no more than permissive. The first substantial link between the two separate systems of public education was created in 1907 in the form of the free place system, enabling a small proportion of pupils from the elementary schools to transfer to grammar schools at the age of eleven or twelve (usually up to a quarter of grammar school places were reserved in this way, the remainder being allocated to fee-paying pupils). The opportunities of brighter working-class and particularly lower-middle-class children were improved by this scheme, but those of the older pupils who stayed on in the elementary schools continued in most areas to be severely limited. The 'ladder' created for working-class children was, in fact, very narrow. By the First World War, for example, Stockport provided forty scholarships annually, thirty-five of which went to children attending elementary schools. They were tenable at the local municipal secondary schools, girls' high school and boys' grammar school. A scholarship entitled the holder to free education, a grant of up to £1 a year for books, and an annual maintenance grant of £5 in suitable cases.[44]

These developments strengthened the conception of *secondary* education as *grammar school* education, and left technical and vocational education as sub-secondary. The creation of Central Schools, following the tradition of the 'higher-grade' schools of the late nineteenth century, and experiments in practical education at the top end of the elementary school, offered many working-class children a poor status substitute for the secondary education to which they did not have access. Economic considerations, intelligence tests and the 'social class image of the secondary school and its purpose' all helped to hold back the rate of improvement in the educational chances of working-class children in the decades after 1902.[45] The framework of selective secondary education had been firmly established as, in Lord Eustace Percy's phrase, 'a lift or stairway to the higher storeys of the social structure'.[46] The bright working-class child was caught between the values and life-chances of his own class and those which grammar school education mainly represented. This ladder, in Raymond Williams's analysis, was an 'alternative to solidarity . . . it is a device which can only be used individually: you go up the ladder alone'. It was a substitute for a better common educational provision, a product of a divided society.[47]

The efficiency of the structure was gradually strengthened. Under the 1918 Act the school-leaving age was raised to fourteen, and exemptions were abolished (the age at which children could be exempted altogether, or partly, from attendance, had been raised from ten in 1880 to twelve in 1899 and to fourteen in 1900). The 1918 Act also proposed the establishment of compulsory part-time education for all children between the ages of fifteen and eighteen, though this never materialized – despite subsequent endorsement of the principle both by the 1944 Education Act and by the Crowther Committee's report *15 to 18*, in 1959. The day-release system became the substitute.

In the inter-war period State scholarships to the universities were created. 'Special places' ousted the free place system, increasing the number of places available but introducing the criterion of the means test. The grammar school population increased over the years after 1902 and a greater proportion of free and special places was made available. By 1938, 53 per cent of pupils in grammar schools had free places and 16 per cent had special places. One in twelve children attended a grammar school. More pupils were also encouraged to stay on in the senior forms of the elementary schools or to enrol for courses at local technical colleges and art schools. Dissatisfaction with the existing opportunities continued, however. One of the most outspoken criticisms was in a Labour Party policy statement produced by R. H. Tawney in 1922, which expressed the need both for the improvement of primary and elementary education and also for

the development of public secondary education to such a point that all normal children, irrespective of the income,

class, or occupation of their parents, may be transferred
at the age of eleven+ from the primary or preparatory
school to one type or another of secondary school, and
remain in the latter until sixteen.[48]

Advances in educational psychology, and particularly in
intelligence testing, provided additional support for the
principle of selective secondary education by emphasizing
the varying needs of the adolescent personality and consequently the need for different kinds of schools. The report
of the Hadow Committee on *The Education of the Adolescent*
in 1926 reflected both of these currents of opinion. Its
recommendation for the division of education into two
separate stages was the culmination of previous tendencies
in educational reform. It laid down the ideological foundations for the legislative changes which were to follow in
1944. Some reorganization of schools began immediately in
some areas, but the outbreak of war in 1939 interrupted the
process. The war also brought to light a number of insuffi-
ciently recognized deficiencies. The poor physical and intellectual condition of most evacuee children from the big
cities, for instance, dispelled many illusions as to the
adequacy of the piece-meal modifications which had so far
been introduced.

As part of wartime planning for reconstruction came the
report of the Norwood Committee, which contained a plan
for the provision of free secondary education, tripartite in
arrangement, catering for three different 'types' of pupil –
the grammar school for those children 'interested in learning for its own sake', the secondary modern school for those
who 'deal more easily with concrete things than with ideas',
and the secondary technical school for those 'whose abilities
lie markedly in the field of applied science or applied art'.[49]
Selection for secondary education was to take place at the
age of eleven and was to be based on diagnostic 'intelligence' tests. With the passing of the 1944 Act the legacy of
inter-war proposals, reforms and experiments became an
articulated national system, covering primary and secondary
education as well as full- and part-time training in colleges
of further education, technical, commercial and art colleges

and in evening institutes. School welfare services (dating back to 1906) were also extended – including free milk, free or subsidized school meals, free dental and medical inspection, grants for travel and clothing, and special schools and facilities for handicapped children. To match these developments an extensive programme of rebuilding was set in motion, and there was a large increase in the numbers of teachers admitted for training. Apart from the inevitable transitional difficulties, therefore, the basic objectives of expansion now seemed secure.

Throughout the 1920s and 1930s, while instruction in 'the three Rs' continued to dominate the classroom, debates about the content of education ranged over wider issues, such as school discipline and classroom organization. Curriculum and other reforms were being called for by educationists and by organizations such as the New Education Fellowship. Major advances, however, were few. In the primary school, where economic pressures were less restricting, some changes were under way. The popularization of the psychoanalytic study of childhood, and the internationally influential work of such educational thinkers and pioneers as Maria Montessori and John Dewey resulted in the adoption of more flexible and 'open' patterns of school organization, and in the encouragement of more expressive and child-centred modes of learning.[50] In the post-war years similar developments have also spread into the secondary schools, and are reflected, for instance, in the extension of creative activities, interdisciplinary inquiry and group activities, the relaxation of rigid streaming, experiments in school democracy and psychological counselling.[51]

One of the main objects of the 1944 Act was to secure an educational system which would provide equal opportunities for children from all kinds of social background. It rapidly became clear, however, that the three different types of secondary school were not in fact offering equal opportunities at all. The schools, quite naturally, offered different kinds of training for children who had 'passed' or 'failed' at eleven-plus: this was the whole point of the system.

It was out of this historical background that the two dominant themes in educational debate emerged in the

1950s and 1960s – the comprehensive school, and relationships between school and society. The comprehensive
school, pre-schooling, compensatory education, educational
priority areas and urban aid were all in one way or another
intended to alleviate educational and social underprivilege.

Evidence of social class bias in selection for grammar
schools gave a new focus to the controversy about equal
opportunities. Jean Floud and her colleagues revealed in
1956 that while 59 per cent of the eleven-year-olds from
business and professional homes in south-west
Hertfordshire and 18 per cent from similar backgrounds in
Middlesbrough had found grammar school places, the
proportion of children from unskilled working–class families
who went to grammar schools in these two areas was only 9
per cent.[52]

From the *Early Leaving* report published by the Central
Advisory Council for Education in 1954, a generation of
educationists and sociologists investigated and underlined
the small proportion of unskilled and semi-skilled workers'
children who achieved a grammar school or university
education.[53] Between the mid-1950s and the mid-1970s a
range of official reports, research projects and sociological
and educational literature examined detailed aspects of the
educational penalties under which working–class children
laboured. The Newsom Report on *Half our Future* (1963)
looked specifically at the education of pupils aged thirteen to
sixteen 'of average and less than average ability', and in
doing so looked at the educational handicap that many
schools catering for working–class children constituted. The
Robbins Report on *Higher Education* in the same year
analysed in detail the relatively untapped 'pool of ability'
that working–class children represented. In 1964 J. W. B.
Douglas, in his extremely widely read *The Home and the
School*, demonstrated the effects of a large number of
adverse conditions – poor housing, irregular health, larger
families, fewer contacts between parents and school and a
number of other social class differentials.[54] Others probed
the same network of relationships between school and
achievement on the one hand, and social class, the home and
related factors on the other hand. The authors of *From*

Birth to Seven in 1972 produced one of the most sophisticated analyses of the effects of social class background,
family size, parents' education and other differential social
conditions, on children's reading and arithmetic attainment,
and on their 'social adjustment' in school, confirming how
directly children's performance in schools reflected their
social condition.[55] Basil Bernstein, from the late 1950s,
sought to explain how these social realities were translated
into school performance through the machinery of language
and early patterns of socialization. He suggested that social
classes had characteristic speech codes, which resulted in
different abilities to cope with the demands of the formal
educational system. He also pointed to the failure of many
schools to respond to the needs and interests of working-
class families. All of this led in the 1970s to more detailed
analyses of how schools worked, how their curriculum was
constructed and which subjects were accorded 'high' or
'low' status, and how schools favoured one section of the
community rather than another.[56]

We are concerned at this point only with education's
increasing importance in interpretations of how 'society'
functioned and should function. We cannot look at many
related and important issues. Although, for example, the
question of the independent public schools was a subject of
a Commission which reported in 1968 and of other attempts
to focus attention on the fact that public schools remained
cornerstones of social privilege,[57] they were in no way central to debates about education in this period. Widespread
discussion did take place about many aspects of school
structures, size, management and curriculum. From the
1960s, for instance, date many of the schemes which
resulted in curriculum changes in schools – Nuffield science
and modern languages, for example. Although many of these
developments, as well as reactions to them in the late 1960s
and 1970s, are important to discussions of education, we
cannot here pursue their relationship to the theme of school
and community.

One development that is vital to this theme was the
evolution in the late 1960s of the 'educational priority area'.
Out of growing awareness in the United States and Britain

37 *Primary education in the 1970s*

of the relationship between social conditions and school performance emerged the concept of 'positive discrimination'. The Plowden Report on *Children and their Primary Schools* in 1967 proposed the establishment of educational priority areas into which extra resources and effort could be channelled. Areas were designated, and preferential financial help was given – including in the form of allowances for teachers in E.P.A. schools, with the aim of reducing teacher turnover. Under an Urban Aid programme inaugurated in 1968 funds were also made available for inner-city improvements – and some of these funds went into additional pre-school provision in poor areas. A number of E.P.A.

'action research' projects, under the directorship of A. H. Halsey, one of the leaders of the new sociology of education in the 1950s and 1960s, explored how positive discrimination could best enrich the educational experience of children in E.P.A. schools and areas. Although in Britain and the United States the notion of 'compensatory' education was being viewed with suspicion,[58] the E.P.A. projects in London, Birmingham, Liverpool, the West Riding and Dundee were concerned in different ways with establishing close relationships between the school and the rest of the community. Explorations of new kinds of realistic curricula in Liverpool,[59] for example, and of school–home liaison in Deptford, indicated possibilities of weakening the traditional isolation of the school from the outside world. They were not so much exercises in compensation as in collaboration.

Local authorities began to experiment in the 1970s with 'community schools', turning primary and secondary schools into places where the community was welcome and encouraged to come – involving parents in school activities, siting libraries, welfare offices and community activities on school premises, and creating new types of relationships amongst teachers, pupils, parents and the community at large.[60]

The 'priority area' and the 'community school' rested on a profound awareness of important social changes, especially in the cities. Immigration, in the 1960s particularly, had major repercussions in some areas on schools as well as on housing and welfare. The specific problems of areas with high population turnover were reflected in the need of many schools to grapple with multi-racial, multi-cultural realities on a new scale.[61] Changes in the family, in authority relationships in the community as a whole, and particularly in the status and cultural identity of young people, had an important impact on the work of the schools, weakening (and occasionally breaking) traditional goals and structures. The search for new curricula, forms of school organization and teaching approaches indicated an acute awareness of these and other changes, and responses to them. The conflict, within schools and within the whole education system, between advocates of adaptation to change and advocates of the defence of established values reflected the conflict inevitably present in all parts of a rapidly changing society.

From the mid-1950s the conflict focused most of all on the comprehensive school. Even from 1944 some authorities interpreted the provision of secondary education for all as involving the comprehensive school, either exclusively (as in Anglesey), or within a framework of selective education (as in London or Coventry). Even Labour-controlled author-ities, however, were reluctant to yield to pressures from proponents of the comprehensive school to plan for com-plete comprehensive secondary education.[62] Nationally, the Labour Party did not commit itself to comprehensive schools until after the 1964 election. The following year, circular 10/65 asked local education authorities, which had not yet done so, to submit plans for comprehensive reorgan-ization. At the same time, in the mid-sixties, sections of the Conservative Party had been won over to support for at least a measure of comprehensive organization.

The debate about the comprehensive school had been, and was to continue to be, conducted at various levels. Some supporters, Robin Pedley outstandingly, collected data in the 1950s and 1960s to show how successful existing comprehensive schools were measured by the criterion of examination successes. The comprehensive schools, the argument also went, enabled children who developed late to make real changes – never really practicable between schools, even though transfer had been theoretically pos-sible. The comprehensive school was also (especially as it was initially conceived) large and provided with facilities which offered children wider choices than in separate schools. The comprehensive school, argued its opponents, was in fact a political, egalitarian instrument, and under-mined the traditional, tested values and objectives of the grammar school. It weakened the education of brighter chil-dren, without providing as adequate an education for the non-academic child as did the developing secondary modern school. All discussions of the comprehensive school, it is true, were political or social in the sense that its underlying aim had been conceived in terms both of improved or equal

educational chances, and of the virtues of the social mixing
it implied. As the number of comprehensive schools
increased, sociologists turned their attention to the inner
workings of the schools to see to what extent they did in fact
overcome the social inequalities of educational selection.
Questions of management, curriculum, assessment and
examinations, mixed-ability teaching and individualized
learning and counselling, were some of those under scrutiny
in the 1970s, raising academic considerations and problems
of the social context of schooling.[63]

By the mid-1970s a half of the secondary-school population was in comprehensive schools.[64] In 1976 the Labour
government introduced legislation to compel the remaining
reluctant authorities to abandon selection and introduce
fully comprehensive schemes. The movement to complete
the comprehensive system raised the same objections as
the concept had always done – the limitation of parental
choice, uniformity and the subordination of educational
standards to political ends. From our point of view the
importance of the comprehensive school lies – as does that
of the E.P.A. and related developments – in its relationship
to discussions of community and class. It would be possible
to trace other ways in which these discussions are highlighted in the field of education. Major developments and
issues in the development of the universities, polytechnics
and teacher education, for example, relate to these basic
considerations. So do continuing inequalities affecting girls
in the educational system. The E.P.A. and the comprehensive school, however, were the most publicly debated, and
the most sensitive indicators of attitudes towards education.

By the second half of the 1970s confidence that the new
educational machineries would fundamentally alter social
patterns had seriously diminished. What the E.P.A. projects
particularly had done was to underline the difficulties inher-
ent not only in attempts to act for a reduction of educational
and social underprivilege, but also in the concept itself.
Experience had shown, as a report on the London project
emphasized, that the 'disparity between the performance of
the schools and the developing demands on them has
grown': the difficulties for educational policy had been

intensified, not reduced. The search for equality of opportunity had 'moved on' from one concerned with individuals gaining access to various levels of education, to a greater concern 'with equality of *results* between groups'. Education, the report pointed out, was a means whereby 'society perpetually renews the conditions of its own existence, reflecting the extant and dominant distribution of adult roles. Yet many believe that it should be an agency of social reform, redistributing access to and transforming the nature of adult roles.'[65] The discussion of education reflects a more general social difficulty – that of measuring social advance, deciding criteria for doing so, disentangling the complexities of what at first appears a simple concept. In education, as in housing, welfare, leisure, community participation, or any of the other areas we have discussed, elusive and relative standards apply.

The discussion of education has been only one way of approaching the analysis of people in society, of individuals as citizens, of the nature of community. Changes in civil, political and social rights have been involved in all this complex discussion of social relationships. They have been changes in social institutions and in people's minds. A discussion of citizenship or of community inevitably poses questions about individuals and about groups, about consensus and conflict, about stability and change. The concept of community embraces the family and the classroom, race relations and politics. The concept of citizenship embraces not only political structures and participatory rights, but also how people feel about themselves and their various social roles. In education, as in the other areas, the discussion of such concepts reveals the constant tension between efforts to perpetuate and to transform, to assess the fine balance of gain and loss.

In sociological terms there is no simple way of defining the contours of a society or an institution, no simple way of establishing a portrait of schools or of interest groups, no simple way of disentangling what society seems to consist of from what people think it consists of. As we have seen in many cases there are rival perspectives, and ambiguous conclusions. While there are insights, there are also reasons for caution, and there is a need to be aware that sociological analyses may be neither the whole truth nor final. The same is clearly true of historical statements. There is no simple way of establishing cause and effect, no simple way of establishing the causes of industrialization or of political reform, no simple way of disentangling what a historical process seems to consist of from what we read into it from the present. There is a similar need for care and caution. The sociologist and the social historian are both aware of changing social tensions, and are both attempting to clarify how society perceives, defines and acts upon such tensions.[66] Words like society, community and citizenship have little meaning without both of their contributions.

Notes

1 T. H. MARSHALL 'Citizenship and social class', in *Sociology at the Crossroads and other essays*, pp. 73, 86 (London, 1963).
2 SAMPSON *The New Anatomy of Britain*, p. 656.
3 See P. STANWORTH and A. GIDDENS 'The modern corporate economy: interlocking directorships in Britain, 1906–1970', *Sociological Review*, XXIII (1), p. 5.
4 JOE ROGALY 'Why our troubles are the worst', *Financial Times*, 2 September 1975, p. 2.
5 *Britain and the Common Market*: texts of speeches made at the 1962 Labour Party Conference by the Rt Hon. Hugh Gaitskell, M.P. and the Rt Hon. George Brown, M.P. together with the policy statement accepted by the conference, pp. 3–23.
6 See, for example, an election speech by Powell on the Common Market in JOHN WOOD (ed.) *Powell and the 1970 Election*, pp. 112–18 (Kingswood, Surrey, 1970).
7 Membership form. See also J. E. DANIEL *Welsh Nationalism: what it stands for* (London, n.d.)
8 See LIBERAL PARTY OF WALES *A Parliament for Wales* (Newtown, Mont., 1949).
9 H. J. HANHAM *Scottish Nationalism*, p. 179 (London, 1969).
10 WELSH RECONSTRUCTION ADVISORY COUNCIL *First Interim Report*, p. 6 (London, 1944).
11 PETER HALL 'The Wilson Years – 1: Our changing lives', *New Society*, 25 March 1976, pp. 657–8.
12 *New Society*, 18 March 1976, p. 609.
13 See STUART HALL 'The Muggers'. Script for an Open University Film Course D101/00 'Making Sense of Society'.

14 KEITH JOSEPH 'Britain: a decadent New Utopia', *The Guardian*, 21 October 1974, p. 7.

15 RAYMOND WILLIAMS *Television*, pp. 21–2 (London, 1974).

16 See TOM FORESTER 'Newspaper sales', *New Society*, 16 October 1975, p. 151.

17 BRIAN GROOMBRIDGE *Television and the People*, pp. 7, 15 (Harmondsworth, 1972).

18 RALPH ROSS and ERNEST VAN DEN HAAG *The Fabric of Society*, p. 168 (New York, 1957).

19 POLITICAL AND ECONOMIC PLANNING *Citizenship and Television*, p. 22 (London, 1965).

20 RAYMOND WILLIAMS *Keywords*, pp. 65–6 (London, 1976).

21 See, for example, BRIAN JACKSON *Working Class Community* (London, 1968), and HOGGART *The Uses of Literacy*. For surveys of sociological studies, see FRANKENBERG *Communities in Britain and* COLIN BELL and HOWARD NEWBY *Community Studies* (London, 1971).

22 STUART HALL 'Between two worlds', in THEO BARKER (ed.) *The Long March of Everyman*, p. 278 (London, 1974).

23 FRANK BECHHOFER 'A sociological portrait: income', *New Society*, 14 October 1971, pp. 707–9.

24 See MICHAEL MEACHER 'The coming class struggle', *New Statesman*, 4 January 1974, p. 7.

25 KEN COATES and RICHARD SILBURN *Poverty: The Forgotten Englishmen*, p. 35 (Harmondsworth, 1970).

26 PETER TOWNSEND 'Poverty as relative deprivation: resources and style of living', in WEDDERBURN *Poverty, Inequality and Class Structure*, pp. 17–30.

27 Among the national organizations responsible for promoting such groups were the Race Relations Commission, Shelter, Save the Children Fund, Task Force and the Child Poverty Action Group. Many received finance under the Government's urban aid and community development projects.

28 BARBARA WOOTTON *Contemporary Britain*, pp. 34–5 (London, 1971).

29 ANTHONY CROSLAND *Socialism Now*, pp. 178–9 (London, 1974).

30 Report of the Committee on Local Authority and Allied Personal Social Services (Seebohm) Cmnd. 3703 (London, 1968).

31 *People and Planning*, Report of a Committee on Public Participation in Planning (Skeffington) (London, 1969).

32 PAUL HARRISON 'The neighbourhood council', *New Society*, 12 March 1973, p. 73.

33 THOMAS L. BURTON 'Current trends in recreation demands', in *Recreation Research and Planning*, p. 27 (London, 1970).

34 JOHN WATSON 'Cinema economics', *New Society*, 12 September 1974, p. 677.

35 TOM FORESTER 'The pop follies', *New Society*, 1 April 1976, p. 27.

36 OFFICE OF POPULATION CENSUSES AND SURVEYS *Population Trends*, 1976, reported in *New Society*, 1 April 1976, p. 21. The data apply to 1973.

37 BRIAN RODGERS 'Leisure and recreation', in PETER COWAN (ed.) *Developing Patterns of Urbanization*, p. 90 (Edinburgh, 1970).

38 NICHOLAS DEAKIN *et al. Colour, Citizenship and British Society*, p. 22 (London, 1970). This book summarizes and updates E. J. B. ROSE *et al. Colour and Citizenship* (London, 1969).

39 For a discussion of the relevance of the urban dimension to immigration and minorities, see ERNEST KRAUSZ *Ethnic Minorities in Britain*, Ch. 4 (London, 1971); JOHN REX and ROBERT MOORE *Race, Community and Conflict* (London, 1967). Also PETER WALKER 'Race and the Inner City: An Open Letter to the Prime Minister', *New Statesman*, 18 June 1976, pp. 804–5.

40 SHEILA PATTERSON *Dark Strangers*, pp. 329, 335 (London, 1963; 1965 Penguin edition).

41 See DILOP HIRO *Black British, White British*, pp. 241–4 (London, 1971; 1973 Penguin revised edition).

42 See, on these aspects, HIRO *Black British, White British*, Ch. 3; DAVID MILNER *Children and Race* (Harmondsworth, 1975); ALAN G. JAMES *Sikh Children in Britain* (London, 1974); DEAKIN *Colour, Citizenship and British Society*, Ch. 12.

43 DEAKIN *Colour, Citizenship and British Society*, p. 22.

44 THISELTON MARK *Modern Views on Education*, pp. 82–3 (London, n.d.)

45 D. V. GLASS 'Education', in MORRIS GINSBERG (ed.) *Law and Opinion in England in the 20th Century*, pp. 330–2 (London, 1959).

46 Quoted in ibid., p. 336.

47 RAYMOND WILLIAMS *Culture and Society*, pp. 317–18 (London, 1968; 1961 Penguin edition).

48 R. H. TAWNEY (ed.) *Secondary Education for All*, p. 7 (London, [1922]).

49 BOARD OF EDUCATION *Curriculum and Examinations in Secondary Schools*, pp. 2–3 (London, 1941).

50 See R. J. W. SELLECK *English Primary Education and the Progressives, 1914–1939* (London, 1972).

51 See CHARITY JAMES *Young Lives at Stake* (London, 1968).

52 J. E. FLOUD (ed.), A. H. HALSEY and F. M. MARTIN *Social Class and Educational Opportunity*.

53 For the sequence of this discussion, and relevant extracts from the literature, see HAROLD SILVER *Equal Opportunity in Education*.

54 See J. W. B. DOUGLAS *The Home and the School* (London, 1964).

55 RONALD DAVIE, NEVILLE BUTLER and HARVEY GOLDSTEIN *From Birth to Seven* (London, 1972).

56 See, for example, some of the contributions to MICHAEL F. D. YOUNG (ed.) *Knowledge and Control: new directions for the sociology of education* (London, 1971).

57 See PUBLIC SCHOOLS COMMISSION *First Report*, Vol. I: *Report* (London, 1968); RUPERT WILKINSON *The Prefects: British leadership and the public school tradition* (Oxford, 1964); J. WAKEFORD *The Cloistered Elite* (London, 1969).

58 See A. H. HALSEY (ed.) *Educational Priority*, Vol. I: *E.P.A. Problems and Policies* (London, 1972), Ch. 2, 'Poverty and American Compensatory Education'; BASIL BERNSTEIN 'Education cannot compensate for society', in OPEN UNIVERSITY *School and Society* (London, 1971).

59 See ERIC MIDWINTER's account of the Liverpool project in *Priority Education* (Harmondsworth, 1972).

60 For an account of the best known of these schools, Countesthorpe College, Leicestershire, see JOHN WATTS (ed.) *The Countesthorpe Experience* (London, 1977).

61 See DEAKIN *Colour, Citizenship and British Society*, Ch. 7.

62 RICHARD BATLEY, OSWALD O'BRIEN and HENRY PARRIS *Going Comprehensive* (London, 1970) contains accounts of different reactions by the Labour Party in Gateshead and Darlington.

63 See DAVID HARGREAVES *Social Relations in a Secondary School* (London, 1967); the journal *Forum* for this period contains regular discussions of these issues.

64 See CAROLINE BENN and BRIAN SIMON *Half Way There*, p. 102 (London, 1970; 1972 Penguin edition).

65 J. H. BARNES and H. LUCAS 'Positive discrimination in education: individuals, groups and institutions', in JACK BARNES (ed.), *Educational Priority*, Vol. 3: *Curriculum Innovation in London's E.P.A.s*, p. 239 (London, 1975).

66 Some useful contributions to this discussion include

ELIZABETH VALLANCE (ed.), *The State, Society and Self-Destruction*, Ch. 1 (London, 1975); KAI T. ERIKSON 'Sociology and the historical perspective', in MICHAEL DRAKE (ed.) *Applied Historical Studies* (London, 1973); E. J. HOBSBAWM 'From social history to the history of society', *Daedalus*, Vol. 100, no. 1 (1971).

Guide to further reading

The suggested reading below covers the main themes discussed in this book, but does not follow the pattern of the chapters. We have tried to indicate books which are neither too specialized nor too inaccessible. We have given details of sub-titles where these help to clarify the character of the books listed. In most cases the first date of publication is given, and also – where we have thought this important – the date at which a revised edition has appeared. A very large number of these books are available in recent editions, and in paperback, but it has not been possible to include all this information. Additional suggestions for reading on other themes or of a more detailed or specialized kind can be traced in the footnotes at appropriate points in the text.

I STATISTICS

This edition of *Modern English Society* contains no statistical tables. Readers wishing to consult either historical or up-to-date statistics are advised to refer to the following sources.

A *Government publications*

Annual Abstract of Statistics.
Social Trends.
The Censuses of Population, Industry and Production.
More detailed information on, for example, education, employment, health, housing, social security, crime and taxation, is published by the Government department concerned. The booklet, *Government Statistics: a brief guide to sources*, describes what is available.

B *Major academic publications*

MITCHELL, B. R. and DEANE, P. *Abstract of British Historical Statistics* (London, 1962).

BUTLER, DAVID and SLOMAN, ANNE *British Political Facts 1900–1975* (London, 1976).

COOK, CHRIS and KEITH, BRENDAN *British Historical Facts 1830–1900* (London, 1976).

HALSEY, A. H. (ed.) *Trends in British Society since 1900* (London, 1972).

C *Paperback guides*

CENTRAL STATISTICAL OFFICE *Facts in Focus* (Harmondsworth, 1972).

SILLITOE, ALAN F. *Britain in Figures: a handbook of social statistics* (Harmondsworth, 1971).

SERGEANT, GRAHAM *A Statistical Sourcebook for Sociologists* (London, 1972).

D *Annual almanacks*

Keesing's Contemporary Archives (for news of national events reported in the press).
The Statesman's Year Book.
Whitaker's Almanack.
CENTRAL OFFICE OF INFORMATION *Britain: an official handbook.*

2 THE INDUSTRIAL REVOLUTION AND AFTER

ASHTON, T. S. *The Industrial Revolution 1760–1830* (London, 1948; revised edition 1962).

BEALES, H. L. *The Industrial Revolution 1750–1850* (London, 1928; reprinted 1958 with new introductory essay).

CHAMBERS, J. D. and MINGAY, G. E. *The Agricultural Revolution 1750–1880* (London, 1966).

DEANE, PHYLLIS *The First Industrial Revolution* (Cambridge, 1965).

FOSTER, JOHN *Class Struggle and the Industrial Revolution* (London, 1974).

GEORGE, DOROTHY *England in Transition* (London, 1931).

HARTWELL, R. M. *The Causes of the Industrial Revolution in England* (London, 1967).

LASLETT, PETER *The World We Have Lost* (London, 1965); *Household and Family in Past Time* (Cambridge, 1972): see particularly editor's introduction.

THOMIS, MALCOLM I. *Responses to Industrialisation: the British Experience 1780–1850* (Newton Abbot, 1976).

3 TOWNS

ARMSTRONG, ALAN *Stability and Change in an English County Town: a social study of York 1801–51* (London, 1974).

ASHWORTH, W. *The Genesis of Modern British Town Planning* (London, 1954).

BOWLEY, MARION *Housing and the State 1919–1944* (London, 1945).

BRIGGS, ASA *Victorian Cities* (London, 1963).

BURNETT, JOHN *Plenty and Want: a social history of diet in England from 1815 to the present day* (London, 1966).

CHAPMAN, STANLEY D. (ed.) *The History of Working-Class Housing* (Newton Abbot, 1971).

CULLINGWORTH, J. B. *Housing in Transition* (London, 1963).

DYOS, H. J. *Victorian Suburb: a study of the growth of Camberwell* (London, 1961).

ENGELS, FRIEDRICH *The Condition of the Working Class in England* (first published in German, 1845).

GAULDIE, ENID *Cruel Habitations: a history of working-class housing 1780–1918* (London, 1974).

LONGMATE, NORMAN *King Cholera* (London, 1966).

MARTIN, GEOFFREY *The Town* (London, 1961).

PAHL, R. E. *Patterns of Urban Life* (London, 1970).

PFAUTZ, HAROLD W. (ed.) *Charles Booth on the City* (Chicago, 1967).

REX, JOHN and MOORE, ROBERT *Race, Community and Conflict* (London, 1967).

ROYAL COMMISSION ON THE DISTRIBUTION OF THE INDUSTRIAL POPULATION *Report*, Cmnd 6153 (London, 1940).

WICKHAM, E. R. *Church and People in an Industrial City* (London, 1957).

4 TRANSPORT

DYOS, H. J. and ALDCROFT, D. H. *British Transport: an economic survey from the seventeenth century to the twentieth* (Leicester, 1969).

HADFIELD, CHARLES *The Canal Age* (Newton Abbot, 1968).

ROBBINS, MICHAEL *The Railway Age* (London, 1962).

SAVAGE, CHRISTOPHER I. *An Economic History of Transport* (London, 1959).

SIMMONS, JACK *Transport* (London, 1962).

Traffic in Towns: the specially shortened edition of the Buchanan Report (London, 1963).

5 INDUSTRY AND ECONOMY

ALLEN, G. C. *The Structure of Industry in Britain* (London, 1966).

ASHWORTH, WILLIAM *An Economic History of England 1870–1939* (London, 1960).

BURNS, TOM (ed.) *Industrial Man* (Harmondsworth, 1969).

CHAMBERS, J. D. *The Workshop of the World: British economic history from 1820 to 1880* (London, 1961).

KERR, CLARK et al. *Industrialism and Industrial Man* (Cambridge, Mass., 1960).

POLLARD, SIDNEY *The Development of the British Economy 1914–67* (London, 1973).

6 SOCIAL AND ECOMONIC HISTORIES – GENERAL

CARR-SAUNDERS, A. M. *et al. A Survey of Social Conditions in England and Wales as Illustrated by Statistics* (Oxford, 1958).

CLARK, G. KITSON *The Making of Victorian England* (London, 1962).

FYRTH, H. J. and GOLDSMITH, M. *Science, History and Technology*; Book I: 1800–1840s (London, 1965); Book II: 3 Pts. 1840s–1960s (London, 1969).

HOBSBAWM, E. J. *Industry and Empire: an economic history of Britain 1700–1914* (London, 1969).

MARSH, DAVID C. *Changing Social Structure of England and Wales 1871–1961* (London, 1958; revised edition 1965).

MATHIAS, PETER *The First Industrial Nation: an economic history of Britain 1700–1914* (London, 1969).

MUSSON, A. E. *Trade Union and Social History* (London, 1971).

PYKE, MAGNUS *The Science Century* (London, 1967).

RODERICK, G. W. *The Emergence of a Scientific Society in England 1800–1965* (London, 1967).

TAYLOR, F. SHERWOOD *The Century of Science* (London, 1941).

7 WORK AND INDUSTRIAL RELATIONS

BLAU, PETER M. *Bureaucracy in Modern Society* (New York, 1956).

BLAU, PETER M. and SCOTT, W. RICHARD *Formal Organizations: a comparative approach* (San Francisco, 1962).

366 Modern English Society

BLAUNER, ROBERT *Alienation and Freedom: the manual worker in industry* (Chicago, 1963).

BROWN, E. H. PHELPS *The Growth of British Industrial Relations* (London, 1959).

BURNS, TOM and STALKER, GEORGE M. *The Management of Innovation* (London, 1961).

FRIEDMANN, GEORGES *The Anatomy of Work* (London, 1961).

GOLDTHORPE, JOHN H. et al. *The Affluent Worker: industrial attitudes and behaviour* (London, 1968).

HOBSBAWM, E. J. *Labouring Men: studies in the history of labour* (London, 1964).

MAYHEW, HENRY *London Labour and the London Poor* (London, 1861–2); Selections edited by JOHN H. BRADLEY (London, 1965).

MCGREGOR, D. *The Human Side of Enterprise* (New York, 1960).

TAYLOR, LEE *Occupational Sociology* (New York, 1968).

8 DEMOCRACY AND SOCIAL MOVEMENTS

BEVAN, ANEURIN *In Place of Fear* (London, 1952).

COHEN, STANLEY and TAYLOR, LAURIE *Escape Attempts: the theory and practice of resistance to everyday life* (London, 1976).

COLE, G. D. H. *A Short History of the British Working-Class Movement 1789–1947* (first published in one volume, London, 1932; revised edition 1948); *A Century of Co-operation* (London, 1944).

FRASER, W. HAMISH *Trade Unions and Society: the struggle for acceptance 1850–1880* (London, 1974).

PELLING, HENRY *A History of British Trade Unionism* (London, 1963).

RIGBY, A. *Alternative Realities* (London, 1974).

THOMPSON, E. P. *The Making of the English Working Class* (London, 1963).

WILLIAMS, RAYMOND *The Long Revolution* (London, 1961).

9 POPULATION

BANKS, J. A. *Prosperity and Parenthood: a study of family planning among the Victorian middle classes* (London, 1954).

DRAKE, MICHAEL *Population in Industrialization* (London, 1969).

GLASS, D. V. and EVERSLEY, D. E. C. (eds.) *Population in History*, especially Part II (London, 1965).

MALTHUS, THOMAS ROBERT *Essay on Population* (first published 1798).

WRIGLEY, E. A. *Population and History* (London, 1969).

WRONG, D. H. *Population and Society* (New York, 1961: revised edition 1963).

10 SOCIAL STRATIFICATION AND SOCIAL MOBILITY

BELL, COLIN R. *Middle Class Families: social and geographical mobility* (London, 1968).

BOTTOMORE, T. B. *Classes in Modern Society* (London, 1965).

COATES, KEN and SILBURN, RICHARD *Poverty: the forgotten Englishman* (Harmondsworth, 1970).

COLE, G. D. H. *Studies in Class Structure* (London, 1955).

GLASS, D. V. (ed.) *Social Mobility in Britain* (London, 1954).

GOLDTHORPE, J. H. *et al.* *The Affluent Worker in the Class Structure* (Cambridge, 1969).

JACKSON, J. A. (ed.) *Social Stratification* (Cambridge, 1969).

RUNCIMAN, W. G. *Relative Deprivation and Social Justice* (London, 1966).

RUTTER, MICHAEL and MADGE, NICOLA *Cycles of Disadvantage* (London, 1976).

WEDDERBURN, DOROTHY (ed.) *Poverty, Inequality and Class Structure* (London, 1974).

WESTERGAARD, JOHN and RESLER, HENRIETTA *Class in a Capitalist Society: a study of contemporary Britain* (London, 1974).

11 EDUCATION

BECK, J. et al. *Worlds Apart: readings for a sociology of education* (London, 1976).

BENN, CAROLINE and SIMON, BRIAN *Half Way There: report on the British comprehensive school reform* (Harmondsworth, 2nd edition 1972).

BERNBAUM, GERALD *Social Change and the Schools, 1918–1944* (London, 1967).

CHANAN, GABRIEL and GILCHRIST, LINDA *What School is For* (London, 1974).

COTGROVE, S. F. *Technical Education and Social Change* (London, 1958).

HALSEY, A. H. (ed.) *Educational Priority*, vol. I (London, 1972).

LAWSON, JOHN and SILVER, HAROLD *A Social History of Education in England* (London, 1973).

MACLURE, J. STUART *Educational Documents, England and Wales, 1816–1963* (London, 1965).

RAYNOR, JOHN and HARDEN, JANE *Cities, Communities and the Young: readings in urban education*, 2 vols (London, 1973).

SILVER, HAROLD (ed.) *Equal Opportunity in Education: a reader in social class and educational opportunity* (London, 1973).

SILVER, PAMELA and HAROLD *The Education of the Poor: the history of a National school 1824–1974* (London, 1974).

SIMON, BRIAN *Studies in the History of Education 1780–1870* (London, 1960; retitled *The Two Nations and the Educational Structure*); *Education and the Labour Movement, 1870–1920* (London, 1965).

YOUNG, MICHAEL F. D. (ed.) *Knowledge and Control* (London, 1971).

12 THE FAMILY AND SOCIALIZATION

ARIES, PHILIPPE *Centuries of Childhood* (London, 1972).

ELLIOTT, KATHERINE (ed.) *The Family and its Future* (London, 1970).

FLETCHER, RONALD *The Family and Marriage in Britain* (Harmondsworth, 1962; revised edition 1966).

GRAVESON, R. H. and CRANE, F. R. *A Century of Family Law, 1857–1957* (London, 1957; revised edition 1965).

LOMAS, PETER (ed.) *The Predicament of the Family* (London, 1967).

MCGREGOR, O. R. *Divorce in England* (London, 1957).

MUSGROVE, FRANK *The Family, Education and Society* (London, 1966).

NEWSON, JOHN and ELIZABETH *Patterns of Infant Care in an Urban Community* (London, 1963); *Four Years Old in an Urban Community* (London, 1968); *Seven Years Old in the Urban Environment* (London, 1976).

TOWNSEND, PETER *The Family Life of Old People* (London, 1957).

YOUNG, MICHAEL and WILLIMOTT, PETER *The Symmetrical Family* (London, 1973).

13 YOUTH AND YOUTH CULTURE

FYVEL, T. R. *The Insecure Offenders: rebellious youth in the welfare state* (London, 1961).

LAING, DAVE *et al.* *The Electric Muse: the story of folk into rock* (London, 1975).

LEECH, KENNETH *Youthquake: the growth of a counter-culture through two decades* (London, 1973).

MELLY, GEORGE *Revolt Into Style: the pop arts in Britain* (London, 1970).

MILLS, RICHARD *Young Outsiders: a study of alternative communities* (London, 1973).

MUSGROVE, FRANK *Youth and the Social Order* (London, 1964); *Ecstasy and Holiness: counter culture and the open society* (London, 1974).

NUTTALL, JEFF *Bomb Culture* (London, 1970).

14 WOMEN

COOTE, ANNA and GILL, TESS *Women's Rights* (London, 1974).

GAVRON, HANNAH *The Captive Wife: conflicts of house-bound mothers* (London, 1966).

HEWITT, MARGARET *Wives and Mothers in Victorian Industry* (London, 1958).

JEPHCOTT, P. *et al. Married Women Working* (London, 1962).

KAMM, JOSEPHINE *Hope Deferred: girls' education in English History* (London, 1965).

KLEIN, V. *Britain's Married Women Workers* (London, 1965).

MILL, JOHN STUART *The Subjection of Women* (1869); WOLLSTONECRAFT, MARY *A Vindication of the Rights of Women* (1792); published together in Everyman edition.

MYRDAL, A. and KLEIN, V. *Women's Two Roles* (London, 1956).

OAKLEY, ANN *Sex, Gender and Society* (London, 1972).

PINCHBECK, IVY *Women Workers and the Industrial Revolution, 1750–1850* (London, 1930).

RAPOPORT, RHONA and ROBERT *Dual Career Families* (London, 1971).

SULLEROT, EVELYNE *Woman, Society and Change* (London, 1971).

YUDKIN, SIMON and HOLME, ANTHEA *Working Mothers and their Children* (London, 1963).

15 COMMUNICATIONS AND MASS MEDIA

ALTICK, RICHARD D. *The English Common Reader: a social history of the mass reading public 1800–1900* (Chicago, 1957).

GLASGOW UNIVERSITY MEDIA GROUP *Bad News*, vol. I (London, 1976).

HALLORAN, J. D. *The Effects of Mass Communication* (Leicester, 1964).

HOGGART, RICHARD *The Uses of Literacy: aspects of working class life with special reference to publications and entertainments* (London, 1957).

PILKINGTON, SIR H. *Report of the Committee on Broadcasting*, Cmnd 1753 (London, 1962).

SMITH, A. C. H. *Paper Voices: the popular press and social change 1935–1965* (London, 1975).

TRENAMON, J. and MCQUAIL, D. *Television and the Political Image* (London, 1961).

TUNSTALL, JEREMY *Advertising Man* (London, 1964).

WILLIAMS, RAYMOND *Communications* (London, 1966); *Television, Technology and Cultural Form* (London, 1974).

16 POLITICAL PARTIES AND VOTING

BEER, SAMUEL H. *Modern British Politics* (London, 1965).

BLONDEL, J. *Voters, Parties and Leaders* (Harmondsworth, 1963).

BUTLER, DAVID and STOKES, DONALD *Political Change in Britain: the evolution of electoral choice* (London, 1969; edition of 1974).

FINER, S. E. *Anonymous Empire: a study of the Lobby in Great Britain* (London, 1958).

MCKENZIE, R. T. *British Political Parties* (London, 1955; revised edition 1963).

MCKENZIE, R. T. and SILVER, ALLAN *Angels in Marble; working class conservatives in England* (London, 1968).

GOLDTHORPE, J. H. *et al. The Affluent Worker: political attitudes and behaviour* (Cambridge, 1968).

GUTTSMAN, W. L. *The British Political Elite* (London, 1963).

PELLING, HENRY *A Short History of the Labour Party* (London, 1961); *The Origins of the Labour Party, 1880–1900* (Oxford, 1965).

ROSE, RICHARD (ed.) *Studies in British Politics* (London, 1966).

WOOTTON, GRAHAM *Pressure Groups in Britain 1720–1970* (London, 1975).

17 SOCIAL POLICY AND ADMINISTRATION

BRUCE, MAURICE *The Coming of the Welfare State* (London, 1961).

CHECKLAND, S. G. and E. O. A. *The Poor Law Report of 1834* (London, 1974).

DONNISON, D. V. and CHAPMAN, VALERIE *Social Policy and Administration* (London, 1965).

FRASER, DEREK *The Evolution of the British Welfare State* (London, 1973).

GILBERT, BENTLEY B. *The Evolution of National Insurance in Great Britain: the origins of the Welfare State* (London, 1966).

GREGG, PAULINE *The Welfare State: an economic and social history of Great Britain from 1945 to the present day* (London, 1967).

JONES, KATHLEEN *Mental Health and Social Policy 1845–1959* (London, 1960).

JORDAN, BILL *Poor Parents: social policy and the 'cycle of deprivation'* (London, 1974).

LONGMATE, NORMAN *The Workhouse* (London, 1974).

MARSHALL, T. H. *Social Policy* (London, 1965).

MIDWINTER, E. C. *Victorian Social Reform* (London, 1968).

MOWAT, CHARLES LOCH *The Charity Organisation Society 1869–1913* (London, 1961).

PARKER, JULIA *Social Policy and Citizenship* (London, 1975).

PINKER, ROBERT *Social Policy and Social Theory* (London, 1971).

ROBERTS, DAVID *Victorian Origins of the British Welfare State* (New Haven, 1960).

SMELLIE, K. B. *One Hundred Years of English Government* (London, 1937); *A History of Local Government* (London, 1946; revised edition 1957).

Social Insurance and Allied Services (Beveridge Report) (London, 1942).

TITMUSS, RICHARD M. *Essays on 'The Welfare State'* (London, 1958); *Commitment to Welfare* (London, 1968).

WOODROOFE, KATHLEEN *From Charity to Social Work in England and the United States* (London, 1962).

WOOTTON, BARBARA *Social Science and Social Pathology* (London, 1959).

18 SOCIAL SURVEYS AND COMMUNITY STUDIES

ABRAMS, MARK *Social Surveys and Social Action* (London, 1951).

ABRAMS, PHILIP *The Origins of British Sociology: 1834–1914. An essay with selected papers* (Chicago, 1968).

BANKS, J. A. (ed.) *Studies in British Society* (London, 1969).

BOTT, ELIZABETH *Kinship and Social Networks* (London, 1957).

CULLEN, MICHAEL J. *The Statistical Movement in early Victorian Britain* (Hassocks, 1975).

DENNIS, N. *et al. Coal is our Life* (London, 1956).

FRANKENBERG, RONALD *Communities in Britain* (Harmondsworth, 1966).

KERR, MADELINE *The People of Ship Street* (London, 1958).

KLEIN, JOSEPHINE *Samples from English Cultures* (London, 1964)

LASSWELL, MARGARET Wellington Road (London, 1962).

MADGE, JOHN *The Tools of Social Science* (London, 1953).

MOSER, C. A. *Survey Methods in Social Investigation* (London, 1958).

OPPENHEIM, A. N. *Questionnaire Design and Attitude Measurement* (London, 1966).

ROSSER, COLIN and HARRIS, CHRISTOPHER *The Family and Social Change* (London, 1965).

ROWNTREE, B. S. and LAVERS, G. R. *Poverty and the Welfare State* (London, 1951).

SIMEY, T. S. *Social Science and Social Purpose* (New York, 1969).

TOWNSEND, PETER *The Family Life of Old People* (London, 1957).

WILLIAMS, W. W. *The Sociology of an English Village* (London, 1957); *Country Village: Ashworthy* (London, 1963).

WILLMOTT, PETER *The Evolution of a Community* (London, 1963).

WILLMOTT, PETER and YOUNG, MICHAEL *Family and Class in a London Suburb* (London, 1960); *Family and Kinship in East London* (London, 1957).

19 SOME IMPORTANT FIGURES

BOTTOMORE, T. B. and RUBEL, MAXIMILIEN (eds.) *Karl Marx: selected writings in sociology and social philosophy* (London, 1956).

BRIGGS, ASA *Social Thought and Social Action: a study of the work of Seebohm Rowntree 1871–1954* (London, 1961).

FINER, S. E. *The Life and Times of Sir Edwin Chadwick* (London, 1952).

HAMMOND, J. L. and BARBARA *Lord Shaftesbury* (London, 1923).

LAMBERT, ROYSTON *Sir John Simon 1816–1904 and English Social Administration* (London, 1963).

LEWIS, R. A. *Edwin Chadwick and the Public Health Movement, 1832–1854* (London, 1952).

SIMEY, T. S. and M. B. *Charles Booth, Social Scientist* (London, 1960).

20 HISTORY AND SOCIOLOGY

BERGER, PETER *Invitation to Sociology: a humanistic perspective* (New York, 1963).

BOTTOMORE, T. B. *Sociology* (London, 1962).

BRIGGS, ASA 'Sociology and History', Ch. 5 in WELFORD, A. T. *et al.* (eds.) *Society* (London, 1962).

CARR, E. H. *What is History?* (London, 1961).

CONNERTON, PAUL (ed.) *Critical Sociology* (Harmondsworth, 1976).

DOUGLAS, JACK *Understanding Everyday Life: toward the reconstruction of sociological knowledge* (London, 1971).

DOUGLAS, MARY *Natural Symbols* (London, 1973).

ERIKSON, KAI T. 'Sociology and the Historical Perspective', in MICHAEL DRAKE (ed.) *Applied Historical Studies* (London, 1973).

FLINN, M. W. and SMOUT, T. C. (eds.) *Essays in Social History* (London, 1974).

MARSH, D. C. (ed.) *The Social Sciences: an outline for the intending student* (London, 1965).

MILLS, C. WRIGHT *The Sociological Imagination* (New York, 1959).

NISBET, ROBERT A. *Social Change and History* (New York, 1969); *The Sociological Tradition* (London, 1967).

THOMPSON, KENNETH and TUNSTALL, JEREMY *Sociological Perspectives: selected readings* (Harmondsworth, 1971).

21 OTHER READING

(a) *Religion*

ARGYLE, MICHAEL *Religious Behaviour* (London, 1958).

GILBERT, A. D. *Religion and Society in Industrial England: church, chapel and social change 1740–1914* (London, 1976).

ROBERTSON, ROLAND (ed.) *Sociology of Religion* (Harmondsworth, 1969).

(b) *War and its aftermath*

CALDER, ANGUS *The People's War: Britain 1938–45* (London, 1971).

MARWICK, ARTHUR *The Deluge: British society and the First World War* (London, 1965).

MOWAT, CHARLES LOCH *Britain Between the Wars 1918–1940* (London, 1955).

SISSONS, MICHAEL and FRENCH, PHILIP *Age of Austerity 1945–1951* (London, 1963).

(c) *Leisure*

DUMAZEDIER, JOFFRE *Towards a Society of Leisure* (New York, 1967).

PIMLOTT, J. A. R. *The Englishman's Holiday: a social history* (London, 1947).

RODGERS, BRIAN 'Leisure and Recreation', in COWAN, PETER (ed.) *Developing Patterns of Urbanization* (Edinburgh, 1970).

ROWNTREE, B. SEEBOHM and LAVERS, G. R. *English Life and Leisure: a social study* (London, 1951).

WALVIN, JAMES *The People's Game: a social history of British football* (London, 1975).

(d) *Race*

DEAKIN, NICHOLAS *et al.* *Colour, Citizenship and British Society* (London, 1970).

GLASS, RUTH *Newcomers* (London, 1961).

MILNER, DAVID *Children and Race* (Harmondsworth, 1975).

PATTERSON, SHEILA *Immigration and Race Relations 1960–1967* (London, 1969).

(e) *Bibliographies*

BLACKSTONE, TESSA *Social Policy and Administration in Britain: a bibliography* (London, 1975).

WESTERGAARD, J., WEYMAN, A. and WILES, P. *Modern British Society: a bibliography* (London, 1976).

Index

388 Index